The Realm
of the Punisher

The Realm of the Punisher

Travels in Duterte's Philippines

Tom Sykes

Signal Books
Oxford

First published in 2018 by
Signal Books Limited
36 Minster Road
Oxford OX4 1LY
www.signalbooks.co.uk

A catalogue record for this book is available from the British Library

ISBN 978-1-909930-72-8 Paper

Cover Design: Louis Netter

Typesetting: Tora Kelly

Cover Image: Louis Netter
Map: Pavalena/shutterstock.com
Images: p. 1 Library of Congress, Washington DC; p. 53 Al Ramones
& Domie Quiazon/Wikimedia Commons; p. 115 Tom Sykes; p. 182
PPD/Cado Niña/Wikimedia Commons
Printed in India by Imprint Press

For Sarah Sykes, my dear mother and a remarkable woman. Sorry for making you worry during these sometimes risky trips to the Philippines over the last nine years.

CONTENTS

FOREWORD

When asked to provide a foreword to this book, I did not hesitate to say yes, for Tom Sykes' work helps illuminate the context surrounding the emergence of one of the most controversial figures in the contemporary global political scene.

In thinking of what to write, I have drawn liberally from an essay I did for the journal *Global Dialogue* (Vol 7, Issue 2, 2017), which has kindly given me permission to share these thoughts in this preface.

1789 and 1989

With the victory of the Nazi counterrevolution, Joseph Goebbels famously said, 'The year 1789 is hereby erased from history.' Along the same lines, could one argue that the rising fascist movements in the US, Europe and elsewhere seek to erase 1989 from history?

1789 heralded the French Revolution. Similarly, for Francis Fukayama and others, 1989 marked the apogee of liberal democracy. In what Fukuyama termed 'the end of history,' the defeat of communism in Europe and right-wing authoritarian regimes across the developing world marked 'an unabashed victory of economic and political liberalism [...] and the universalization of Western liberal democracy as the final form of human government.'

Fukuyama's nascent utopia was soon challenged by anti-liberal movements, mainly religious-inspired forces like political Islam in the Middle East and ethnic exclusivist ones in Eastern Europe. But no movement or individual has been more brazenly contemptuous of liberal-democratic ideals than Rodrigo Duterte, elected President of the Philippines in May 2016 by an insurgent movement.

Eliminationism

Duterte's signature program has been his war on drugs, which to date has claimed as many as 20,000 lives. This is no ordinary law-and-order campaign. Carried out with a fanaticism bordering on the ideological and justified with ideas reminiscent of pseudo-scientific Nazi racial theory, the campaign has stripped a whole sector of society of the rights to life, due process or membership ian society. Duterte has all but written drug users and drug dealers – a group said to comprise three million of the country's population of 103 million – out of the human race. With a typical rhetorical flourish, he told the security forces: 'Crime against humanity? In the first place, I'd like to be frank with you: are they human? What is your definition of a human being?'

Justifying killings 'in self-defence' by the police, Duterte insists that using *shabu* – the local term for meth, or methamphetamine hydrochloride – can 'shrink the brain of a person, who therefore is no longer viable for rehabilitation'. Calling drug users the 'living, walking dead' who are 'of no use to society', he insists they are 'paranoid' and dangerous. Duterte has offered police a blank cheque to kill drug users, whether or not they resist arrest. Indeed, to any policemen who might be convicted of killing drug users without justification, he has offered an immediate pardon 'so you can go after the people who brought you to court.'

In spite of, or because of, these views, Duterte – who after all promised during his campaign that he would 'fatten the fish' in Manila Bay with bodies of thousands of criminals – remains immensely popular, with a fanatical following of netizens who launch cyber assaults on people who dare criticize his regime's extra-judicial executions. His recent attacks on the Catholic Church, to which some 80 per cent of Filipinos belong, and on God, whom he has called 'stupid', have hardly dented cross-class appeal.

The Roots of *Dutertismo*

What are the roots of Duterte's mass appeal? True, his identification of drug users as the plague of society resonates widely. But there are more profound causes. Duterte's hold on society reflects deep disenchantment with the liberal-democratic regime that followed Ferdinand Marcos' overthrow in February 1986, the so-called EDSA Uprising. In fact, the failure of the 'EDSA Republic' – named after the Manila highway where mass protests were mobilized to topple the Marcos dictatorship – was a condition for Duterte's success.

Duterte's path was paved by a deadly combination of elite control of the Philippines' electoral system, continued concentration of wealth, neoliberal economic policies and Washington's insistence on foreign debt repayment. By the time of the 2016 elections, a yawning gap had opened between the EDSA Republic's promise of popular empowerment and wealth redistribution, and Philippine reality: massive poverty, scandalous inequality and pervasive corruption. Add to this the widespread perception of inept governance during President Benigno Aquino III's administration, and it is not surprising that more than sixteen million voters, some 40 per cent of the electorate, saw the tough-guy, authoritarian approach which Duterte had cultivated for thirty-plus years as mayor of the southern frontier city of Davao as precisely what the country needed. As the novelist Anthony Doerr said of pre-war Germans, Filipinos were 'desperate for someone who can put things right'.

Moreover, the EDSA Republic's discourse – democracy, human rights and rule of law – came to seem a suffocating straitjacket for many Filipinos overwhelmed by a sense of powerlessness. Duterte's discourse – a mixture of outright death threats, coarse street-corner language and frenzied railing, combined with disdainful humour directed at an elite he called *coños* or cunts – proved an exhilarating formula for his audience, who felt themselves liberated from stifling hypocrisy.

A Fascist Original
Duterte's campaign of extermination, his mobilization of a multiclass base and his concentration of power has left the Philippines' US-style separation of powers in tatters. These features of his reign mark him as a fascist – but of an unusual kind. If the conventional fascist takeover starts by violating civil liberties, moves to a grab for absolute power, and then to indiscriminate repression, Duterte reverses that sequence, first ordering wholesale killings, then moving on to assault political liberties and the country's political institutions, finally ending with a lunge for absolute power. This is *blitzkrieg* fascism, of which the last phase is now in progress – that is the revision of the constitution to radically enhance the power of the president under the guise of federalism.

THE REALM OF THE PUNISHER

Though a novice at foreign policy, Duterte has demonstrated an instinctive grasp of the dynamics of Philippine nationalism. Moves like calling former US President Obama a 'son of a bitch' – after the then-American president had criticized Duterte's extra-judicial executions, and his openness towards China – seemed politically risky, given that pro-Americanism has been deeply entrenched in the Philippines. Surprisingly, however, Duterte's moves provoked very little protest, instead eliciting much internet support. As many have observed, ordinary Filipinos may feel admiration for the US and its institutions, but there is also a strong undercurrent of resentment at US colonial subjugation of the Philippines, at the unequal treaties that Washington has foisted on the country and at the overwhelming impact of the 'American way of life' on local culture. Here, one need not delve into Hegel's complex master-servant dialectic to understand that the 'struggle for recognition' has been an undercurrent in the US-Philippine relationship. Duterte has been able to tap into this emotional underside of Filipinos in a way that the left has not. Like many authoritarian predecessors elsewhere, Duterte has been able to effectively splice together nationalism and authoritarianism.

Populist in Rhetoric, Fascist in Substance
Though much of his rhetoric is populist, however, Duterte makes no pretence that he will use the masses as a battering ram for redistributive reform. Rather, like classic fascists, he seeks to balance class forces while projecting an image of being above class conflict. During his campaign, Duterte promised to end contractual labor, curb the mining industry and turn over to small coconut farmers the taxes unjustly collected from them by the Marcos regime; but those promises have remained largely unfulfilled while the country's key elites have positioned themselves as his allies. But while in the long term, delivering social and economic reforms will be central to maintaining support for his authoritarian project, the lack of progress so far seems unlikely to significantly dent Duterte's popularity in the short or medium term.

For the moment, opposition to Duterte among the elite and state institutions is weak. Similarly, the Catholic Church hierarchy, formerly a strong advocate of human rights, has been hesitant to take on a popular leader; the Church lacks credibility due to internal corruption and to its bull-headed stance on family planning. What opposition from the liberal elite there is has come from isolated figures – including Senator Leila de Lima, now jailed on trumped-up charges that she is on drug lords' payroll and from some of the media, notably the internet news agency Rappler that Duterte has threatened to shut down. Opposition is growing, however, in the ranks of civil society, and the inflation that is now wracking the economy owing to the rise in excise taxes to fund his ambitious infrastructure program is likely to contribute to its spread over the longer term.

Duterte, Philippine Society and Sociology

Duterte may be politically reprehensible, but his personality and its contradictions have drawn much interest from social scientists. Some have asked about the intersection of socio-historical trends and personality. A recent *New York Times* profile described how Duterte was greatly affected when a Jesuit priest sexually molested him in high school — a revelation that Duterte himself raised during the 2016 election campaign. Later transferred to Los Angeles, the offending priest went on to sexually abuse children, with no effort on the part of his superiors to discipline him or turn him over to the law (though the Jesuits were finally forced to pay a $16 million settlement with the victims). Given the psychological damage that is likely to have been inflicted, is the Philippines now paying for the crimes of a child predator?

Sociologists might also ask, in philosopher John Gray's words, how 'what we see as the unalterable features of civilized life vanish in the blink of an eye'. Especially after the 1986 EDSA Uprising, the Philippines was regarded as a showcase of liberal democracy. Many argued that in overthrowing Marcos, Filipinos reasserted long-standing values they had internalized during the American colonial period, of individual rights, due process and democracy. The liberal-democratic constitution of the EDSA Republic seemed to crystallize these national political values. But suddenly, in the space of less than a year, most Filipinos express strong support for a man whose central agenda is the extra-judicial execution of a certain category of human beings; many have served as Duterte's 'willing executioners,' to borrow Daniel Goldhagen's description of Germans during the Nazi era, or at least as his 'willing accomplices'. To some, seeing many compatriots cheering Duterte on in his bloody campaign is incxplicable as well as tragic. To others engaged in the behavioral sciences, however, it seems time to shed the assumptions that our people are civilized beings or creatures with compassion; instead perhaps we must approach contemporary Philippine society with the same lens that Goldhagen proposed for studying Germany during the Nazi period:

> [T]his period can be approached [...] with the critical eye of an anthropologist disembarking on unknown shores, open to meeting a radically different culture and conscious of the possibility that he might need to devise explanations not in keeping with, perhaps even contravening his own common-sense notions, in order to explain the culture's constitution, its idiosyncratic patterns of practice, and its collective projects and products. This would admit the possibility that large numbers of people [...] might have killed or been willing to kill others [...] in good conscience.

Comparative Genocide

Meantime, the body count continues to mount. Duterte's war on drugs has already claimed more victims than most genocidal campaigns in Southeast Asia's recent history, behind only Pol Pot's extermination of nearly three million Cambodians in the 1970s, and the 1965 massacre of nearly a million Indonesians following a failed coup against the Sukarno government. Duterte told the country in 2016, with characteristically sinister humour, that 20,000 to 30,000 more lives might have to be taken to cleanse the Philippines of drugs. Having learned to take Duterte seriously even when he seems to be joking, many observers expect this figure to be an underestimate.

Finally, Duterte must not be seen in isolation. He is just one of a number of figures who seem to have suddenly emerged to shake to its foundation the post-World War II liberal order. These personalities include Donald Trump, Victor Orban of Hungary, Narendra Modi of India and Recep Erdogan of Turkey. To effectively counter the authoritarian populist or fascist trend these figures represent, one must first understand them. In this regard, Tom Sykes' book is an excellent contribution when it comes to Duterte. It sheds valuable light on how such a popular leader could emerge from the thicket of Philippines politics and why he literally continues to get away with murder.

Professor Walden Bello, University of the Philippines Diliman
Manila
26 July 2018

THE REALM OF THE PUNISHER

PART 1:
1985-2010

71. The native Filipino prefers cock-fighting to work. Philippine Islands.
Copyright 1902 by C. H. Graves.

1. PEARL OF THE ORIENT

The first I ever heard of the Philippines was from my grandad. I was six, he was sixty. I was surprised how warmly he spoke of the place. He wasn't known for his warmth.

'Took shore leave in Manila with the navy. Back in '41. We were well looked after. Bloody modern as you like. Elevators that went *whoosh*. Also rather pretty. Palm trees, mangoes, that sort of thing.'

Grandad always spoke in these telegram-like sentences, as if giving orders. While he talked, he'd scratch at his cropped white hair, bold and bright as the target spots of the searchlights he used on HMS *Formidable* to bamboozle kamikazes.

He showed me black and white pictures of Manila and told me how it had been beautified by the American architect Daniel Burnham. According to Burnham's plans, the US colonial authorities widened the tangled streets into acacia-shaded boulevards, dredged the inner city estuaries and grew gardens between handsome villas with *capiz* (oyster shell) windows. Grandad claimed Manila was cleaner and greener than British cities of the time.

For an officer of the Royal Navy, Manila's pleasures were varied and affordable. Grandad frequented the Manila Hotel, another Burnham brainchild. Surrounded by its own custom-built park, this 500-room Art Deco spectacle had champagne suites, string quartets and celebrity guests. One evening, Grandad spotted the imposing bulk and moustache of Mr Ernest Hemingway holding hands with an attractive blonde woman, but was too shy to approach them. Grandad's memory was probably correct – later I found out that, in February 1941, Hemingway flew into Manila with his then wife Martha Gellhorn, the notable war correspondent, *en route* to Beijing to report on the Sino-Japanese War.

Grandad showed me the silk suits he'd bought from Chinese-Filipino tailors in Intramuros, the walled city built in the late sixteenth century by the Spanish colonizers of the Philippines. He told of lazy afternoons at a café famed for its *bibingka* (rice cakes) that took hours to prepare, and of long nights on the azoteas of colonial bars filling his belly with ice-cold *tuba* (coconut wine) and his pipe with fine local tobacco.

The Army and Navy Club in Luneta Park was the place to go for poker, pink gins and beautiful women. Grandad said he resisted the latter temptation. Not that the six-year-old me really understood such adult things. At the club on Sundays, you could play polo, golf and tennis with the British and American officers. To cool off in the evening, the members would swim in the translucent, indigo waters of Manila Bay, the flower-crested island of Corregidor gleaming in the distance.

Although he was later to scowl at the multiculturalism that reshaped post-war Britain, Grandad marvelled at the diversity of pre-war Manila. He joked with the fast-talking Indian-Filipino traders descended from Sepoys who'd deserted during the British occupation in the 1760s. He was impressed with the erudite, Western-educated *mestizos* of mixed Spanish, Chinese and Malay descent. He bantered with Greek and German and French captains of ships packed with coffee, sugar and hemp bound for Europe, China and the US.

After these nostalgic flights, there was always a point when the glee would slip from Grandad's eyes. His sneer would expose brown, jagged teeth.

'All went to shit in Manila,' he'd growl. 'Japs invaded after Pearl Harbor. Wrested it from the Yanks. Place got hairier than bugger's carpets.' Years later, I discovered that 'bugger's carpets' was 1940s slang for sideburns. 'Made it a bloody shambles,' Grandad would continue. 'Damned ruthless the Japs, the lot of 'em. Killed the men. Raped the women. Bloody animals.' At this juncture, Grandad would snuff out the rest of his glass of Laphroaig and flop back in his armchair.

Grandad didn't elaborate on the Japanese invasion, but later aged nine, I learned more by listening to stories from other veterans. A great uncle who'd fled Hong Kong after it fell to the Japanese was detained in the Philippines on his way to Australia. He became one of the few British POWs amongst mostly Americans in the horrific New Bilibid Prison, Manila. When I asked him for more details he slowly replied, 'I'm sorry, Tom, I just can't go back there.'

To Grandad's chagrin, my parents sent me to a progressive state middle school run by ex-hippies where we sang Bob Dylan's anti-war songs in assembly rather than the usual hymns about God, joy and ploughing fields. Grandad was pleased, though, when I started researching a project on the Pacific War. The schoolbooks said that the Japanese, as part of their plot for world domination, had surprise-attacked American forces based in the Philippines. One of my ex-hippie teachers pointed out that, in fact, the US was an imperial power too, hence its presence in the Philippines in the first place. Manila changed hands twice during the war and, by the end of it, was one of the world's most damaged cities. I found an old book of photos of the Battle of Manila, 1945, when the Americans recaptured the Philippines and dealt a mortal blow to the Japanese Empire. The scratchy monochrome of the pictures made them all the more disturbing:

A shell-shocked GI, pupils dilated behind wide-lens glasses, staggering zombie-like through rubble, holding a wounded little Filipina in his arms.

Another GI kneeling to fire a flamethrower, the outline of a Japanese just visible within the cloud of fire. His brother-in-arms looking on coolly, foot resting on a shell case.

Filipino civilians executed by fleeing Japanese, lying face down, limbs and backs curved into the pliable postures of rag dolls.

More corpses: Japanese commandos strewn around a bullet-holed truck. One leaning against an oil drum, arm reaching desperately for help that isn't there. Another, on his back, wearing a death grin, floating in a lake of oil-black blood.

One side of the Old Congress Building pristine, the other side crumbling like the facial droop of a stroke victim.
Finally, a bird's eye view of the city after the Japanese surrender – eerie, blank, nothing left but ash and foundations. Easily mistaken for post-A-bomb Hiroshima.

These shocking pictures jarred with the exotic images of pre-war Manila I had in my head from Grandad. Now I understood his sadness. It was also important for a young boy to know about these things in order to understand the brutality of the world. I imagine those notorious stills from the Vietnam War – *that* Viet Cong guerrilla about to be shot in the head, *that* nine-year-old girl running naked and napalm-scorched – had a similar impact on those who saw them in the 1960s.

At school, I had a history teacher called Mr Turnbull whose nose was bent because a policeman broke it in 1968. He'd been one of the 6,000 at Grosvenor Square protesting against the Vietnam War. A charismatic speaker, he got me interested in Asian liberation movements of the Cold War era. I didn't tell Grandad about that. He hated the political left as much as he hated the Japanese. I came to admire Ho Chi Minh, who led the struggle for Vietnamese self-determination, routing first the Japanese and then the French. After that, his socialist model of development appalled the United States, which was trying to enforce its own market system upon the world. It's little known that Ho had begun his career as a fan of the US. His initial plans for an independent republic of Vietnam quoted its Constitution extensively. Ho never wanted a confrontation with the Americans, but the Americans saw him as an evil communist tyrant who had to be stopped. They failed, of course, and Ho stands out in history as the only national leader ever to have beaten the US in open warfare, even though he didn't quite live to see the last of its troops flee Saigon in 1973.

I also learned about the Huks, the Filipino Marxist guerrillas who, like the Vietminh, had daringly repelled the Japanese. After the war, they took on the shady, US-backed regime of President Ramon Magsaysay. Aiming to stop feudal landlords from cheating and abusing peasant farmers, the Huks robbed banks, planted bombs and assassinated politicians. By 1950, they were gathering on the outskirts of Manila.

I didn't tell Grandad about my research into the Huks either. Marxists and imperial Japanese were equally unwelcome in the idyllic 'Pearl of the Orient' of his memories. I know now that Grandad's Manila was run by and for rich, white Westerners like himself, and sustained by the kind of monstrous exploitation the Huks railed against.

'And a bloody good thing too,' Grandad might have added.

2. WHOSE PHILIPPINES?

While Grandad's affection for the Philippines sparked my curiosity about the country, my perspective on its history, culture and society would come to differ from his. In 1996, I went to study history – amongst other A-Levels – at Havant College in a suburb of Portsmouth. After class one day, I got talking to a German exchange student called Werner. 'I went to watch thiss film last night,' he hissed, 'and it was a-bloody rubbish!'

He had only himself to blame – he'd gone to see *The Thin Red Line*. This pompous sham of a movie is one of the few I've walked out of, even if it was on a subject that interested me: the Battle of Guadalcanal, a crucial clash in the Pacific War. Despite some arresting cinematography, not a lot happens beyond a horde of Hollywood stars relating specious homilies in voiceover about life, death, love, bravery and so forth.

'Only 'cos your lot lost,' snorted Ryan, a tracksuit-clad *townie*, which was snobbish nineties slang for *brash working class youth*. Like me, Ryan had a grandfather who'd served in the Royal Navy during the war. Since then, two generations of British males had been raised to revere those who'd shielded Britain from the Nazis. Pop culture reinforced this. As infants, we'd spent our pocket money on toy soldiers, comics set in the D-Day landings and polystyrene Spitfires that raced off on the breeze when thrown from the beach. Many of the lad-oriented films of my youth, from *Raiders of the Lost Ark* to *Saving Private Ryan*, had Nazi antagonists. When England played Germany at football, the tabloid papers would superimpose Tommy helmets onto the heads of Stuart Pearce and Paul Gascoigne. Stereotypes drawn from the Nazi cult were applied to normal, modern German people – they were ruthless, irritable, humourless, despotic and as efficient as their public transport systems.

'I do not know what you mean by "your lot",' Werner replied. 'Those crimes had nothing to do with me, I wass not born then. And every country in the world has been in wars to be ashamed of, yours also.'

'What you on about, mate?' Ryan glared.

Werner glared back. 'The British Empire. Thiss is an example, no?'

'The British Empire was sorted.'

'Really? The colonies? The slavery? The famines?'

'Look mate, I'm gonna deck you in a minute...' Ryan took a step forward but Werner held his ground. If they'd got physical, I wouldn't have known who to bet on. While Werner had the tubby cheeks and prescription spectacles of an archetypal geek, his torso was muscle-studded and he had four inches' height on Ryan's spare, featherweight boxer's physique.

After an uneasy instant while it seemed someone was preparing to throw the first punch, Werner continued his spiel, perhaps thinking this was a battle better won with words. 'I am just asking you to be a little fairer here. I am not saying what happened in my country wass right, it was a-bloody rubbish, you know. The damage England did to other countries is also true. Not that you boys are to blame for that either.'

Ryan made a brushing gesture with his hands. 'Not worth it,' he said and sloped off to the bike sheds for a cigarette.

Werner got me thinking. What if he was right and the population of a country shouldn't be liable for the actions of its rulers? The assumption of the nationalist or the patriot is that their government always represents and serves its people. Can that be said of dictatorships like Nazi Germany or the USSR that, by definition, don't rule by public consent? Can it be said of many democracies given that a party can win an election with a third or less of the popular vote? And even if, say 99 per cent of Britons in 1780 supported slavery or the same percentage of Germans loved Hitler in the 1930s, why should progressive young people like me and Werner, who weren't alive then, be held responsible for such outrages? Furthermore, what if Werner was right and almost every state has cadavers in its military-imperial cupboard? And following that, what if there are no firm boundaries between 'them' (the baddies) and 'us' (the goodies), especially if 'them' and 'us' merely refers to the ruling elites of nation states?

I went on to find proof for Werner's points. Britain, France and Portugal, among others, were responsible for the deaths of 30-60 million Africans during the Atlantic Slave Trade. Settler colonization from the 1600s to the 1900s in what we now call the United States wiped out 90 million Native Americans through disease and outright butchery. In the nineteenth and twentieth centuries, 60 million Indians perished in famines the British authorities could have prevented. Belgian company bosses in the Congo Free State killed another 10-15 million indigenes between 1885 and 1908. Yet, in the popular discourse, these atrocities – if they get an airing at all – are seen as bagatelles next to the Nazi extermination of 10 million European Jews, gypsies, disabled people and homosexuals, not to say the breaches of the Geneva Convention by the Japanese in World War II. Why? One reason is that history is written by the winners, as shown by the candid admission of Curtis LeMay, the US general in charge of the bombardment of Japanese cities in the war, that, had the Axis powers won the conflict, he'd have been hanged for war crimes.

Furthermore, there are gaps in the histories written by those who won World War II and stopped the Holocaust. They forget that the 'liberal democracies' not only appeased Hitler but supported him. Most of his ideas about race came from top universities in Britain and the US – some twenty American states had banned interracial marriage and sterilized 'undesirable' people long before the Nazi Party existed. Throughout his reign, Hitler had a portrait of Henry Ford on the wall of his office – fitting, since Ford had funded the US publication of the *The Protocols of the Elders of Zion*, a fake news report on a Jewish conspiracy to take over the world. Anglo-American firms from IBM to Ford to the Bank of England did business with Germany throughout the war. In the 1930s, my local newspaper, the Portsmouth *News*, was friendly to fascism – one op-ed was headlined 'HITLER THE MAN

To Lead Germany to Liberty!' Notable Britons and Americans who agreed with Nazi ideology included Edward VIII, Charles Lindbergh, Errol Flynn and Winston Churchill. Although he's painted as saviour to Hitler's antichrist, in truth Winnie would have got on famously with the *führer*. He detested socialism, communism and trade unions. He also detested Indians enough to deny them aid during the 1943 famine, writing at the time, 'Why hasn't Gandhi died yet?' Gandhi survived, but 4 million of his compatriots didn't. Earlier in his career, Churchill had praised British concentration camps in the Boer War, promoted the gassing of Kurds in Iraq (sixty years before Saddam Hussein actually did it) and reckoned racist mass-murder broadly a good thing. 'I do not admit,' he wrote, 'for instance, that a great wrong has been done to the Red Indians of America or the black people of Australia. I do not admit that a wrong has been done to these people by the fact that a stronger race, a higher-grade race, a more worldly wise race to put it that way, has come in and taken their place.'

I found out – and not from the college-approved reading lists – that money was the common driver of modernity's genocides. African slaves were needed for the lucrative mines and plantations of the New World. Native Americans were evicted from economically valuable land across the same continent. Indian peasants starved because the Raj was intent on selling the grain on the world market. The Congolese were either worked to death – or executed for not working hard enough – in the extraction of rubber for export to resource-hungry Europe. While the Holocaust didn't bring any commercial benefit – rather it became a huge burden on the German war effort – it was rooted in economics because the pervasive bigotry towards European Jews hinged on their perceived wealth, avarice and commercial acumen.

My history teachers said we'd learned lessons from these tragedies. 'Never again' was the favoured phrase. I wasn't so sure. Capitalism was still alive and, since the Cold War had ended, now almost ubiquitous. Surely, there'd be more slaughter for greed. A few years later, some of the same states responsible for the imperial crimes above would be violently plundering Iraqi oil. When Bush and Blair said they were on a humane mission of mercy, history suggested otherwise.

Our set texts for history stated that the Cold War was all about the democratic US reacting to the provocations of the totalitarian USSR. When I read other scholars not on that list – for example, Chomsky on neo-imperialism and Nkrumah on neo-colonialism – I found another angle: under the cover story of the Red Menace, the American-led First World had tried to crush nationalism in the Third World the better to loot the Third World's resources and make it a market for First World products. Millions more had died in that process – in Vietnam, Cambodia, Indonesia, Korea, Chile, Guatemala and elsewhere.

When I went on to the University of East Anglia in 1998, I learned that the Philippines had been the first prey of American imperialism. For 333 years, the archipelago had been a Spanish colony ruled by perfidious friars who stole all the land, forcibly converted the natives to Roman Catholicism and introduced a racist caste system that largely meant the darker you were, the worse you'd be treated. Then in 1898, the US allied with Filipino revolutionaries to overthrow the Spanish regime. American diplomats hinted to rebel leader Emilio Aguinaldo that, after the job was done, the Filipinos would be free to set up an independent republic. However, the US went back on this pledge and decided that occupying the islands would be better for everyone, especially the US. Its merchants wanted rice, hemp, cocoa and tobacco, not to say access to the China market. Its strategists desired a military foothold in the Far East. Its 'race scientists' held that *Homo philippinensis* – the indigenous Filipino – was too savage and backward to be allowed to choose his own destiny. 'Your new caught sullen peoples/Half-devil and half-child,' as Rudyard Kipling depicted them in 'The White Man's Burden', his panegyric to the intervention.

But the Filipinos didn't want to swap one bunch of colonial masters for another. An asymmetrical war began that would bear chilling parallels with Vietnam and Iraq. According to the historian Howard Zinn, Brigadier General Jacob Smith instructed his troops to kill any

Filipino of either gender over the age of ten. 'I want no prisoners,' he added. 'I wish you to kill and burn. The more you kill and burn the better it will please me.' The Americans used torture by water-boarding for the first time. 'His sufferings must be that of a man who is drowning, but cannot drown,' said Lieutenant Grover Flint.

After three years of fighting, a quarter million or more Filipinos lay dead: a genocide by anyone's standards. As Mark Twain wrote at the time, 'We have pacified some thousands of the islanders and buried them; destroyed their fields; burned their villages, and turned their widows and orphans out-of-doors.'

At the end of my second year at UEA, I had my own encounter with US imperialism, although it wasn't nearly as damaging as the Philippine-American War. I went for a brief holiday in San Francisco, my first stop Chinatown. It was spookily quiet. Old men played chess under the pea-green canopies of a pagoda. Most of the shops were closed, yet it was a Tuesday. I bought a newspaper, but it offered no clues.

I then saw a policeman with a handlebar moustache lowering the Stars and Stripes to half-mast. It was an affecting symbol of defeat, an anti-Iwo Jima.

'Excuse me,' I asked, 'could you tell me why you're taking that flag down?'

'Haven't you heard?' the cop bellowed, his eyes fireballs of wrath. 'America has been attacked! American airplanes have been hijacked! Many thousands of Americans are dead! This is too big-scale for a Timothy McVeigh kinda thing, so foreigners *must* be behind it!'

I walked away from the cop and into what had once been Jack Kerouac's favourite bar. The widescreen TV was showing what has become the most famous video footage in history: *those* planes crashing into *those* buildings. It's almost banal now, we've all seen it so often. But at that moment, at 11:30am on 11 September 2001, I was seeing it for the first time, and there was something frighteningly new about it. So new as to be unreal. Indeed, later on in my trip a Canadian tourist would tell me that, when he first saw it, he expected

James Bond to leap from the cockpit of one of the planes just before the moment of impact.

The caption on the screen read AMERICA UNDER ATTACK – PLANES CRASHED INTO WORLD TRADE CENTER, NEW YORK. The footage was replaying on a loop. I ordered a beer and sat near an office worker whose collar was loose around his scarlet throat. He kept shaking his fist at each replay, shouting, 'I don't wanna see it no more!' Why was he putting himself through it then? Perhaps he was simultaneously attracted to and repulsed by the cyclic image of destruction. He wasn't the only one: more people were coming into the bar, ordering drinks and then shouting at the TV. Someone was holding an 'extra' edition of a local newspaper. I'd never seen an 'extra' before. The front page was a still from what we were watching on the screen. The headline simply read BASTARDS!

The office worker got precariously to his feet. 'I bet the ragheads did it,' he said and left.

This was not the first time the US had faced suicide attacks from Islamic jihadists. During the Philippine-American War a *Moro* (Muslim from the southern island of Mindanao) assassin would work himself up into a state of *amok* (meaning 'insane rage' and the origin of the English idiom 'run amok') by spending all night with a piece of copper wire tied around his testicles. When he was sufficiently angry, he'd charge at the nearest American soldier and do as much harm as he could with a sword before getting himself shot, usually with a Colt .45 automatic, a sidearm invented expressly to fend off the *Moros*.

The Philippine conquest announced the twentieth century, the American century. Now, though, we were very much in the twenty-first. Now suicide attacks were happening on American soil, in the nub of American power. Was change afoot?

When I came home, I found a book called *Language of the Street* by Nick Joaquin on a stall at Norwich market. The autumn weather unusually fine, I went down to the university lake, sat on the grass and read the text in one sitting. After what I'd gleaned from a British Navy officer, here was a *Manileño's* take on Manila. Joaquin showed me a richly distinctive culture that paradoxically owed much to foreign influence. I learned about the evolution of Tagalog – the main language of the Philippines – from its early appropriations of Spanish to its absorption of Americanisms such as *genoowine* (a compliment paid to a woman with fair skin). With a cool equilibrium that contrasted with my anti-imperialist fervour, Joaquin argued against renaming the streets of his home town for nationalistic reasons because 'Manila has been a Malay city, a Spanish city, an American city, and is now a Filipino city … a people as young as we have surely need of every bit of memory that can surely make us feel more intensely *us*.' He went on to explore the panorama of Filipino rituals, from Christian-inspired mock crucifixions and festivals in which pigs were dressed up as saints, to the Aztec facets of the Day of the Dead celebrations. (For 250 years, the Philippine colony was adminstrated by the Spanish viceroyalty in Mexico.)

Thanks to the new medium of the internet, I learned more about the contemporary Philippines too. The country was becoming the cultural powerhouse of Southeast Asia. The Eraserheads, a band dubbed the 'Philippine Fab Four', sold a million albums worldwide and earned followings in Japan, Singapore, Australia and the US. The Filipino film industry began winning awards at Cannes. English language writers like Joel Toledo and José Dalisay scooped grants, fellowships and prizes across Europe and the US. (Dalisay had been a David T.K. Wong Creative Writing Fellow at UEA during my first year, and I was annoyed to find this out only in my second year, after he'd left.) All this sounded like a renaissance, but I found no allusion to it in the Western media. It seemed that if an Asian creative wanted to get reviewed in the press or discussed in seminar rooms over here, he or she should have the good sense to come from India, China or Japan, and not the Philippines.

Among my fellow students, a different narrative emerged about the post-colonial world. Southeast Asia was rebranded to them as a waypoint on the new Grand Tour. Stuffing their backpacks with parental credit cards and copies of Alex Garland's *The Beach* – the *On the Road* of my generation – Western kids flew thousands of miles to experience 'cultural otherness'. What this actually entailed was large amounts of drinking and drug taking, and almost getting seduced by a misleadingly attractive female impersonator.

But when I came to ask backpackers specifically about the Philippines, it turned out most hadn't been there. They said it was too far – a whole four-hour plane ride! – from peninsular Southeast Asia. The few who had gone bypassed Manila for pleasure spots such as Boracay Island, which they hailed as 'like something out of *The Beach*'.

I searched for more books about Manila. I found *The Tesseract*, the novel Garland wrote after *The Beach*. While there's no denying *The Tesseract*'s narrative velocity and structural innovation, it offered few insights into history or culture. Like a shanty town built from salvaged materials, Garland's Manila is a rickety composite of American movie tropes. Before the epic-slo-mo-hostage-crisis-shoot-out-finale, we're shown bloodstained hotels that recall Stephen King or the Coen Brothers. The moustachioed, matchstick-chewing mobster Don Pepe is straight out of a Spaghetti Western. The references to Spanish-named locations ('Sierra Madre') evoke cowboys, Indians and Mexican bandits. Moments of slapstick violence such as the bungled shooting of a cat could have been lifted from a film by Garland's contemporary Quentin Tarantino. Also Tarantino-esque is the book's splicing of pop culture (junk food, comic books, video games) with sensationalized tragedy (a baby attacked with acid, a woman driven mad with grief after losing her child to septicaemia).

Published a few years before *The Tesseract*, James Hamilton-Paterson's *Ghosts of Manila* is an arguably darker vision still. His Philippines is 'the Khmer Rouge in Disneyland', full of barbarity, perversion, rotten luck, broken dreams and psychotic felons. But while the horrors sketched in *Ghosts of Manila* (the illicit corpse trade, police protection of foreign paedophiles, a corrupt official giving a blind man a driving licence in return for a bottle of whisky) struck me as believable, I was less convinced about *The Tesseract*. When the book deals with the histrionics of Filipino Catholicism, for example, it feels more like one of Martin Scorsese's expletive-addled quests for redemption. In one unlikely sequence, a homeless boy hurls abuse at a good-natured Irish priest: 'Jesus Christ! … I'm not asking about the mind of God or your fucking leg!' You can almost hear the Brooklyn accent.

After reading these fictions, I wondered if any society anywhere could really be that disastrous, depressing and dangerous? Then again, these *were* fictions and not necessarily beholden to verisimilitude – is that ever fully attainable in any writing anyway? – so maybe it was naive to expect them to convey to me 'how it really is' in that part of the world.

And so these novels, Granddad's memories, history books, photographs – these were all versions of the Philippines, different 'Philippineses', if you like. There were contradictions between them and I wasn't sure which one to believe. There was only one way to settle it – I'd have to find my own Philippines.

3. HOW TO WRITE

Manila is a city of contrasts *what city hasn't that been said about?*, an interesting *didn't everyone's English teacher tell them never to use that adjective?* blend of old and new, East and West, rich and poor, calm and busy *so more or less every contrast imaginable, then*. After decades of stagnation, at last Manila is on the up *because its neoliberal rulers are resigned to the Philippines' natural place as an economic colony of wealthier nations – hurrah!* The middle classes are growing *they always seem to be no matter which country or historical period* and life is steadily getting better for the poorest *the good old trickle-down theory; these narratives of progress!* The national character *what a ludicrously essentialist concept – as if every single Filipino behaves exactly the same way by the accident of being born in roughly the same place* is typified *that's probably too smart a word for this hack* by inexhaustible politeness, an easy-going manner and an infectious joie de vivre. Not for nothing has Manila been called *use of the passive voice excuses the writer from actually bothering to source the following quote* 'the land of smiles' *most of Southeast Asia seems to have that soubriquet, and it's a patronising and infantilizing one*. Filipinos love to eat *only people with eating disorders don't* and they delight in playing basketball, singing karaoke and watching American science fiction movies *any mention of home-grown cultural forms or are they all dependent on those wealthy nations again?* At the same time, religious zeal is strong among Manileños *tautology alert!* who participate in holy rituals that will seem bizarre to the outsider *the opaque Oriental mind at work*.

Manila's key tourist attractions *yes, that's it, reduce the multiplexities of a 400-year-old global city to a scattering of stuff to spend your money on* are hidden gems *travel writing cliché #2,395* mostly located in and around the intriguing, ornate and atmospheric *hollow adjectives galore* colonial Spanish quarter of Intramuros *the assumption here is that little or nothing built since 1600 will be of interest to visitors*.

On the other hand, the multinational banks and smart hotels of the business district of Makati will undoubtedly remind the Western visitor of Manhattan or the City of London *foreigners eh? They try to imitate us but not very well.* Here you can feast on everything from sushi to McDonald's *oh the fruits of globalization!* thanks to investment from the U.S., Japan, Netherlands and Singapore *keep ramming home that Pepsicolonization point.*

Backpackers *for they are the lifeblood of tourism in any Third World country* prefer to stay in areas with a little more character such as Ermita, which has cleaned itself up since its days as a notorious sex tourism hub *mention only this aspect of Ermita's history rather than the more complimentary – and less spicy – stuff: it started as a settlement of Australoid people around 5,000 years ago; expanded from trade with China and Southeast Asia during the medieval Tondo period; was made into a religious hermitage by the Spanish conquistadors; exchanged goods, customs and ideas with Mexico and almost every part of Asia over the next 300 years; was briefly occupied by the British in the 1760s; and was renovated by the Americans in the early 1900s into a colonial quarter of posh dwellings and exclusive clubs.* Nearby Malate boasts *another massively overused travel writing verb* excellent nightlife options including The Hobbit House, a *Lord of the Rings*-themed bar staffed entirely by Filipino dwarves and midgets *an exotically othered yet reassuringly Western pop culture-tinged choice of venue.*

Be warned – Manila isn't all exotic fun. *Really? There's more to it than getting drunk with comedy little people?* Not everyone has benefited from development. Many have been left behind. *The old passive voice again, this time to exculpate the rich from leaving the poor to rot. And the poor don't even get a mention. And how many is many?*

Some useful facts in brief: The famous brown envelopes come from Manila. *Actually they don't – only the hemp that was used to make them came from Philippine bananas.* Everyone loves Manny Pacquiao. *Bit more accurate, though a blanket statement.* Filipinos have a natural predisposition towards nursing and answering queries on telephones. *They don't, they just go where there are jobs available, like migrant labourers anywhere.* They are innately attracted to unprepossessing, older Western men. *Again, this might be more to do with the economic incentives.*

I'd been on my laptop for four hours and this was the best I'd come up with: an 800-word spoof of my mediocre guidebook to the Philippines plus sarcastic annotations. The deadline for my first column for *Quill*, a Malaysian travel magazine, was accelerating towards me like a drugged Soviet sprinter. After graduating from UEA, I'd backpacked across Asia, disturbed by the poverty and authoritarianism of nominally socialist societies such as Vietnam and West Bengal. Sadly, my cash ran out before I got to the Philippines. Back in Britain I wrote up a dozen travel features that I'd sold to websites and magazines in both Asia and the West. These had caught the attention of Deirdre Wong, editor of *Quill*, who'd offered me the role of the magazine's 'Englishman in Manila' correspondent. So here I was now, indescribably fortunate to at last be in the Philippines and getting paid to write about it. The problem was I didn't know how to write about it.

I looked over my doggerel again. If I carried on the article in this vein but deleted the annotations, Deirdre might well accept it at face value without grasping the irony. She probably approved copy riddled with 'cities of contrast' and 'hidden gems' every day.

It was getting close to the end of my third day in Manila. For the umpteenth time, like someone operating a microfiche reader I wound back through my recent memories, pausing on and magnifying those I might use for my column. The pre-dawn taxi ride from the airport to my new home here in Quezon City – one of the sixteen conurbations making up the urban region known as Metro Manila – via the 100-foot high Skyway road, the darkness hiding the city below and the skies around us. The little boy in me squealing, 'We're flying through space!' Morning kindles, I spy colossal billboards – RED HOT SALE, WE ARE YOUR SECURITY PARTNERS, LOAD NA DITO, TRUE MONEY – and condos under construction, cloaked in green webbing. On to Katipunan Avenue, the boisterous motorway named after the secret society that triggered the 1896 uprising against the

Spanish. My taxi trades horns with a tinted SUV, skims a teen in a Jay-Z T-shirt. Hawkers in flip-flops dawdling between the windows of jeepney buses modelled on wartime US jeeps and covered in flamboyant graffiti and Catholic imagery. Hip-hop blaring from KFC and McDonald's. Roadside barbecues. Basketball courts.

None of this was glamorous enough for my column. I leafed through the current issue of *Quill* and the barely concealed advertorials with headings like 'Georgetown – Ultimate Romantic Getaway' and 'South Korea's Top Ten Wellness Spas'. Just get on and pen something formulaic like this, I ordered myself.

I stood up and crossed the parquet floor of my new study. I opened the sliding door to the balcony just an inch. It was like suddenly turning the volume up on some avant-garde orchestra. Blasting in from Katipunan were the random, high-tempo honks of car horns that made me imagine a thousand free jazz saxophonists all overblowing at the same time. Beneath it a bass-off between engines of varying sizes all with their own distinctive drones. The tinny high-hats of builders bashing hardened steel nails. Crass nursery rhyme jingles from carts selling cheese-flavoured ice cream.

Smells as well as sounds came through the gap. Acrid exhaust smoke dominant, next to ammonia-like urine and the piercing saline of fish balls, tempura and *kikiam* (pork and veg enveloped in bean curd) bubbling in crocks of lard. I opened the door further and noticed a sulphuric whiff that was unfamiliar to me. (I would later discover that this was likely a crystal meth lab (local name: *shabu*). It was coming in from beyond the art deco-ish buildings on the other side of Katipunan, possibly from as far as the jade-coloured hills of Antipolo, in hazy soft focus due to the smog and clotting darkness.

Could I put into my article what I was hearing and smelling right now? No, my molly-coddled readers wouldn't like it. Readers don't want the truth, or at least not the kite-boarding and cocktail-supping readers of a commercial travel mag. They want reasons to, as the French philosopher Guy Debord said of modern tourism, 'go and see what has been banalized'.

21

I yanked the door shut and the racket vanished.

One of the contributing bricks to my writer's block was made of pure, unalloyed betrayal. In the hotel I'd booked for my first night in Manila, I'd bumped into an American exchange student who advised moving to the Katipunan area. 'You'll live like a king,' he said. I took him on trust and found an online ad for 'Loyola Heights Condominium, nr Katipunan'. I paid the deposit electronically and moved in the next day to find myself directly behind a profoundly busy, noisy and polluted road. Whether I kept the windows closed or not, every morning brought a new film of dirt on to all the flat's surfaces.

My phone played a Buddhist chime. I'd chosen that particular ringtone to try and reduce my stress. When I saw who the email was from, my stress rocketed.

Dear Tom,

How are you progressing with the article? I do hope you have settled into Manila OK.

Warm regards,

Deirdre

I replied:

Dear Deirdre,

I should have it with you by tomorrow. Taking a quick break now and will crack on with it again soon.

Best,

Tom

But I didn't do that, I went to the pub.

4. INTERNATIONAL RELATIONS

I liked F. de la Rosa Street. Its mild traffic, studenty coffee shops and foliage splotching over the pavement were a world away from Katipunan's noxious din. My condo straddled the two roads – and worlds.

I set off in the direction of Ride N Roll Bar. I hadn't been there yet but I'd spied it on my travels around Loyola Heights, my new *barangay* (neighbourhood). A tricycle pulled up beside me. 'Hey sir, get in,' said a wheezy voice. The driver had an extinguished cigarette slotted into a gap in his teeth.

'I like to walk,' I said, continuing to walk.

He accelerated and drove alongside me at my pace. 'But sir, rain coming.'

I accepted his offer not because of the weather. His line of work was tough and badly paid, and he needed my business. I had to bend almost into foetal position to fit inside the tiny sidecar. As we got going, the driver turned to me and I caught the scent of hard liquor on his breath. He said something, but I didn't catch it for the rumble of the engine.

'I'm sorry?'

'You are coming from Australia or America, my friend?'

'England.'

'Ah, Larry Gorgon!'

'What?'

'I said Larry Gorgon.'

I couldn't fathom who or what Larry Gorgon was. I visualized a Jewish-American comedian with vipers for hair.

'Here in Philippines already you can have many woman, Larry Gorgon. Keep you fit. How many children, sir?'

'None.'

'None? Sorry for you, Larry Gorgon.'

Ride N Roll had sanded floorboards, minimalist furniture and fans' paintings of Yoda, Luke Skywalker and the Death Star from the *Star Wars* films. As I came in, I was approached by a thirtysomething man with a pigtail sticking out the back of a beanie hat. He spoke amphetamine-fast. 'I'm Al. I'm the owner. How are you? Why are you in the Philippines? Is it your first time here? What do you think of Manila?' He didn't give me time to answer any of these questions.

'I'm Tom,' I squeezed in.

'What do you do?'

'I'm a writer.'

'American or Australian?'

'I'm a citizen of the world, Al.'

He peered at me in confusion.

'Okay then, Britain.'

He remained perplexed.

'England.'

'Ah, home of Public Image Ltd?'

'The same.'

'Tom, you should meet another writer, a poet.' He showed me to a table where an intense-looking guy with John Lennon glasses and long hair tied back samurai-style was sitting at a laptop. He wore a T-shirt with a distorted, moddish Union Jack on the front. 'Joel, this is Tom, a writer from England.'

Joel pressed the tips of his fingers together to form a steeple shape. 'Please, please sit down. A beer?'

I pointed at a gold San Miguel sign above the bar. 'I'll have one of those please. It's Spanish, right?'

'Nooo,' said Joel in a hurt tone. 'It is a Filipino company, more than 100 years old. I believe they now brew a version of it in Spain, though.'

'Oh I see. It's what we call a "premium lager" in the UK, which basically means it's more expensive than other beers.'

'Did you know that in 1945, when the Americans were liberating us from the Japanese, they took a huge risk knocking out a machine gun nest opposite the San Miguel brewery just so General MacArthur could safely enter and enjoy a beer?'

'No I didn't.'

'So you come from England,' beamed Joel, lighting a cigarette. 'I would love to go there. A friend of mine has been to Ireland only for a writers' workshop.'

'What did he make of it?'

'*She*. She said they're like Filipinos. They have the same religion, they like singing and they over-drink like us. Tom, do you like a band called Modern English?'

'Can't say I've heard of them.'

Joel scowled. 'They were a great English band of the 1980s, my time. What about The Smiths?'

'I like them, but aren't they a bit parochial? I'm surprised they resonate with Filipinos.'

'You kidding? Morrissey's poetic is universal. Every outsider can appreciate his sentiments. We may not know where "Dublin, Dundee or Humberside" are, but the chorus we can enjoy: "Hang the DJ".' Joel sang a few lines of 'Panic' in a sturdy voice. 'You come from a good country, Tom. You must love being English, no?'

'Not massively. There are some good things – like The Smiths – and some bad things like...' I trailed off. The list was too long. If it hadn't been, I would have stayed. 'So good and bad things, as with anywhere.'

'See, we Filipinos are divided. We are spread across 7,000 islands, all with our disparate cultures and attitudes. We have twenty-one languages too, many with their own literary traditions that go way back. The *Darangen* epic poem of the Manao people in the south is pre-medieval, but nowadays the centre of our literary scene is Manila, where we write either in English or Filipino.'

'How do Filipinos outside of Manila feel about that?'

'Ha! Some are very resentful. They talk about "Manila Imperialism" because it is hard to get published and reviewed unless you come to this city and use its local lingoes. Of course you have no chance of recognition abroad unless you write in English. You could stay it all stems from the 1930s when our government introduced a "national language", Filipino. It was based on Tagalog, which is spoken in and around Manila. This continues to annoy some Visayans, Ilocanos, *Moros* and others in non-Tagalog communities.'

'Can anything be done to reduce this resentment?'

'I think it's important that we unite to find a common identity. This is why I am a nationalist.'

'I get that. You're a new country and you don't have much in your past to be ashamed of... yet. In Britain we still need to answer for our historic crimes: slavery, the empire, Tony Blair.'

Joel pointed a friendly rather than accusatory finger at me. 'You say "our", Tom, but these bad things of the past were not personally your fault.'

I had a flashback to Werner the German exchange student. Perhaps it took perceptive foreigners like he and Joel to force me to think harder about myself and my own culture. 'Exactly,' I said. 'They were done by rulers in the name of ordinary people. The rulers gained from these crimes, the ordinary people didn't.' Al slid another bottle of San Miguel my way. 'Anyway, don't mean to get heavy. We've only just met. Let me buy you another beer.'

'Thanks and no problem, Tom. If you can't have these kinds of discussions at the bar where can you have them? Tell me, can you understand my accent?'

'Yes fine, although I had a problem with the tricycle driver back there. He asked my nationality and then called me "Larry Gorgon". Who is that, do you know?'

Joel laughed like the clatter of a road drill. 'I think he was trying to say "Harry Potter". The only two things most Pinoys – Filipinos – know about England is your Harry Potter and your Mr Bean.'

'I see. Then the driver said something about how I would get many women. Funny, I've never regarded Harry Potter as a sex symbol.'

'Potter is young, smart and well-heeled. But most important of all, he is white. That is what girls – and boys – like here because of the *casta* system.'

That word *casta* stirred a memory of a hierarchical chart I'd found in a Philippine history book back in England. At the top of the chart were the *peninsulares*, those born in Spain who formed the colonial ruling class. The ranks below them were crudely defined by parentage – those born in the Philippines to two 'pure' Spaniards were called *Filipinos* or *insulares*, which made them superior to *tornatrás* (those of mixed Spanish, Chinese and Malay heritage) who, in turn, were a cut above *Sangleys* (100 per cent Chinese ancestry). At the bottom of the pile were indigenous *indios* (Christianized native Malays) and *negritos*, meaning 'little black people' in Spanish.

'*Casta* is still an issue in the Philippines?' I asked Joel.

'I would say yes. Nowadays if you are quite dark and you stroll around Manila, you may get a rich person come up to you and ask, "Are you for hire?" They will assume you are a lowly domestic servant.'

'So race is bound up with class.'

'Tom, can I ask you: what is Britain in relation to the UK, England and Ireland? It puzzles me.'

'We can blame history for that. Today the legally recognized state is the United Kingdom of Great Britain and Northern Ireland.'

Joel frowned. 'Strange. My friend said the Irish were fiercely proud of their independence.'

'That's because she went to Southern Ireland. All of Ireland was a British colony for centuries and when the south declared independence we – well, the rulers of Britain – hung on to the north because a majority there remained loyal to Britain. It didn't stop the loyalist Protestants mistreating the nationalist Catholics in the north.'

'Which is why the terrorism started?'

'Yes. So Great Britain is the island comprising England – where I come from – Scotland and Wales. Britain without the "Great" is just England and Wales. When we add Northern Ireland we use the term the United Kingdom or UK.'

'I understand,' Joel said in a wavering tone that suggested that he didn't fully. He was right not to – I couldn't think of another country so small whose administrative structure was so needlessly Byzantine.

'Great Britain and the United Kingdom are, I'd say, artificial constructs. I mean, most Welsh people don't feel British, they feel Welsh, if they feel anything. Most Scots are Scots first, British second. And then British liberals and leftists aren't the least bit interested in calling themselves British, English or anything else. In fact, the British people who are proudest of being British tend to live in Spain, which makes you question the validity of the whole set-up. The only beneficiaries of the set-up are the powerful who have cultivated the idea of Britishness for their own ends. You know, the British Empire, British values, British war heroism etc.'

'Hegemony,' said Joel.

'It has nothing to do with gardening,' I said, hoping he'd get the feeble pun. He did, and drilled with laughter once more. He then ordered some food. I was surprised when Al brought us platters of spam, black pudding, hog roast and pork scratchings.

'You've tried this?' Joel squirted a polythene bag of vinegar over the little spindles of pig skin.

'It's a traditional English pub snack,' I said.

'How traditional?'

I didn't want to speculate. Lots of things the British consider traditional are modern inventions, like Great Britain itself, which only started in 1707. The same can be said for everything from Morris dancing (whose rules were only formalized in 1899) to the ploughman's lunch (devised to boost cheese sales after World War II).

'You want some, Tom?'

'Thanks, I've already eaten. Actually, all this stuff reminds me of English fare.'

'Then here is more common ground between England and the Philippines. *Wasak!*'

'What does *wasak* mean?'

'It literally means "destroy", but we use it as a slang superlative like "amazing" or "cool".' He looked past me over to the door of Ride N Roll. 'Oh. Coach Jay, my colleague at the university where I teach, is here with some of his athlete buddies. Do you mind if they join us? They are a bit *testosterone*, if you catch my drift?'

Jay had a hefty, rectangular head with a marine corps crew-cut. With him was a lanky youth called Toto and a flabby fifty-year-old wearing a prayer cap, whom Jay introduced simply as a member of the Muslim royal family of Mindanao, an island in the southern Philippines. They were all dressed in tracksuits.

'Let's get some fuckin' brews,' said the royal. Unexpectedly, he had the nasally Midwestern American voice of a jock from a 1980s Brat Pack movie, picked up so I would later learn from a basketball scholarship to the University of Minnesota. He ordered Red Horse – the harshest and strongest of all the beer I've come across in the Philippines. Without so much as a hello, he asked me if I was from Australia or the US.

'England,' I sighed.

'England? But you sound more British to me.'

'England is *in* Britain.'

'How the fuck does that work?'

I explained exactly what I'd explained to Joel just ten minutes ago.

'They all got their own soccer teams, England, Wales, Scotland and shit. I saw it on ESPN.'

'They do.'

'But they ain't independent states? They are all part of *this* United Kingdom?'

His cronies chuckled. Joel picked at the label on his beer bottle.

'Yes.'

'And you have a queen not a king, and it's called a kingdom?'

'Yes.'

'But it's a piss-small country. Why divide it into smaller fuckin' pieces like that?'

More giggles. I was feeling hectored – and for trying to explain something I didn't even agree with. Would the royal be just as willing to mock the historical accident of the Philippines being composed of thousands of contrasting islands? I thought not.

'Do you really talk like that?' said the royal.

'What do you mean?'

'Like you're talking now. Are you doing a funny voice *now*?'

'No, this is my normal voice. This is how I speak.'

'Fucked up, man. I only heard that kinda accent before in *Lord of the Rings*. I thought you UK English people spoke like Americans and that you just made up that accent for the movies.'

'Here's what I like about England,' cut in Jay. 'At college we used to get drunk and watch your *Monty Python's Life of Brian*. That bit where they're all getting crucified. Oh man, that still cracks me up.'

'No,' said the royal through a burp. 'That's gay shit, that is.'

'How's that?' sneered Jay.

'All their stuff in England is gay.'

'Thanks Your Highness,' I said through gritted teeth.

'Welcome,' he said through another burp. 'Like that soccer we was just talkin' about.'

'I don't think so,' said Jay. 'Those soccer guys are top athletes.'

'I saw somethin' else English on ESPN. Cricket or somethin'?'

'You hit a ball through a hoop on the ground,' said Toto.

'No, that's croquet,' I said.

Jay's eyes sparked with recognition. 'I know, *I* saw that on ESPN, too!' He got to his feet and waddled like a penguin while hurling his arms about in Pete Townsend windmill fashion. This was his impression of bowling.

'That really is the gayest sport in the whole wide world,' slurred the royal.

'So how long does a cricket game last?' asked Jay.

'Five days sometimes,' I said.

'What, twenty-four-hours a day for five days? Or you have time-outs?'

'They take breaks for lunch and afternoon tea.'

The royal banged his hands against his temples. 'Afternoon tea? Now that *is* gay.'

'Anyway guys,' said Joel, bolting to his feet and offering his steeple gesture. 'Great to see you all. I am afraid Tom and I must go now. Goodbye and *matutulog na ako.*' Joel nodded at me and then changed the direction of his nod towards the door.

The royal tutted and waved to us patronizingly.

When we were outside Joel turned to face me. He was blushing. 'I think you need to learn some Filipino, Tom. Repeat after me. *Putang ina mo.*'

'*Putahn in a more.*'

'It's an *ang* sound. *Putang ina mo.*'

'*Putang in a more.*'

'No it's *mo. Mo.*'

'*Putang ina mo.*'

'Perfect.'

'Now I know some Filipino,' I grinned. 'What's it mean?'

'Your mother is a whore.'

'Steady on, Joel, I thought we were friends.'

'No, no, this is the worst thing you can say to a Filipino. You should say it when you meet guys like that. Homophobic snob assholes every last one of them.'

I found this hard to swallow. He'd been almost monastically meek while these 'assholes' had been dishing out abuse. Yet as soon as we were away from them, he'd unleashed his fury. 'So why didn't you say that to them back there?'

'Not worth the stress, my friend. You will learn this about my country while I learn more about yours. See you tomorrow night?'

'Maybe. As long as His Royal Highness isn't there again.'

When I got home, I sat down in front of my unfinished column and had an intoxicated revelation. To avoid going daft with boredom writing about fish pedicure for *Quill*, from now on I'd pitch other stories about social and political issues to the appropriate magazines here and abroad. There wasn't anything in my contract with *Quill* to prevent that.

5. RED IS GREEN

Since before moving to Manila, I'd been a fan of the work of Renato Constantino, a Marxist historian whose magnum opus, *A History of the Philippines* (1975), I thought a fine literary achievement. In the materialist mode, it explains the economic and ideological determinants of key events in Philippine history from Spanish colonization to Japanese occupation in lucid, elegant and rousing prose. Constantino died in 1999, so I wouldn't get an interview with him now. However, I discovered that the Constantinos had become something of a radical political dynasty and that Renato's grandson, Red, was very much alive. He was an environmentalist who'd set up a fleet of electric-powered jeepney buses intended to address Manila's chronic pollution problem. I'd approached *Red Pepper*, a political magazine in London, and they'd commissioned me to interview him.

I travelled to Fred's Revolucion, Red's flamboyant, Marxism-themed bar in the district of Cubao. Affable and baseball-capped, Red invited me to sit down at the bar with him, posters of Lenin and Che Guevara looking down on us.

'You launched your fleet in 2007,' I said. 'Has it been successful?'

'Depends on how you define "success"! In Manila we plug our jeepneys into the mains and the moment you use electricity you reduce emissions. We're ultimately aiming for self-sufficiency by using an anaerobic biodigester which will turn waste into energy. So as the city grows, so does the waste it produces and hopefully so does our fleet. In Tacloban City, we energize our fleet with a solar-powered system and a geothermal-powered grid for back-up.'

'How did you get the idea for the project?'

'After years working for policy and political change for organizations like Greenpeace, I wanted to do something more concrete and practical. We chose jeepneys because they're iconic in the Philippines and help working-class people get around. We're not interested in demonstration schemes – we make alternative transport commercially feasible and technically. The point of our fleet is to set an example so others can come in and do similar things to us, if not better. Then together we can improve the environment.'

'Would you say you were an ethical employer?'

'Our jeepney drivers are unique in the entire country because they get a fair salary, work reasonable hours and receive housing, pension and health benefits. 99.9 per cent of other drivers in the Philippines lease their vehicle for a set amount like 1000 pesos a day. Once the driver has paid off the 1000, he can keep the excess for himself. It's a bad scheme that compels drivers to work crazy hours and break all the traffic rules by picking up and disgorging passengers from any part of the road just so they can earn what they need.'

'Have you come into conflict with vested business interests? I'm thinking particularly of big oil.'

'Not yet. We're focusing on the public transport sector and currently pose no threat to fossil companies. Anyway, our challenge to big business is this: if you really believe in going green then stop the corporate social responsibility nonsense and go to your shareholders with longer term plans. Ramp up operational efficiencies, buy an assembly line and make bazillions out of it. If, for instance, you're Jollibee [the Philippines' largest fast food chain], use electric vehicles for your entire home delivery service.'

'What does the Filipino left make of your advocating reform of capitalism by calling for companies to get greener?'

'Some on the left take a Ché Guevara pose and call for the overthrow the oil companies in ways that are ultimately safe to the system. The system can easily absorb rhetoric and protests that don't demonstrate to people that alternatives are possible or which don't undermine the basic tenets of the set-up.'

'I notice you have pictures of Ché Guevara and Lenin on your wall.'

'Ah, but look closely at the picture of Lenin and you'll see that he has a little Angry Bird – from the computer game – on his forehead.

We like to have fun here and it keeps away the boring, humourless revolutionaries. The problem with large sections of the left now is that they ignore the relationship between ecology, the economy and class.

'Historical materialism – the Marxist method – has always been about ecology. Marx argued that the environment is the basis upon which all economies are run and that the metabolism of nature is in conflict with the metabolism of capital. That remains a powerful analysis, I think.'

'But some Marxists would argue that the solution is revolution rather than working within existing power structures.'

'You need to create the conditions for revolution. Our jeepneys are part of a wider initiative to reorganize local economies so that they can grow and produce and meet workers' needs. All the technologies for achieving this exist right now. The challenge is in application. But some on the left look unfavourably on this.'

'They see it as reformist?'

'Who the fuck cares whether it's reformist or revolutionary? Are we still waiting for the thunderclap, the revolution around the corner? This waiting is an excuse to do nothing and that's dangerous because, unlike national liberation or human rights, the fight against climate change has a deadline. There's no stopping it completely, but we can act to reduce the amount of chaos it will cause when it comes. And it will come.'

6. PANIC IN THE SI-MALL-ATION

Robinsons Galeria mall's south-facing wall was stippled with brand names inviting punters to thrilling experiences within: Toys 'R' Us, Robinsons Cinemas and – to my mild amusement – a place called Tom's World. I waited at a double door while a pistol-packing female security guard with a hygiene mask hanging from a broken nose dipped her truncheon into my backpack. She found no jihadist bombs and let me in.

Inside I met Joel, who'd trimmed his samurai locks down to a short back and sides and was sans his specs, and his four-year-old daughter Jenilyn, who wore a brace on her teeth and plaits in her hair.

'Oi oi, mush,' he said, giving me a firm handshake. 'What do you want to do then?'

'When I'm in Britain,' I said, 'I'd rather put my head under a steamroller than go to a shopping mall, but I feel like so much of Philippine life happens in these places that I ought to investigate further.'

'All in the interests of research, mate,' winked Joel. 'Then we can get trolleyed after, yeah?'

We entered Tom's World, a simulation of an American funfair – or, more accurately, a simulation based on a Filipino's idea of an American funfair replete with mini-basketball games, machines that command you to twerk and a selection of luminous-hued foodstuffs that will shorten your life. As befits good ol' American capitalism, you spend a fortune on the attractions, winning – if you're lucky – tickets that can be traded in for prizes, except that it takes at least two hours – and thousands of pesos – before you've earned enough tickets for a measly pencil eraser that, while it bears the face of an American cartoon character, has probably been manufactured in China by children Jenilyn's age and for a fraction of the money you've spent on trying to win it.

Anyway, I swallowed my scepticism and joined in with my companions. We whooped at our abject failure to throw the little basketballs into the little hoops. I ordered a pus-coloured soda while Joel and Jenilyn went into the kids-only Austin Land, a world-within-Tom's World whose scaled-down model dogs, cats, bridges, roundabouts and swimming pools were all made from spongy plastic, as if designed for criminally insane people who might do themselves or others harm if exposed to sharp or hard objects. The asylum analogy was validated by yet another armed guard – a real one – patrolling the rubbery approximation of a picket fence that encircled all Austin Land.

While Jenilyn frolicked and Joel oversaw her, I read my battered old book, *United States Colonies and Dependencies Illustrated* by the American newspaper tycoon William D. Boyce. I found out that simulations had been around a while in Manila. Writing in 1914 at the height of US colonial control, Boyce is thrilled that the swanky boulevard of Calle Escolta was a little slice of Manhattan in the Orient: 'The Broadway of Manila ... has motion-picture shows galore and a light opera company from England twice a year.' Furthermore, the chocolate ice-cream sodas vended on Calle Escolta were so authentic that one US sailor couldn't resist drinking five in a row while on shore leave. Perhaps twenty-first-century Tom's World was a logical evolution from Edwardian Escolta. The distinction was that Escolta was designed to sate the desire of American expats for American products while Tom's World was designed to sate Filipinos indoctrinated to desire American products.

As I read on, Boyce's zest for Yankeefied Manila faltered. His nag that 'the market is full of good things to eat', but that the problem is 'poor cooking and poor service', implied defects in the copy. Maybe it was too much for a staunch Western supremacist to accept that his beloved homeland could ever fully and wholly be grafted on to the shadowy Orient. Boyce's doubts, printed a century ago, aroused doubts in me, right now in 2010, about the closeness of Tom's World to some 'original' theme park in Boston or Baton Rouge. If the prizes on offer here were made in China how much of the squishy topography of Austin Land – a reference to Austin, Texas? – was also manufactured outside the US? And how many of the apparently all-American arcade games – from Iraq-sited, first-person shoot 'em ups to recreations of illicit drag races on the streets of Miami – were in fact created in Japan and South Korea, nations with their own histories of US victimization? Might, therefore, an electronic reproduction of a classic American activity – whether machine-gunning Arabs or driving dangerously fast – devised by a Japanese and then exported to the Philippines count as a simulation of a simulation of a simulation?

As my head started to hurt, Jenilyn skipped over, Joel following. 'I'm hungry,' she panted. '*Star Wars!*' She pointed to an eatery across the floor called the Sci-Fi Café. Its windows were decked with *Star Wars*, *Batman*, *Terminator*, *Alien* and *Ghostbusters* memorabilia. We sat opposite some students trying on Storm Trooper helmets while one of the *Lord of the Rings* films clanged, roared and whooshed from a flatscreen above our heads. The punning menu added to the ambience. After mulling over 'The Chickenator', subtitled 'fried chicken and Java rice guaranteed to have you saying "I'll be back"', I plumped for 'Planet of the Shrimps'. Jenilyn and Joel both ordered 'Jabba the Hot Dog'. While we munched I made eye contact with the denizens of this otherworld: the blue flashing headlight of a 1:1 scale model R2D2, the loony gander of a suitcase-sized Joker based on Jack Nicholson's rather than Heath Ledger's portrayal and the steel-framed squint of a ragdoll Major Toht, the Gestapo antagonist of *Raiders of the Lost Ark*.

Jenilyn dropped the remains of Jabba onto her plate and started swinging her legs under the table. 'Bit creepy here,' she whispered. 'Isn't it?'

'Agreed,' I said.

We took another taxi up the road to Shangri-La Plaza, a classier mall with a chichi five-star hotel protruding from it like the pot belly of an executive, the sort of executive who might stay in such a hotel, indeed. Though Jenilyn was tired, Joel needed groceries from Rustan's Supermarket. To get there we had to negotiate a labyrinth of peculiar amenities.

A corrective to Tom's World and the Sci-Fi Café, the food court conveyed a romantic idea of rustic Philippines: baby palm trees, garden furniture, watercolour illustrations of *lechons* (suckling pigs) on spits, waiting staff in *barong tagalogs* (traditional embroidered shirts) and Maria Clara dresses. TVs showed slo-mo parochial food porn – an exquisite-looking woman in pre-Hispanic headgear at a rural *fiesta* tearing tender pork off the bone and pouring silky eggs into sizzling noodles.

And the puns kept coming. Oriental Seoul, Manilachon (a conflation of Manila and *lechon*), Serious Dough (pizza), Karate Kid (Japanese food) and Sisig Hooray! (*Sisig* is fried pig's head and liver.)

As we took each escalator up each gigantic floor, I noticed that Jenilyn – who, Joel had told me, was just starting to read and write – was as transfixed by the names as I was. She double-took at a supermarket called Payless. 'Dad, is that where you don't pay no money at all?'

It was a fair question. 'Payless' could have meant 'pay-less' as in no payment required, but it was unlikely – we were deep inside the overactive guts of a neo-liberal tiger economy, not outside a food bank in Britain. 'I think they're trying to say that customers pay a little less for things,' said Joel.

There was potentially a whole episode of *Boardwalk Empire* in the sign that read 'Capone's Dental Health Shop'. The Sugarhouse Bakery was refreshingly honest about the unhealthy nature of its products. The same could be said for The Marlboro Shop, which brazenly vended every smoking accoutrement conceivable plus T-shirts celebrating the brand. A laundromat called Lord of the Rinse was just, well, brilliant. Why a bar specializing in foreign beers was called Smoky Bastard, I couldn't fathom. I assumed Beyond Ablution Massage was so-called in case punters got the idea it offered services of a less holy sort.

We passed boutiques vending everything from pump-action shotguns to bubble tea, drum kits to self-help guides, French bread to Japanese robot dogs. Three times we were assailed by more gorgeous women – trouser-suited and *mesa*-breasted – pressing us to put down a deposit on a yet-to-be-built deluxe apartment. They'd gesture to a table top scale model of the proposed condo. It looked to me like the dioramas I used to play toy soldiers on when I was Jenilyn's age.

One floor housed a medical-themed mall-inside-the-mall. On either side of its glacé-tiled corridors were petite booths where you could get an FMRi brain scan, your blood pressure checked, your bones X-rayed or *Fear and Loathing in Las Vegas* quantities of drugs, albeit pharmaceutical ones. GET YOUR FLU SHOT NOW!!! a poster instructed. Why had an optician's outlet been named 'The American Eye Centre'? Perhaps if you put the word 'American' into a title people will trust it. The same principle might apply to 'Irish' pubs and 'French' restaurants.

So far, so intriguing. But then I made the mistake of fixing on the shoppers and my mood wilted. A slim granny on a bench trowelling *halo-halo* dessert into her mouth, beans and coconut shavings stuck to her chin. A baffled family of four clinging to an overflowing shopping trolley forced stationary by a broken wheel. Nuns in full habit around a Formica lunch table, eyes latched to phones, teeth nibbling on wraps. A bevy of toddlers staring hushed at the spasms of an automated massage chair. A glamorous teenaged couple – her with her hands around his torso, him oblivious to her, tapping away at a tablet. I thought of a quote from Iain Sinclair about J.G. Ballard's last novel *Kingdom Come*, partly set in a shopping mall: 'We've gone insane in a way that leaves us in a tranquilized, robotic state. The future is boredom reaching the point when it has to be rescued by terror.'

The people around us certainly looked tranquilized and robotic. Was terror imminent? I thought of a short story called 'Aviary' by Lysley Tenorio about homeless kids who gatecrash Greenbelt Mall in Makati – the homeless are banned from malls in the Philippines as they are in Britain – and vandalize shops and restaurants as a form of class revenge. Then I recalled the geographer David Harvey's research into grand architectural projects from the suburbanization of American cities after World War II to the reinvention of nineteenth-century Paris as a 'city of light' of roomy boulevards and fragrant lakes. The down side is that these projects are vulnerable to capitalism's quirks. Boom and bust. What goes up must come down. The dream of a new Paris crumbled in 1868 under the weight of over-speculation. A century later, America slumped and uprisings ripped up its cities.

I grew anxious. Was Shangrila Plaza another grand project ready for an uprising? My throat dried. My breathing went irregular. I had a stinging in my nose like I'd eaten too much mustard. 'Joel,' I drawled. 'We need to... we should leave now.'

'What's wrong, mate?'

'Just feeling quite... ill.'

'Sure, we'll get the groceries later,' he said and turned on his heel to head back the way we'd come.

As soon as we get out of this place, I hissed to myself, I'll know whether this is a panic attack or a revolution. I'm all for revolutions, just not ones that might hurt me.

On the escalators down, Joel and Jenilyn remained rapt by the signs and symbols while I took breaths through my nose and expelled them from my mouth. As we exited through the double doors, a man in a balaclava and biker's leathers strode towards us. Is this it? I thought. Will he brandish a Kalashnikov and declare class war on the *Manileño* bourgeoisie? Should I start begging now? Tell him that, while I broadly agree with his political attitudes, I'm not sure machine-gunning people shopping for three-piece suites is the best route to emancipation?

No, instead he removed his balaclava and patted Jenilyn on the head. 'Hey there Tinkerbell,' he said in a sing-song voice, 'where is Peter Pan?'

7. WE NEED A HERO

In the Rizal Shrine, once the swanky *bahay na bato* (stone house) home of José Rizal, national hero of the Philippines, I got on my tiptoes to see over the spectators who'd linked hands to form a bastion around the hardwood-framed window. I could now spot the José Rizal Day crowd below in José Rizal Street, chanting 'José Rizal! José Rizal!', banners bobbing with José Rizal's portrait on them. The signature defiant eyes, fine-line moustache and wavy side-parting form an image that's as important to Filipinos as Che Guevara's was to Western students in the sixties.

Some of the crowd were mimicking Rizal by donning black fedoras, white shirts and black waistcoats. Others carried a colossal PVC model of Rizal's head, glossy and stylized like a fast food mascot – more Colonel Sanders than Captain-General Bolívar.

I stepped back from the window. I've never been one for cults of personality or for merging with hundreds of bodies, but I had to suffer it for my art – Deirdre wanted a touristic piece for *Quill* and I wanted to explore Rizal's political significance today for a website back in the UK.

To deserve this much attention 120 years after your death you have to be remarkable. And Rizal *was* remarkable. He travelled widely, practised ophthalmology, wrote successful novels (as a student he won first prize in a Spanish-language writing competition ahead of dozens of Spanish entrants), was well-versed in Western philosophy, knew twenty-two languages (he translated Hans Christian Andersen into Tagalog) and was the leading orator of the Propaganda Movement that peacefully agitated for concessions from the Spanish state, amongst them free speech, secular education, equality under the law for Filipinos and Spaniards, and the right to send elected representatives to the Spanish parliament. It's one of the less funny ironies of Philippine history that Rizal, who was committed to nonviolence, was publicly executed by the Spanish in 1896 on fake charges of fomenting a putsch. His death wasn't in vain – it inspired the first ever anti-colonial revolution against a European empire in Asia.

Rizal is central to Filipino culture. His face is on the money, hundreds of roads and landmarks are named after him, and his novels *Noli Me Tangere* (*Touch Me Not*, 1887) and *El Filibusterismo* (*The Reign of Greed*, 1891) are set texts in schools and colleges.

I felt a tap on my shoulder. It was Gary, who sits on the management committee of the Rizal Shrine. He wore a long-sleeved T-shirt emblazoned with I MIGHT NOT BE GOD BUT I'M SOMETHING SIMILAR. Next to him was a gnomish old woman all in white with a sedate – perhaps sedated – beam on her face.

'Hello Sir Tom,' said Gary. I was still getting used to this honorific. Where I came from, the only men who earned the right to put 'Sir' in front of their names were geriatric thespians, slippery business leaders and washed-out parliamentarians who spent their days asleep on the back benches. However, here in the Philippines 'Sir' was a form of address that conveyed respect towards anyone who might deserve or warrant it. As Clark Lee, an American war correspondent stationed in Manila in 1941-2, discovered, the 'frequent use of the word "sir"' was less a 'symbol of servility' and more 'a hold-over from the polite Spanish "señor"'.

Gary introduced me to Mrs Bigay. 'She is one of the *Rizalistas* you asked for,' he said. 'She is the one who prefers to talk in Bicol language. I will translate for you, if you will accompany us to my office?'

Mrs Bigay told me she was born into the *Rizalista* faith – others call it a cult – soon after its founding in 1936. Since then she'd travelled every year from Bicol to attend Rizal Day here in Calamba, thirty miles south of Metro Manila. A month ago she'd been diagnosed with a heart condition, but her doctor had let her attend this year's festivities.

'How exactly do you worship Rizal?' I asked.

'I have a shrine in my home with an etching of him next to an altar for Jesus. His teachings are similar to the Christ's. When I have a problem I make a wish to Rizal and he usually grants it. We *Rizalistas* wear white because we must express our purity within on the outside.'

'What are Rizal's values?'

'The Ten Commandments of Rizal are the same as the Bible's. He is also for defending our nation and against injustice, especially towards women. Rizal was the second son of God after Jesus. He was a miracle worker or how else could he have known so many languages and healed the sick?'

'Is it acceptable to be married more than once, as Rizal was?'

'That is propaganda. He had only one wife, Josephine Bracken. There is a song to this effect.'

'How many *Rizalistas* are there in Bicol?'

'More than 1,000. There are followers in seven provinces.'

Mrs Bigay went on to tell me that non-*Rizalistas* have called her *wasiwas* (crazy) and likened her to a flag, loose and wild in the wind. 'We may get bullied,' she said, 'but the government accepts us as a genuine religion.'

'Where is Rizal now?'

'He is still alive somewhere.' She closed her eyes, perhaps in prayer.

I was tempted to get her take on the urban legends about Rizal. The most sensational one is that he was Jack the Ripper, although the proof is circumstantial at best. His stay in London coincided with the Whitechapel murders and his medical training meant he'd be capable of carving the prostitutes up in that notoriously methodical way. Mr Ripper was purportedly a ladies' man, as was Rizal. And finally, the killings ceased around the time Rizal moved on to France.

More insulting is the allegation that Rizal was Adolf Hitler's dad. Again, the evidence is sketchy. While studying in Heidelberg in 1888, so the story goes, Rizal bedded Austrian chambermaid Klara Pölzl and she bore a child who grew up not exactly to follow in his father's footsteps – Hitler, of course, was more interested in slaying than liberating marginal groups and his berserk bid for world domination was rather different to Rizal's moderate campaign for a freer Philippines. Be that as it may, the legend-spinners cling to the observation that both men had dark eyes and side-partings. A fair sum of men between the 1860s and the 1940s had dark eyes and side-partings, but that doesn't mean they were all blood related. Supposedly, another shared trait is short stature. Not true: Hitler was five foot nine and Rizal five foot two, meaning that both men were above average for their time and ethnicity.

Before bidding me farewell, Mrs Bigay said to me through Gary, 'Watch for Rizal, he will make himself known to you and us all someday.'

I pushed to the front of the crowd. Men and women with Calamba Rotary Club ID cards round their necks carried a twelve foot-tall bronze effigy of Rizal. The rosettes of orchids affixed to his stomach were redolent of the Christian saviour.

Rizal's deification – and the fusion of alternative religion with political revolt it involves – is nothing new in the Philippines. In 1622, Tamblot, a native priest from Bohol, was visited by a *diwata* (pagan goddess) who advised him to quit Catholicism and erect a temple in her honour in the hills. She promised that he and his flock would be freed from paying tributes to the Spanish if they burnt down churches, desecrated images of the Madonna with spears and assaulted Spanish officials with rocks, crossbow quarrels and sharpened sticks. It took 1,000 troops to quell the insurrection.

Four decades later, a man called Tapar from the wedge-shaped isle of Panay was told by a demon that if he took up arms against the colonial administration, the mountains would come to life and aid his struggle. Any casualty on the rebel side, the demon continued, would be resurrected and Spanish musket balls would turn in the air like boomerangs and strike Spanish soldiers instead of Tapar's followers. Tapar established a shadow church, appointing himself God and three of his followers Christ, the Holy Ghost and the Virgin Mary. None of the demon's promises came to fruition and Tapar was put to death after some in his cult stabbed a Spanish friar.

In 1762, while Manila was under occupation by the Royal Navy, Diego Silang declared himself 'Christ's *cabo* mayor' and led an insurrection in the town of Vigan. He wanted the Church to devolve power to the indigenes. Although he convinced the British to make him Governor of the Ilocos provinces, they wouldn't support him militarily against the Spanish. He was assassinated by a close friend whom the Church bribed to betray him.

Such insurgencies show how, across Philippine history, mainstream Christianity has generally been on the side of the powerful, justifying the political status quo as God's infallible will, above and beyond rational scrutiny. The epitome of this process was the 333-year-long Spanish 'friarocracy'. By the time of the US occupation, Father Gregorio Aglipay had founded an independent, Filipinized Church out of solidarity with the anti-Spanish revolution and as a direct challenge to the pre-eminence of the friars. However, according to Luis H. Francia, the established Church supported the Americans' decision to sell 160,000 hectares of friar-owned estates to 'wealthy elite families and a few corporations' rather than 'to those who most needed them'. Since independence, Church leaders have largely backed the government of the day, with the exception of the 1970s when a small group of bishops came out against Martial Law. Today, as the investigative journalist Aries C. Rufo has revealed, the Philippine Church has arguably more influence over politics than ever, and is embroiled in numerous graft and sexual abuse scandals.

The throng swelled and I got claustrophobic. As I pushed my way through the bodies, I had the unsettling conjecture that I was amongst a herd of conformists all blindly believing the same thing: the fundamental, unassailable merits of one human being.

But not every Filipino lionizes Rizal. As the historiographer Reynaldo Ileto avers, Rizal was co-opted by the American colonizers as the 'correct' national idol for the Philippines. He was the politically expedient choice because he didn't live long enough to oppose the US and his sticky end confirmed American convictions that the Spanish Empire was so degenerate that it had to be usurped by a kinder, gentler power such as... the US. Rizal also favoured a slow, gradualist approach to independence, which suited American rhetoric about one day equipping Filipinos to rule themselves. The problem was that while the Americans were saying this, they were helping themselves to the Philippines' resources, imposing an American-style education system, introducing American English as the lingua franca and locking up anyone who had the cheek to demand self-determination. What the Americans bleeped out – or didn't know – was that Rizal had been less than fawning about their country when he'd been there in 1888: 'America is undoubtedly a great country, but she has many defects.' He also protested the quarantining of passengers on the boat he arrived on because the port authorities had falsely declared that a cholera epidemic was raging in Asia. This was a ruse to stop Chinese and Japanese immigrants disembarking. While Rizal commended the US for its quality of life and industrial progress, he abhorred its veneration of money and its subjugation of minorities: '[It] is the land par excellence of freedom but only for the whites.'

The recuperation of Rizal flouts the fact that, in his lifetime, he was chided for being soft on colonialism by other nationalists like Andrés Bonifacio and Emilio Aguinaldo, who preferred the armed route to liberation. For this reason, neither Bonifacio nor Aguinaldo could ever be the right kind of champion for the Americans.

Aguinaldo is as contradictory a figure as Rizal. A talented general, he led the resistance against the Spanish – whose army he beat on land while the US Navy routed their fleet at sea – and then, when the Americans had gone back on their word to grant Philippine independence after the Spanish had yielded, he took on the US – and lost. But as his correspondence shows, he would have laid down his guns in exchange for the Philippines becoming an American protectorate inside which his own *ilustrado* class would retain its supremacy. Indeed, his declaration of independence on 12 June 1898 was modelled on that of the US in 1789, except that it was prefaced with, 'Under the protection of the Mighty and Humane North American Nation, we proclaim and solemnly declare...'

Had the Americans negotiated, they'd have got their foothold in Southeast Asia, no blood spilled. They might then have canonized

Aguinaldo instead of Rizal as the figurehead of the new, free-but-not-actually-free Philippines. Not all Filipinos would have cheered that. Some had seen Aguinaldo as a sell-out ever since December 1897 – this being before the US entered the conflict – when he'd accepted 400,000 pesos from the Spanish Governor to go into exile in Hong Kong. Later, his Machiavellian amorality would again dent his chances of national sainthood, even if it saved his neck a few times. After he surrendered in 1901, the Americans spared his life in return for his allegiance, When the Japanese marched into the Philippines in 1942, he swore allegiance to them too. After the war, he was forgiven for collaborating and lived to ninety-four.

What could I take away from all this about Rizal, Aguinaldo and iconography? Hero worship is silly and usually predicated on a fiction? Ideas like *nation*, *nationalism* and *national hero* are highly ambiguous? As Renato Constantino writes, Rizal, Aguinaldo and the other bourgeois *ilustrados* had a narrow conception of nationalism. Their struggle was not for the liberty and equality of *all* Filipinos at *all* levels of society. No, Aguinaldo was a snob who wanted his country run exclusively by wealthy gentlemen like him. And, as we've seen since the Philippines achieved formal self-determination in 1946, the *national interest* might be more accurately described as the interests of a native elite in league with the elites of the US and other moneyed nations exercising undue sway over the Philippine polity and economy. Not so nationalistic then.

The sun was high now. I felt like my face and arms were being cauterized. I finally got through the crowd and entered the car park behind the Rizal Shrine. I saw a trio of student-age lads all wearing T-shirts with Rizal's face rendered in photographic negative style against the red, white, blue and golden sun design of the Philippine flag. One of them said something to me in Filipino.

'I'm sorry?' I said, mopping my brow with a tissue.

The other two laughed and slapped their foreheads. The guy said something else in Filipino. More mirth from the other two. It was unusual for Filipinos to address a Westerner in Filipino and then mock him for not comprehending. What was this about? My breaching of the consensus by not dressing up like Rizal or having his image on my apparel? My being a foreigner, pure and simple?

As I got into the car, I tried to repress my irritation. If only those kids knew that I was a foreigner with a relatively sympathetic take on their country. If only they knew that I broadly shared their politics, assuming that, like other Filipinos, their nationalism went hand-in-hand with leftist ethics. But if I could somehow make them know any of this would it make any difference? They might just be bigots.

8. ANIMAL AVENUE

There are many good reasons to walk. It's the freest form of transport and not just in the sense that it costs nothing. When you walk, you're freed up to see more of the world thanks to a degree of peripheral vision not available through the narrow frames of car or plane windows. When you walk, you have more control over your own pace. You can pause for as long as you like without fear of being whisked to the next destination by your pilot or driver. It's also easier to interact with your environment when you're on foot. When in a private car or on public transport you can only get so close to passers-by you want to talk to or places you wish to explore.

As walkers, we're free to go wherever our legs can take us. We're unrestricted by roads, train tracks, flight paths or other routes imposed on us. For the Situationist intellectuals of the 1960s, walking in random directions (they called it the *dérive*) across Paris was a political act. Napoleon I had built the *grand boulevards* of that city wide enough so that the army could be mobilized against revolt, and the Situationists thought that aimless wandering could subvert such oppressive urban planning. More ambitiously, they held that the anarchic spontaneity of the *dérive* could chip away at the logic of capitalism, based as it is on obedience, banality and conformity.

Coming from a similar if less militant angle, the Filipina travel writer Rechilda P. Manahan claims that roaming the streets of Manila is a desirable alternative to the only kind of roaming the Filipino middle classes are used to: from shop to shop. 'I felt a real concern,' she writes, 'for a generation which was being shaped in the consumerist culture of the mall, completely oblivious to the rest of reality.' According to Jaime C. Laya, who wrote the introduction to Manahan's account of peregrinating around the capital's historic sites, *Street-Bound: Manila on Foot*, walking was *de rigueur* for all classes of *Manileños* just a century ago, from the gentry promenading along the seaside Malecon Drive (now Bonifacio Drive) to the paupers using their feet because they couldn't afford cars or horses.

However, there's one glitch in what I've just argued about the freedom of the walker: the presence of too many damn cars. When I stepped on to Katipunan Avenue one lunchtime, these natural enemies of pedestrians everywhere stalked me from all directions, their engines rumbling like the bellies of famished predators, their bumpers shining like flesh-tearing teeth. Had Charles Darwin lived long enough to visit twenty-first -century Manila, he may have studied Katipunan as a day-and-night arena for lethal competition between diverse species of vehicle and pedestrian. The latter is very much the prey. When trying to cross the road you're at the mercy of elephantine SUVs. You can only hope they'll slow down in time and flash their beady eye-lights, a signal that gives you permission to flee from them. The pedestrian must defer to the motorist because *he* – and it usually is a he – is king of the jungle, the first in the food chain. When he's taking an age to reverse out of a tricky corner you must wait for him. When you step into his path, he has the evolutionary boon of a thunderous horn to scare you off. And an adaptive trait that no walker has a chance of withstanding is the menace of Sudden Unintended Acceleration (SUA), wherein Mitsubishi sports cars abruptly shunt forward from a standstill position and run over bystanders. While no-one is sure whether a design flaw makes the cars accelerate of their own volition or whether it's the fault of the driver treading on the wrong pedal, there's no debate about the fact that, according to CNN Philippines, nineteen Filipino pedestrians have thus far died from SUA.

Throughout my time living behind Katipunan, I masochistically scanned the news for recent tussles in this survival of the fastest. A massive pile-up had demolished several cars and a trendy café. An official of the National Prosecutors' League had ploughed into two teenagers, killing them instantly. A street kid had been squashed by a yuppie reversing his Toyota Fortuner out of the International House of Pancakes.

Efforts at conserving the pedestrian species are easily foiled.

When the traffic police – the game wardens, as it were, of Animal Avenue – pull someone over for hunting they'll say something like 'I am Jeric Raval' or 'I am Joseph Estrada'. Jeric Raval is a film star, the Filipino Arnold Schwarzenegger, and Joseph Estrada is the Mayor of Manila who was himself a film star in the 1970s and 1980s. The naive motorist will assume the cop has a personality disorder. The savvy motorist will know that this is coded language for a bribe. The amount you must donate depends on the fame of the celebrity cited.

As I moved charily along Katipunan, ribbons of bougainvillea brightened the traffic islands and Spanish flags burst across the skywalk. By mid-afternoon when the fumes had built up to a pasty mist, these flowers would shine through – a propitious image, for me at least. All the bad smells of Katipunan – sewage, particulates, burning plastic – were somehow offset by the seductive scent of *siopao* (rice flour buns) and chicken balls frying in pavement skillets. Well-groomed men in shorts sold helium balloons of Disney characters. Skin-whitened, jewel-studded old homemakers stopped and asked me if I needed assistance. Students of Ateneo de Manila and the University of the Philippines thronged in Mexican-style *cantinas*, their laughter competing with the chunky riffs of The Eraserheads and other OPM (Original Pinoy Music) bands. The students' bonhomie was infectious – it always cheered me up.

It was on that particular ramble that I almost got killed. As the pavement levelled out into two parking spaces outside the Philippine Society of Gastroenterology, a Subaru Forester reversed towards me at full pelt. I dodged into the adjacent space, the vehicle missing my kneecaps by a millimetre.

I then went over to the Subaru and banged my fist on the tinted driver's window. The fury was burning up from the pit of my stomach and into my eyes. Until then I'd thought 'seeing red' was just a metaphor. Now I was *actually* seeing red. It was as if I'd put on a pair of anaglyph 3-D glasses with both frames coloured scarlet. I stood there shaking, panting, the self-control bleeding out of me. My free will was evaporating into the air like steam from street food.

Instinct overrode any concern for safety, consequence or the law. I wasn't thinking, I was feeling, and the feeling was this: a fucking idiot has almost killed me and he will suffer.

I banged again on the window, my knuckles numbing. The window zipped down. Inside were well-dressed yet profoundly scared people. Big shots: off-duty lawyers, actors or executives. They cringed, mouths wide as coal pits. 'I'm so sorry, sir. So sorry, sorry, sorry…' They may have wondered who on Earth I was. The only white, unarmed carjacker in Manila?

It was a pitiable sight. I was appalled by my own capacity to frighten. Whatever switch had flipped in me flipped back. It was like instantly sobering up from a state of intoxication. I un-balled my fist, which was broiling with pain now the adrenalin was gone.

PART 2: 2014

9. THE COMFORT
WOMAN

My contract with *Quill* ended in April 2010, just before the election of Benigno 'Noynoy' Aquino as President of the Philippines. He promised recovery from the pork barrel scandals, summary executions and attempted *coup d'état* that had sullied the Gloria Arroyo administration. Unable to find any other work that would sustain my modest lifestyle in Manila, I moved back to the UK where I was able to sell Philippines-based travel stories to airline magazines and some 'hard' news features to *Private Eye, New Statesman, New Internationalist* and other, more cerebral titles. After I began studying for a PhD in the recent history and culture of Manila, the University of Portsmouth hired me as a lecturer in creative writing. My faculty was generous enough to fund a research trip back to Manila in the summer of 2014.

'Comfort women' is the chilling euphemism for Asian females who were forced into sexual slavery by Japanese soldiers in World War II. Between 100,000 and 250,000 were coerced into 'army brothels' in the Philippines, China, Korea and the other parts of Asia the Japanese conquered. Some victims were as young as eleven. Only 30 per cent survived their ordeal.

I had to dodge past two surly Alsatians on leashes before entering the modest offices of Lila Pilipina, a support group for the 174 Filipina survivors of Japanese wartime abuse. I waited in a room with a dining table in its centre. It looked like the lounge of a bourgeois Filipino home, albeit with photos, banners and text boards on the walls telling the story of the organization. I jotted down some key dates. Although I knew a fair bit about the Pacific War, there was a fissure in my awareness about the comfort women, which I hoped to fill with the coming interview.

After a few minutes, a slender middle-aged woman in glasses came in, leading an old woman – also slim and bespectacled – by the hand. They sat down, the older woman taking longer about it.

'Good afternoon,' said the middle-aged woman. 'You must be Tom. I am Rechilda Extremadura and this is Estelita B. Dy.' As I tried to think of a polite way of finding out Estelita's age, Rechilda came to the rescue. 'She is eighty years old and has been a member of our group since 1993.'

I sat with them and switched my recorder on. 'I'm grateful that you've agreed to talk to me. I don't want you to get upset so please just share with me whatever you're comfortable sharing with me.' I cursed myself – 'comfortable' was not the most diplomatic adjective to use.

Estelita preferred to speak in Filipino, so Rechilda translated for me. At the outbreak of the Pacific war in 1941, Estelita was twelve and living with her family on the southern island of Negros. The family was well-to-do, her father a sugar farmer, her mother the owner of a *sari-sari* (convenience) store. When the Japanese occupied the island they closed the sugar mill and forced the Dys to relocate to Candoni, in the south, where they continued farming but with scant resources: one *carabao* (water buffalo), one cow and seventeen chickens. At first, relations with the occupiers were cordial – Estelita's father would trade eggs and chickens for salt and soy sauce.

In 1943, the Japanese sent Estelita to an airfield in Bacolod City. She was given a half kilo of rice a day for labouring in a human chain to gather stones from a riverbed that were needed to mend an airstrip. After a year of this, a US plane flew over and dropped messages telling Estelita and her colleagues that it was futile working for the Japanese. This was the first inkling she had that the Allies were winning the war.

Estelita was sent back to her family farm to help grow cassava and sweet potatoes. One afternoon, while she was bringing some of the produce to the market, she saw a Japanese truck pull up. Soldiers jumped out. After noticing one of the soldiers staring at her, she ran away, but tripped and fell over. The Japanese dragged her by her hair to the truck. A dozen other Filipinas were inside. They were not allowed to speak to each other.

A single tear formed in Estelita's left eye and bumped down over the wrinkles on her cheek. Her voice crackled. I started to say to Rechilda, 'She doesn't have to go on.' But Estelita went on.

The truck took her and the other women to the Dalisay army camp. A soldier led her into a large house and upstairs to a room with a table and a bed within. The soldier shoved her onto the bed and raped her. She screamed, tried to resist, but her assailant was too strong. When he was finished, another soldier came in and did exactly the same to her. When she tried to roll off the bed and escape, he seized her by the arms and smashed her head against the table.

When Estelita awoke some hours later, a fellow comfort woman was standing over her. 'It's best you don't fight back,' she said, 'or they'll kill you.' From then on, Estelita would close her eyes and put her hands over her ears every time she was raped. She was just thirteen years old.

After three weeks of being violated several times a day, she heard a commotion outside the house. She looked out of the window. The Japanese soldiers were packing up their equipment. 'The Americans are coming,' they shouted. That night the soldiers fled to the mountains. Estelita ran out of the house and all the way home to her family. They were sitting around the kitchen table weeping.

'We thought you were dead,' her father said to her.

She was never able to tell him what had happened to her in the room in the large house. It would have brought shame on the family. Her parents had explained her absence to the neighbours by pretending she'd been on holiday. A few weeks later, Estelita gathered enough courage to tell her mother the truth. Although sympathetic, her mother warned her to stay quiet about it. 'What the Japanese did to you is not your fault, my child,' she said. 'Still, Filipinos will think you have been tainted by the Japanese, so hated are they now.'

After the war, Estelita moved to Manila and married. To the day of his death, her husband knew nothing of her time as a comfort woman.

Estelita dabbed a tissue at more tears. I wasn't sure what to say next. Rechilda put her hands around Estelita's and said, 'The Japanese paid the Philippines reparations in 1956. This did not include anything for the "comfort women". All we are asking for now is an apology. We hear they are soon to give the Korean women one.'

'Have the Japanese ever acknowledged women like Estelita?' I asked.

'One ex-soldier came here and testified to the existence of the comfort stations. That is all.'

'How are you funded?'

'We receive 80,000 yens a year.'

'Japanese yens?'

'Yes, surprisingly there is support for us from the Japanese public.'

'Are you aware of other nations during the war that used "comfort women"?'

'No side is innocent. The Nazis had military brothels all across Europe. When the Allies invaded and occupied Germany, the Soviets raped maybe two million local women and the Americans around 190,000, so the estimates say.'

Rechilda went on to explain that Lila Pilipina does not exclusively struggle for victims of the Japanese in the 1940s. 'Since the war, there have been many cases of Americans sexually assaulting Filipinas. They often get away with it due to the Visiting Forces Agreement, which means US personnel are immune to prosecution. Only one rapist, Daniel Smith, has ever been convicted, although he was released after the US government put pressure on our government. The Americans blackmailed us by postponing a prestigious joint exercise with our armed forces until our president agreed to hand Smith over to US custody.'

'Is the situation getting better or worse?'

'I think worse. The Philippine Commission on Women has found that one in five Filipinas experience sexual abuse and that there's been a 50 per cent increase in violence against women only this year.'

'Why does it happen?'

'The ill-treatment of women – and children – is universal. Oftentimes they have less money and influence than men so this leaves them vulnerable. You know that traffickers go into high schools in poor neighbourhoods here? We have a campaign where we tell the students not to sell themselves even if the high amount is tempting. Other problems come when, after a cyclone or earthquake, people lose their homes and their livelihoods. The only way to avoid starving is to sell your children to a paedophile. He will come to the disaster site in person or contact you on the internet. Many of those men pay enough to keep a family fed for months. Many of those men are from *your West.*'

10. DEFERRED DISGUST

In the taxi to my next meeting, I pondered Rechilda's use of that phrase 'your West'. She was right: many Westerners were complicit in sexual crime and exploitation in the Philippines.

Nearing Quezon City, I spotted a homeless girl in only a maize-yellow vest that stretched to her knees. Her coat hanger frame drooped as she picked up a length of bamboo from the ground. She paused, turned her head and peered at me with a 'mind your own business' expression. Blushing, I retrained my eyes on my shoes.

'I'm just a dirty bastard,' a retired welder in a Portsmouth pub had said when I asked why he travelled to the Philippines every year. 'It's all about shagging, mush,' he added. My daydream then cut to the moment – also back in the UK – when I told my friend Ian about accepting the correspondent's job for *Quill*. 'Wouldn't go myself,' he scowled. 'Lot of foreign nonces about, aren't there?'

'Sex tourism and child molestation are not the only things that happen in the Philippines,' I thought, wishing I'd said it to those men at those times. 'And it all depends where you look and what you're looking for.' I closed my eyes and discerned against the blackness a blob of the same maize shade as the girl's vest. Neuroscientists hold that the coloured lights you see when your lids are shut may come either from the outside world as photons or from within yourself in the form of signals generated by your own atoms. Was the ex-welder's perverted vision of the Philippines based on external data or inner peccadilloes?

These men's accusations also implied that the same horrors didn't happen in their homeland. Before meeting Estelita and Rechilda, I'd read a newspaper report that placed both the US and the UK in the top five worst countries for paedophilia – this being some time before Jimmy Savile, Rolf Harris et al. The Philippines didn't make that list. This demolishes any notion that sexual exploitation is a culture-specific problem rather than, as Rechilda had said, a worldwide human one.

And even if, for argument's sake, the Philippines *had* made it on to that list, the material reasons would be more understandable than those behind the inclusion of developed nations. Can *anyone* in Britain – no matter how broke – ever excuse selling their kids for food as some Filipino families are compelled to? Yet such crimes are more common in the UK than in poor countries stereotyped as cesspits of dark carnality.

There was a slither of truth in Ian's statement – gauche as it was – given that Westerners feature in both the supply and demand sides of paedophilia. There's a frighteningly high volume of headlines like these:

> *Australian charged with child abuse in Angeles City.*
> *Policemen arrest two foreigners and a Filipino involved in child pornography and cybersex ring.*
> *British paedophile builds house next to Filipino school.*
> *American couple running orphanage in Philippines charged with human trafficking and child abuse.*

At times, members of the British establishment have helped shore up the Philippine sex industry. In 1970, the hereditary peer Lord Antony Moynihan was facing fifty-seven criminal charges in London, amongst them defrauding a casino and bouncing a cheque on a brand new Rolls Royce. He fled to Manila, befriended President Marcos and constructed a criminal empire that included several whorehouses, one of them within spitting distance of the British Ambassador's home. When Moynihan died in 1991, his siring of two children by Filipina wives – one of whom was a belly-dancer – caused a stir about who'd inherit his seat in the House of Lords. (The Moynihan surname was to return to the news a quarter century later when his daughter Aurora was shot to death in President Duterte's anti-narcotics war.)

The taxi dropped me outside an office block layered like a cake with rows of shaded glass in between rows of overhanging concrete. As I took the lift to the HQ of Ang Ladlad, a small political party advocating for LGBT rights, I hoped I wouldn't be about to find out that 'my West' also plays a part in the suffering of yet another marginalized group.

I was greeted by Bemz Benedito, a transwoman about my age and wearing citrusy perfume.

'I'll start with a question you've probably been asked a lot, if you don't mind,' I said.

'No problem,' said Bemz.

'What caused you to become a trans activist?'

'It was after I suffered harassment in the workplace.'

'Can I ask whereabouts?'

'I was working as a sociologist in one of our universities here. Two academics from India came to visit us. During a tour of Taal Volcano these guys started groping my legs and touching my breasts. They were married men, sixty years old. They should have known better.'

'I should say. Did you complain?'

'Yes I did. One of the Indians told the investigating committee, "I'm sorry, I thought she was a woman, that's why I touched her." It was as if had I been a biological female, their behaviour would have been acceptable. My colleagues were no better. One of them said, "Didn't you appreciate being harassed because it validates your womanhood?" I did not – I felt violated. The supervisor of the project wanted to just sweep it all under the rug.'

'Did anything come of the complaint?'

'There was no legal outcome. I am still considered a biological man under the law here. It says a biological man cannot harass a biological man! At least the Department of Immigration and Deportation banned the Indians for life from coming back to the Philippines.'

'Were they removed from their posts in India?'

'No.'

'Did the case become a news story?'

'Only in the Philippines.'

'So they've been publicly disgraced?'

'Again, only in the Philippines.'

'Behaviour like that should ruin someone, no?'

Bemz shrugged.

'When you started your activism what other mistreatment of trans people did you uncover?'

'We made a documentation for the Congressional Commission on Human Rights about the last ten years of hate crimes against LGBTs. These crimes have increased tenfold. Often those prosecuted only get a manslaughter sentence.'

'Why?'

'A transwoman called Jennifer Laude was found dead in a hotel room in Olongapo City. She'd been drowned in the toilet bowl. A US marine, Scott Pemberton, was detained. The court decided it was a homicide of passion rather than premeditated because Jennifer had concealed her gender identity from him. He was sentenced to ten years only, and with good behaviour it could be five years.'

'If a biological man murders a biological woman is the sentence generally harsher?'

'Yes, normally it is a life sentence.'

'You could argue that the sentence should be higher for hate-driven murders.'

'We are pushing for that. We want the police to investigate more deeply and to recognize patterns of hatred. When the decision was being read out in court we were squirming because the judge referred to Jennifer as a man. The motive given is always either robbery or non-payment for a sexual service. But often the killings are so brutal – there is mutilation sometimes – that the motive *must* be something stronger.'

'Do these murders usually occur when a heterosexual man is shocked to find out that he is with – how can I put this – a woman who was born a man?'

'No. Often the murderer has been dating or sleeping with the victim for some months.'

'Really?'

'One study shows that the savagery of these crimes is down to the killer feeling shame that he is attracted to a transwoman. Often he himself is a repressed, self-hating homosexual. One transwoman in Baguio – who'd been in a long-term relationship with a guy – was not only killed but her organs were cut out and stuffed in her mouth.'

'I guess it might be like these Christian fundamentalist preachers who constantly condemn the LGBT lifestyle, and then they themselves turn out to be having liaisons with rent boys and so forth.'

'Scott Pemberton's lawyers said he had no idea that Jennifer was trans until he touched her crotch. This we don't believe because surveys show that most transgender Filipinos would reveal their identities on a first date.'

'Because they wouldn't want to risk upsetting their date?'

'Exactly. The defence also claimed that Jennifer tried to rob Pemberton, but if that were true he, as a US serviceman, could have arrested her and taken her to the authorities. So why overreact and kill her in that horrible way? Another transwoman, Barbie Reilly, was killed by her boyfriend after a month of courting him. He must have known her gender identity from the get-go, as she was a famous gay beauty queen who appeared in pageants. This killing, again, was dismissed by the police as robbery.'

'But why do these murders happen after, say, a month or year of a relationship?'

'There is a deep hatred of someone who is different.'

'I get that, but if there's deep hatred why would the person engage in a relationship in the first place?'

'He enjoys it at first – mostly the sex – and will get to know the transwoman. They will dine and drink and go out. They may decide to live together. And then a disgust at himself takes hold.'

'Thinking about your political and advocacy work now, what are the big challenges?'

'The big one for us is how do we protect LGBTs? They are often among the poorest in society, they have no economic assistance. If you go back to the period before Spanish colonization, LGBT people – named *babaylans* or "the third sex" – were revered in our society as healers and wise people. When the Roman Catholic Church came here with the Spanish, LGBTs became despised.'

'And the Church is still generally anti-LGBT?'

'Yes. There is a Church-sponsored group of so-called "ex-gays" who profess that LGBT behaviour is just a sinful phase, a disease that can be cured. The main problem for us today is that there are no anti-discrimination or anti-hate crime laws. We have party members in Cebu City whose parents persuaded male friends of the family to rape them to "cure" their lesbianism. They call it "therapeutic sex". This is tolerated in some communities, although of course it is not legal.'

'It doesn't cross these parents' minds that it might be more immoral to invite someone to rape your daughter than to accept that your daughter is a lesbian?'

'No. For them it is a corrective measure justified by their religious beliefs.'

'I take it these people are poor and uneducated?'

'Not really. We are talking about middle-class and rich families. Sometimes they break our anti-abduction laws. This is when an angry parent will file a kidnapping case against the lover of their LGBT child and the police and judiciary cooperate.'

'What is the current administration's attitude towards LGBTs?'

'It has indicated that it will allow civil unions, but has denounced as "useless" the Commission on Human Rights, which has traditionally been prepared to listen to LGBT voices. Having said that, the main cause of homophobia here is the Church.'

'It seems like a Herculean task persuading the Church to change its view.'

'Actually, we no longer have that dream. Where we think we can have an impact is in Congress.'

I left wishing Bemz and her party the best of luck with their intended reforms. I spent the journey home feeling desolate about the two interviews I'd conducted today. There seemed to be a formula of oppression that applied to women, children and LGBTs: they suffered for being powerless, underprivileged, bereft of rights and under the heel of aggressors enabled by the dominant mores, however contradictory these mores were. I tried to console myself with the chance that my reportage on these problems might in some way help people like Rechilda and Bemz to solve them.

11. HOUSING THE EGO

The following day, I rose before dawn to prepare for a long couple of days in the field. While I waited for an egg to boil I looked on my phone at jpegs of some of the 4,200 pairs of shoes Imelda Marcos had purportedly amassed. Imelda's footwear gluttony is about the only thing most Westerners know about the family that has had more impact on Philippine society than any other.

My first awareness of the Marcoses was when they were deposed by a peaceful revolution in 1986. I was seven and hazily remember a video of several US Air Force planes on the BBC *Six O'Clock News*, an exuberant voiceover stating that the Marcos family were escaping to Hawaii.

I took the lift down to the condo's front steps where a charcoal Isuzu car was waiting. I opened its door and found an old geezer with concentric wrinkles like the hedge maze of a country estate. He flinched trying to lift his jeans-clad legs from the footwell.

'You must be Leopoldo. No need to get out.'

Leopold lowered his feet back into the footwell. 'How are you today, Sir Tom?'

'I'm fine. How are you?' I nodded towards his leg.

'I am the one who has gout.'

'I have some painkillers in my bag.'

'I don't trust.' He let out a grotesquely jangling cough like someone putting a pickaxe through a stained glass window. For the rest of our time together, Leopoldo was to cough like that about every five minutes.

As we set off, I grew guilty about making this dilapidated man work for me. Did the tour company I'd hired know about his gout or the causes of his cough?

Katipunan had never been so quiet. As the sun flowered in the murky sky, a handful of bucket-balancing *taho* (a hot tapioca-like tofu drink) sellers and the odd tangerine-toned school minibus came into relief.

'So sir,' coughed Leopoldo, 'you are interested of the Marcoses?'

'Yes, I'm writing about the Marcos-related sites around Luzon.'

'I am the one who was driver for Aspiras. You know he? He close man with Marcos. He die 1999.'

'They were both from Ilocos Norte, right?'

'My province too.'

'And Aspiras was Marcos' press officer.'

'You know our history, Sir Tom.'

I also knew that Aspiras had started his career in the 1950s as an apprentice to Edward R. Lansdale, the CIA counterinsurgency expert who'd helped President Magsaysay quash the Huk uprising.

Before I could ask Leopoldo about working for a man like Aspiras, we veered off the high rise-bullied Roxas Boulevard and onto Vincente Sotto Street, the waters of Manila Bay to our right bleached blonde by the ascendant sun. At the end of the street was an octagonal cluster of double-storey buildings held up by pillars made from cross-grained coconut shells. One of Imelda Marcos' more eccentric creations, the 37 million peso (about US$650,000) Coconut Palace was constructed in 1981 for the sole purpose of accommodating Pope John Paul II. The glitch was that having witnessed the poverty across the Philippines, the pope refused for reasons of good taste to stay in so lavish a venue, even if the chandeliers were made of fruit skin rather than crystal. He then upset Imelda further by holding forth on Negros Island about the myriad sins of capitalism.

Relations soured between the Marcoses and the Catholic Church. Imelda was arrogant enough to think she could afford to estrange the one Filipino institution that is supposed to transcend politics, money and national pride. Is there a link between the size of one's ego and the size and opulence of the buildings one commissions?

67

I got out of the car for a better look. Leopoldo followed me, steadier on his feet this time. As he lit a cigarette, I asked him if he remembered the pope incident. He screwed his face up, his wrinkles contracting closer together so that they formed the same grainy pattern as the coconut pillars. 'It was no problem, as pope go somewhere else. You know we have other personalities stay there after he? Already, Brooke Shields, actress from America, and Gaddafi, leader of Algeria.'

'You mean Libya?'

'Sorry, Sir Tom. Libya.'

Gaddafi's nationality wasn't the only thing Leopoldo had got wrong. Gaddafi never came to the Philippines. In 1976, the Marcoses erected another boondoggle in Manila, the Golden Mosque, in preparation for a state visit by 'the Mad Dog of Tripoli', but the invititation was rescinded after US complaints.

Leopoldo pointed his cigarette at the palace. 'Will you get inside, Sir Tom?'

'Not possible. The vice-president has his office there, I believe.'

A few hundred yards south, past the ochre balconies of the Sofitel Philippine Plaza Manila Hotel, was the Manila Film Center. It was a grody hunk of concrete with zero resemblance to the Athenian Parthenon which had inspired it. The rush to finish construction in time for the 1982 Manila International Film Festival caused 170 plus workmen to fall off the scaffolding and into wet cement. What happened next is disputed. Some say the foreman ordered the surviving men to keep working and pour more cement onto the trapped unfortunates. To this day, their skeletons are preserved inside the walls.

We lunched at a hole-in-the-wall café. Leopoldo ordered *bulalo*, slow-cooked beef marrow bone in a sauce so salty and fatty a mere spoonful of it gave me a hot flush. I settled for the healthiest item on the menu: *kinilaw* (raw tuna in a vinegar dressing). Leopoldo ate fast. Once he'd forked all the meat into his mouth, he picked up the bone with his fingers and chewed at it like a stir crazy hamster attacking the bar of its cage. 'My doctor he say I should not do this,' he spluttered.

'I like too much, though.' He placed on the table a plastic bottle with a NATURE'S SPRING DRINKING WATER sticker on it. 'You want?'

I nodded, my mouth full. He poured two glasses. I took a big lug on mine and felt the scorch of distilled alcohol in my throat. 'That wasn't water,' I winced.

'It is gin from the province,' he said, pronouncing *gin* with a hard *g* like *good* or *guard*. He finished the bottle. I was too polite to ask him if this might in any way impair his ability to drive us the almost 300 miles north to Marcos country.

On Ayala Bridge we foundered in a traffic jam of tricycles, their lawnmower engines and duck-quack horns grating on me. As we edged forward at a rate of an inch every ten minutes, I ruminated on Marcos' plans for a national rail network. If he'd enacted them would I be stuck here right now?

What is it about the popular consciousness that associates trains with tyrants – especially Hitler and Mussolini – and how the locomotives in their tyrannies supposedly ran on time? Whether or not transport punctuality was a Marcos aim, he did set up the first Light Rail Transit (LRT) line in the capital, brought the Philippine National Railway (PNR) company into a broader infrastructure project and, according to his son Bongbong, planned a further eight lines for the Metro Rail Transit (MRT) before he was overthrown in 1986.

We finally got out of Manila around 2 p.m. We crossed a hinterland of car showrooms, billboards so vast you couldn't see their full extent from a car window and industrial units composed of multi-coloured, Lego-like blocks with names like WIMPEX and STANPAK. A lot of new building was going on – proof perhaps that the Philippines' growth rate was almost 4 per cent whereas Credit Crunch Britain's was minus 2.

I was woken by the slamming of Leopoldo's door. I think he slammed it particularly hard with the intention of waking me up. Cold sweat logged my socks and armpits. Filipino drivers tended not to turn on the air-con unless asked, and I hadn't been able to ask because I'd been asleep for the last seven hours. I stepped out into a dimly lit car park to a ringing choir of crickets. A green neon sign blinked HOTEL and WELCOME TO BATAC CITY.

The receptionist wore a cerise silk scarf and an excess of make-up. She slipped me a silver key. 'One single superior room, sir.'

'Do you have a room for him too?' I thrust a thumb at Leopoldo. He'd been yawning and coughing alternately ever since we got out of the car.

'We have.' She led us outside into a spot-lit courtyard and to a sunbed with a bamboo umbrella attached to its back.

'Come on, it's outside!' I hissed. 'You must have something for him inside, no?'

The receptionist goggled at me as if I'd just told her I was the transgender reincarnation of her late grandmother. Clearly round these parts it was routine for a lowly driver to sleep in the open air. 'We are fully booked, sir.'

Leopoldo shook his head. 'This okay, Sir Tom. This okay.' The receptionist looked at Leopoldo and then back at me hopefully. My downcast expression remained.

'Leopoldo, do you want to sleep in my room?'

He and the receptionist looked at each other again. 'No,' he said. 'I cannot.'

'What if he would sleep in reception?' suggested the receptionist.

'He won't get a good night's rest there if it's open twenty-four hours.'

'In our restaurant, sir? Nobody at all would be there until six tomorrow.'

'Do you have a bed he can use?'

'We can find, sir.'

Next morning in the hotel restaurant, a waitress was lifting the lids off trays of rice, *tapa* (dried beef) and harshly salted *bangus* (milkfish). There was no sign of Leopoldo. I went to reception. There was no sign of him there either, although a lad of twenty was crouched over a laptop playing *Candy Crush Saga*. He nodded sluggishly at the door to the courtyard.

Leopoldo was hobbling away from the sunbed, brushing himself down.

'Leopoldo, why the hell did you sleep out here?'

'Aaah, restaurant next to graveyard. Me, I scared of ghosts.'

'Next time we're getting you a proper bed indoors.'

'No no. Here almost luxury. When I work for Aspiras, I use to sleep in *carabao* harness in garden.'

As we ate breakfast, I concluded that the Marcos mob's approach to hospitality said something about their ethical temperament: if you were a social better whom they wanted to suck up to in the hope that some of your prestige might rub off on them, they'd build you a brand new palace or mosque. But if you were one of their skivvies so loyal you'd die for them, they'd condemn you to a space on the ground next to the dogs and the cockroaches.

12. OFFICIAL FIBS

We drove past a *barangay* hall with BATAC: HOME OF GREAT LEADERS on its eave. I flipped my attention to a Philippine Supreme Court report on extra-judicial killings under the presidency of Gloria Macapagal-Arroyo (2001-2010). Of more than 300 murders of journalists and political activists – some of them University of the Philippines students gunned down while investigating the plight of aboriginal peoples in the north – only a fistful had come to court. The popular view was that, like Marcos, Arroyo had been on a mission to wipe out the left. And, like Marcos, she'd imposed Martial Law – 'a state of emergency' was how she'd spun it – but for only three weeks rather than Marcos' nine years.

Making a comparison of scale between the two regimes would be unfair – the Marcoses killed over 3,000 opponents, after all – but I questioned what had been learned from those diabolical days and whether the conditions that bred oppression had changed much. In both cases, the US and its commercial and strategic interests were fully behind the leader; urban poverty caused violent crime; rural poverty fed the Maoist insurgency; racism and marginalization fed the *Moro* Muslim struggle for self-determination – and so on. (Of course, even Marcos' hit list would come to look like small beer beside the 4-10,000 suspected drug pushers and addicts murdered within a year of President Duterte's election in 2016 – more on that later.)

The Ferdinand E. Marcos Presidential Center was a Hispanic mansion with lanterns swinging from stucco arcades. It didn't look that pricey considering its founders had allegedly embezzled US$10 billion from the Philippine treasury.

I was met by an effete young guide called John-Mark who wore pink skinny jeans and an auburn-dyed ponytail. 'Welcome, Sir Tom.' He gently bit his lower lip and cast his eyes away from mine. I read the expression as somewhere between shyness and anticipation.

'Welcome here to our museum that is celebrating a national hero a little like your William Shakespeare or your Tony Blair.' He let out a trebly chuckle after saying the name 'Tony Blair'. I hoped it was a chuckle of sarcasm.

In the vestibule was a twenty-four-carat gold bust of Marcos, head held high, expectant eyes staring into a bright future – well, that was more the effect of having a lamp shining directly into his metal face. That such an imposing object should greet visitors the moment they arrived seemed to be a way of stamping the Marcoses' authority here – we own this place, we control the narrative.

John-Mark led me to a section about Marcos' early days. It was all hagiography laminated and mounted on paperboard. Beneath a sepia mugshot of a flat-cheeked Chinese *mestizo* with big, anchor-shaped eyebrows, a caption read, 'From his father Mariano, Ferdinand learned more than just machismo.' Mariano was, apparently, a 'prominent achiever' who could 'shift effortlessly from English to Ilocano, and even to Spanish.' Ferdinand's mother Josieta was a 'local beauty queen endowed with oratorical prowess'. The dynastic logic was impeccable – Ferdinand was bound to be clever, handsome and articulate because his parents were. These were inherited traits, apparently. I wondered what role nurture had played. 'Do you think Marcos was under pressure from his parents to become a great man?' I asked John-Mark.

'Yes, maybe that. He came from a long line of commanding persons here in Ilocos Norte. His father was a congressman and his grandfather a businessman. His mother's forefathers were Spanish mayors.'

Even Marcos' stormiest critics would agree with the next captions about his success as a law student at the University of the Philippines. Endowed with an exquisite memory, he knew the 1935 Philippine Constitution by heart and scored the highest marks ever in the national bar exams. His stellar performance drew accusations of cheating. He agreed to sit a *viva voce*. He passed that just as decisively.

Next we came to the first blemish on Marcos' record – his imprisonment for murder aged just twenty-one. 'Marcos' father and

Julio Nalundasan were political rivals,' said John-Mark. 'They were both running to be representative for the second district. Nalundasan won the election and was slain by gun. The first suspect was the neighbour of Nalundasan, but after three months it was boiled down to Ferdinand Marcos. The police found the murder weapon in the locker room of the University of the Philippines Pistol Club. Marcos was the president of that club. There was also a star witness, Aguinaldo, who said he saw Marcos do the deed. Marcos was placed in jail and then he wrote an appeal to the Supreme Court.' John-Mark pointed to a pillow-thick stack of brown-white papers in one of the display cabinets. 'Then, thank the Lord, everybody realized he was not guilty and he was made free.'

Whether John-Mark had knowingly misled me or had done so in good faith, I'll never know. Either way his version modulated or excised certain details that appeared in the Supreme Court decision and other accounts. What John-Mark missed was that Ferdinand, Marino, Ferdinand's uncle Quirino Lizardo and others met on 17 September 1935 to plan, essentially, a mob hit on Nalundasan. They wanted to avenge their humiliation by Nalundasan's drudges who'd driven a car around Batac containing a coffin and two dummies with 'Marcos' and 'Aglipay' (the leader of the Republican Party) labels attached to them.

Ferdinand was chosen as the hitman for his skill with a trigger and the likelihood that, if he were caught, his youth would get him a lighter sentence. To gamble everything – his life, his career, his chance of adding something to the Marcos family legacy – must have required extraordinary loyalty to his father.

At 9 p.m. on 20 September, Ferdinand, Lizardo and a lackey, Calixto Aguinaldo, infiltrated the back yard of Nalundasan's house. Aguinaldo stood watch as the other two drew pistols and positioned themselves in parts of the yard from where they could aim at Nalundasan while staying concealed. Aguinaldo suffered a panic attack – or perhaps a moral *volte-face* given that he later testified in court against his bosses. As he fled the scene, he heard a shot fired.

74

Ferdinand had put a bullet in Nalundasan's back as he stood at the window brushing his teeth.

As John-Mark said, Ferdinand was arrested, jailed and later acquitted. However, as the historian Sterling Seagrave speculates, Ferdinand wasn't freed because his guilt was disproved. Rather, the Marcos family's 'special relationship' with Ferdinand Chua, Batac's Municipal Court Judge, persuaded President Manuel Quezon, who depended on the backing of the prominent Chua clan, to grant Marcos a pardon. A familiar case of a well-connected person levitating above the law.

Remarkably, Marcos was able to turn this potentially career-sinking scandal into career-lifting publicity. When he went into politics a few years later, the voters didn't see a callow hoodlum who'd been ordered by his domineering family to commit a sordid and cowardly murder in reprisal for minor cheek. What they saw was a macho gunfighter who'd fought the law and won. To sustain the tough guy image, Marcos never denied the rumours of his culpability.

I tried to see things from the perspective of the twenty-one-year-old Marcos. He *must* have felt at least some remorse over Nalundasan. Like so many innocent young soldiers in so many wars across history, did that early experience of killing another human being offer two possible outcomes? Might he have sworn never to kill again and from then on follow the path of peace in the hope of redemption, like those British World War II tank commanders who became vicars after demob? Or would he somehow come to terms with his remorse, morally square with himself the pain he'd caused, and then be ready to cause more of it? Back in the UK a few years ago, a veteran-turned-peace campaigner told me army training does its best to strip new recruits of their empathy, scruples and compassion. Building the perfect soldier means building a sociopath of sorts.

'Having literally got away with murder,' as James Hamilton-Paterson puts it, Marcos was emboldened to go on and do worse, all the time able to dodge both his conscience and the system. One small-town baby-kisser dead in a Batac back yard prefigured 3,000

Filipino civilians murdered in almost every corner of the republic. No doubt, each time the body count rose, Marcos found a way to self-justify it morally, politically and psychically.

As the problems of the Philippines multiplied, Marcos cranked up the machismo. When a fresh threat to his power popped up, his reaction was to take an ever bigger hammer to it. In 1969, when two insurgencies – that of the Marxist NPA and the *Moro* National Liberation Front (MNLF) – commenced, he preferred aggression to arbitration. According to José Maria Sison, founder of the Communist Party of the Philippines, Marcos' troops used napalm on civilians in Jolo City and deployed a maniacal transvestite lieutenant who claimed to be Christ and practised cannibalism on the *Moros* he captured. Such brutality only fanned further opposition to Marcos.

1970 saw more NPA and MNLF sorties, and the attempted storming of the Malacañang Palace by left-wing students. Marcos wouldn't talk with any of these parties. Instead, his secret police abducted undesirables and subjected them to sexual assault, water-boarding, electrocution in the genitals and beatings with metal bars and rifle butts. Some of 'the disappeared' were caged up like animals, others forced to play Russian roulette. In addition to the dead, a total of 35,000 Filipinos were tortured and 70,000 imprisoned throughout the junta.

The sequence of greater repression followed by greater protest continued until one side had to crack. Ultimately that would be Marcos'. He would have fallen sooner had he not been bolstered by the US. When Marcos won his first and only free election in 1965 (he'd go on to brazenly cheat in all subsequent ballots), 35,000 American soldiers based in the Philippines were becoming central to the Vietnam War effort. A year later, Mr and Mrs Marcos were warmly greeted in Washington, DC. President Johnson was so enamoured of Imelda that he groped her during a dance. In addresses to the American public, Ferdinand confirmed his nation's compact with the US in the tussle against communism. The Philippines, he said, was one of the last outposts of capitalism in a continent fast buckling under the Red Menace.

After that, the US-directed World Bank made favourable loans to Marcos and Filipinos were sent to be trained as soldiers and police officers at US academies. Enlisting American succour may have been in Marcos' DNA, for his grandfather Fructuoso had expanded his rice, coffee and timber concerns thanks to policies instigated by the early US colonial regime. Another influential fan across the Pacific was Ronald Reagan who, unlike Pope John Paul II, had enjoyed the Marcoses' hospitality on a stopover in Manila in 1969. After becoming POTUS in 1981, Reagan dubbed Ferdinand a 'freedom fighter' and shored him up with money, arms and compliments until he was toppled by the People Power Revolution of 1986.

Reagan's assertion that Marcos was 'a hero on a bubble-gum card he had collected as a kid' was fresh in my head as John-Mark and I strolled into a room entitled 'War Years: Valor of the Veteran'. I tried not to smile as I read the captions parroting one of Marcos' most preposterous lies: his 'noble sacrifices for the motherland' by courageously leading a guerrilla unit against the Japanese in World War II.

John-Mark pointed to a clinquant shelf of medals. 'He has the US Congressional Medal of Honor and the Distinguished Service Cross, as well as twenty-five others.' But he was wrong again. As the *New York Times* revealed shortly before Marcos was ousted, the US armed forces have no record whatsoever of bestowing any of these honours.

'Are there any surviving photographs of Marcos with the guerrillas?' I asked.

'We have only this one.' John-Mark pointed to a snapshot of a forage-capped Marcos. It was hardly smoking gun stuff.

'Some people say that Marcos was never a guerrilla,' I said, eyeing the tattered front pages of the *Manila Bulletin* for comparisons of Marcos with Errol Flynn, or suchlike.

John-Mark scowled. 'It is common knowledge. You can read it in the official life of Marcos by Hartzell Spence.' He was referring to a biography Marcos himself commissioned. Spence, an American hack credited with inventing the term 'pin-up', painted Marcos as an Indiana Jones figure who, so Hamilton-Paterson puts it, 'single-handedly wipes out nests of Japanese machine-gunners' and 'carries out daring rescue missions though mortally wounded' plus other hackneyed staples of the boy's own genre.

Extensive research over seventy years has shown that not one of these exploits is true. What is true is that Marcos was drafted into the Philippine Army after law school and fought with the Americans before the Japanese took him POW on the Bataan peninsula in April 1942. Then a curious thing happened: he was set free from the Camp O'Donnell military prison because his family was merrily collaborating with the Japanese. Back in December, his father Mariano had laid on a welcome party for the invaders and gave speeches in their honour right up until he was caught by exactly the sorts of partisans Ferdinand would later pretend to have led. The partisans tied Mariano's hands to two *carabaos* and spurred the beasts. His body was ripped in half.

'Those who doubt,' said John-Mark, sensing that I was one who doubted, 'cannot explain why Marcos was incarcerated by the Japs.'

It wasn't worth gainsaying John-Mark about the guerrilla falsehood – his belief in Marcos' sainthood was held with the bombproof conviction of a brainwashed cultist. Moreover, he was a mellow kid and it would have been mean to upset him. Maybe his employers knew that hiring such a sweet-natured lad would be a shrewd tactic for averting wrangles with more sceptical visitors.

I noted his use of the epithet 'Japs'. I'd read it a lot in books by Filipinos, even in ones published long after the war. It was as if the rage towards the Japanese was still fresh enough to excuse casual racism.

Pulp fiction clichés were as pervasive in the room named 'The Eleven Day Romance of Ferdinand and Imelda' as they were in the war heroism section. On Tuesday 6 April 1954, Imelda swooned as she watched Ferdinand showing off his debating skills in the Senate. When they were introduced in the Senate cafeteria, Ferdinand was smitten: 'It was as if he was hit by temporary paralysis ... He stood motionless staring at her.' He chased her to the beautiful hill station of Baguio during the Easter holiday, but the *dénouement* wasn't quite Barbara Cartland – Ferdinand got down on one knee and presented Imelda with… a marriage licence to sign. Once a lawyer, always a lawyer.

Ferdinand grew more romantically adventurous later. In 1969, the American actress Dovie Beams secretly tape recorded her and Marcos having sex. Among the lowlights were Marcos' desperate pleas for fellatio, his longing for a half-American baby with Dovie and his penchant for singing traditional Ilocano ditties after ejaculation. Copies of the tapes fell into the hands of student militants who broadcast them non-stop on the University of the Philippines' radio station. For someone so muscular at managing his public persona, this was PR self-harm of the bloodiest proportions.

John-Mark laid a soft hand on my forearm. 'Are you ready for the main attraction, Sir Tom?'

13. THE POLITICS OF MUMMIES

Having seen Ho Chi Minh in Hanoi and Chairman Mao in Beijing, I was looking forward to a hat-trick of embalmed Asian leaders by spending some time with what was left of Ferdinand Marcos. According to the Filipino essayist Luis H. Francia, the body on display looks healthy and fresh-faced, and nothing like 'the dictator who died at the age of seventy-two, his features bloated by illness [… and] medication'. The mortician who did the embalming, Frank Malabed, admitted that he spent three weeks beautifying the corpse before it was sent from Hawaii – where Marcos had been exiled for the last three years of his life – to here in Batac.

Still, rumours abound that Marcos was secretly buried deep underground and that what lies on the silk mattress in the casket here in the Presidential Center, dressed up in a white *barong tagalog* shirt covered in phoney medals, is in fact a waxwork model. It would be poetic if this *was* a mannequin rather than the real thing – Marcos was so flamboyantly dishonest in life, why not save up the greatest fib of all for his death?

I didn't know enough about the procedure to answer the question myself. My layman's eyes, though, were wary about the overly smooth, glossy, painted *papier mâché* quality to Marcos' face and his back-combed hair that looked too neat, brittle and black, like the industrially dyed synthetic fibres glued to the head of a doll.

Supposing this *was* Marcos, how much of *him* was left after all the work done by the embalmer? After all, the Marcoses had made an art form of cosmetic modification, from spraying the grass outside official buildings green to Imelda's entourage purportedly injecting themselves with duck embryos to slow the ageing process.

Do those who want to be embalmed have delusions of immortality? Francia suggests that Marcos 'wanted to reign forever' and Hamilton-Paterson claims he constructed 'a superman image of himself' which required 'some degree of belief in it'. Until his early sixties, Marcos was fit and brawny. 'If I'm this well at this age,' he may have thought to himself, 'I can go on forever.' When he came down with lupus and kidney disease, he refused to name an heir. Perhaps he thought there would never need to be one. His advisers colluded in the fantasy – they never discussed his illness even when they noticed him bleeding from his sleeve in 1984.

If someone is preserved post-mortem, it must be hard for their friends and family to accept they are gone forever. And, if that someone has wielded great power, does preserving him mean his country can't let go of his legacy and learn from his mistakes? I pictured the ghost of Marcos rising out of its varnished shell to give the thumbs-up to Arroyo's own endeavours at Martial Law and the current President Aquino's failure to prosecute security forces for the 'disappearances' of opposition activists.

There could have been other, equally cynical motives behind Marcos' embalming. The Marcoses liked to co-opt native traditions in order to counter accusations that they had sold out to US 'dollar imperialism', and mummification might have been an example. The pre-Hispanic tribes of northern Luzon, with which Marcos shared some genes, pursued the practice from about 1200 AD until the mid-nineteenth century. Similar to modern-day techniques, the Igorot peoples would dehydrate the organs with salty water, wash and peel off the skin to prevent worm infestation and smoke, and sun-dry the body until it hardened for posterity. The finished article was exhibited inside a special cave.

'Sir Tom?' said John-Mark, interrupting my musings. 'Do you want to give President Marcos a little wave?' He lowered his gaze obsequiously and made a V-for-Victory sign at the casket. Was he joking or did he genuinely believe Marcos was still sentient – or at least still sentient enough to appreciate a little wave? I didn't give him a little wave – that would have felt just a bit too silly.

Showing me out of the door, John-Mark asked me to 'write only nice things about our town' and handed me a goody bag of Marcos paraphernalia. In it was a book whose title alone implied it wouldn't be a classic of disinterested inquiry: *Ferdinand E. Marcos: A Hero in History*. Flicking through it on the ride out of Batac, I was overwhelmed not by its insights or arguments, but by its plodding, repetitive style and use of innumerable devices to fudge, excuse, caricature and downplay pretty much any criticism that's ever been levelled at Marcos. When discussing Marcos' leadership abilities, the author, former politics professor Remigio Agpalo, is heavy on rhetoric and light on details (presumably because they might prove troublesome as, say, the details of Marcos' soldiering record are): 'Here is a leader who philosophizes on the nature of man, of society, of politics comprehensively.' Marcos was himself a dab hand at platitudes so vacuous they could have been uttered by someone working in higher education management. They certainly don't reveal anything meaningful about his worldview and thereby don't give his detractors anything to get their teeth into.

'Once a champion, always a champion.'

'Freedom is not just declared; it is exercised.'

'The permissiveness of society must be balanced with authoritativeness.'

'There are many things we do not want about the world. Let us not just mourn them. Let us change them.'

My reading was disrupted by two text messages. The first was from Imelda Marcos' 'people' informing me that the eighty-year-old ex-First Lady wouldn't be available for interview. The other bore better news – I could have a few hours with a Ferdinand Marcos lookalike.

14. I WAS FERDY'S DOUBLE

'Tom, please excuse me, but have you ever held a dying child in your arms?' asked Francisco 'Frankie' Salazar as he unbuttoned his shirt outside the Marcos Hall of Justice.

I didn't know what to say. I was unable to turn my gaze from his liver-spotted fingers while they worked their way down his chest, the shirt falling apart to expose a vest and silver crucifix beneath. Where would this undressing end?

'Shall we get in the car?' I pointed behind me to the Isuzu parked crookedly under an orange gazebo with a portrait on it of a melon-headed old dear with bouffant hair and superhero sunglasses. Underneath her twin chins were the words CONGRESSWOMAN IMELDA MARCOS WELCOMES YOU TO LAOAG CITY. *HINDI CORRUPT* [not corrupt].

Frankie pushed his horned, half-rim glasses back up the bridge of his nose and bundled his shirt and tie into his leather satchel. We sat in the rear seats while Leopoldo twisted the ignition. The air-conditioning was chilly against my sunburned face. The fifties rock 'n' roll radio station came back, the opening bars of Chuck Berry's 'Johnny B. Goode' soundtracking a very fifties American scene – a Total gas station attendant in a red uniform and baseball cap high-fiving a youngster in a vintage-style Yale University basketball shirt.

'Excuse me Tom,' said Frankie. 'Please let me continue my point. Would your David *Cam-ah-rron* hold a dying child in his arms?' Unlike younger Filipinos who speak English with an American accent, his pronunciation of the then PM's name was heavily Hispanic, all rolling *r*s and throaty vowels.

'Probably not, no. He isn't…'

'Would your war hero Winston Churchill have the courage to hold a dying child in his arms?'

'He may have done during the war, I really don't...'

'I have held, oh, maybe a thousand dying people in my arms. If you are a good politician, a true politician, you have to be close to your people like this. I could have caught diseases from the blood and the mucus falling from the noses of these poor damned souls, but their families respected me for being unafraid.' He gave me another ludicrously firm handshake. What is it about those men – always men –who have such a forceful grasp? Is it a marker of manliness? A ploy to intimidate a potential adversary? A spasm auguring Parkinson's or some other muscular malady?

Perhaps Frankie thought the shake added sincerity to what he'd just told me. It wasn't going to work. I'd been in a sceptical mood about all things political since my visit to the myth-soaked Marcos mausoleum. Now here I was with a man who claimed to have been Marcos' body double in the early 1980s. How much of what *he* was going to tell me could I believe?

I looked hard at Frankie's face while he lit a menthol Marlboro and struggled to see his likeness to the Great Dictator. Frankie's mistily receding side-combed hair lacked the volume and erectness of Marcos' leonine quiff. His elongated smirk, protruding butterfly-wing ears and too-small, circumflex-shaped eyes could never be mistaken for the younger Ferdie's suave, well-proportioned, Oriental Action Man features.

'How did you first meet Marcos?' I asked, as we left town and hit the coastal Pan-Philippine trunk road.

'I was the protégé of one of his ministers, a man named Reynaldo. During my first term as Mayor of Ascension, Reynaldo took me to a meeting at the Malacañang Palace.'

'What was Marcos like one-to-one?'

'He had the greatest mind in Philippine political history. He appreciated my work in Ascension and asked if I would avail myself of an opportunity to sometimes ride in one of his limousines. How could I turn down such an offer? I did a good job...'

I wanted more details, but I could squeeze out just one syllable before he carried on, speaking over me. 'I did a good job, for the president offered me to become a judge in Cebu. I declined for I did not want to uproot my family and leave this province.' He raised his hands to the ceiling of the Isuzu, turning his palms to face the heavens. 'God's own province!' he declared. By coincidence, the radio was now playing 'Three Steps to Heaven' by Eddie Cochran. Frankie replaced his hands by his side. 'I thank God also that I did not take the role, for the man who did was assassinated in his restroom one week later.'

Frankie's attention was snared by something out the window. He barked in Ilocano and Leopoldo stopped the car. 'Tom, please accompany me.'

He led me to a small breezeblock health clinic. 'As mayor I built this one,' Frankie said with a proud touch of his crucifix. 'In 1988, I went to Brussels and presented to your European Union. I said to them, "I give you two hours to decide whether you want to help the Third World." And when they came back they agreed.'

My doubts were allayed by a sign on the clinic's gate: WITH GREAT THANKS TO OUR GOOD FRIENDS IN EUROPE.

'I built five clinics like these, all free for the poor to avail of.'

That seemed a progressive policy to me, but had Frankie enriched himself from it? How could I ask him without coming over rude? In the event, I didn't need to.

'I know what you are thinking, my British friend,' he said. 'But I am *hindi corrupt*. I mean, if I grafted in my mayoral days, what do I have to show for it now?' He pinched the collar of his vest. 'This is fifty pesos from the market. I am still a country attorney whose peasant clients pay me in chickens. I have just my little house in Ascension, nothing more. I did not send my kids to Harvard or Stanford. You see *they* cannot use any of this against me.'

'Who can't?'

'My opponents in the next election.'

Frankie spent the rest of the drive to Pagudpud beach outlining his bid for a third term as mayor, despite the risks. He was up against the Vizcocho clan, whose dominance of the local judiciary allowed them to peddle crystal meth with impunity. They deployed a hitman against other dealers, nosy reporters and rival candidates like Frankie. On a recent hustings, he'd bumped into the hitman, whom he'd known for decades. 'Are you coming for me now?' Frankie whispered, sliding his hand towards his shoulder holster.

'No,' the hitman replied. 'You're not enough of a threat... yet.'

Unlike the old days, Frankie told me, now candidates could buy votes *en masse* by delivering a new laptop or TV to a *barangay* captain. In return the captain would persuade all his constituents to support the benefactor. 'Except it is not a gift,' added Frankie, 'when it has been paid for out of your own tax money already.'

Had he had any near misses? 'One time these bastards came to my home with shotguns. Praise be to God that I was in Manila that day. They scrammed when they saw my security guards.'

I was surprised by his candour, but I guessed it was all about cultivating the hard man image learned, no doubt, from his idol Marcos. When we could see the wind turbines of Bangui, which look like seventy metre-high Mercedes Benz logos stretching along the coast in a neat row, Frankie unscrewed a bottle of Ginebra San Miguel. 'You like?'

'Bit early for me.'

'This gin has snake bile added to it.'

'Sounds scrumptious. So in the upcoming campaign will you have to buy votes too?'

'No, in God's name no! It is shameful, undemocratic.' Frankie took a slug of the gin. 'And I could not afford it.' He went on to tell me he'd won his previous two elections by spending time in his consitutents' homes, playing with the children, dancing with the women and drinking with the men. One time, he claimed, he consumed ten bottles of gin and went straight into the office at 7 a.m. to begin a fresh day of campaigning. 'You would never catch the Vizcochos getting up close and personal like I do. The daughter who is standing against me has spent most of her life in California, for goodness sake!'

Frankie said that his lowly upbringing brought him esteem from the common man. From the age of ten he worked on his sharecropper parents' tobacco farm before supporting his studies as a priest by working nights as the seminary's janitor. He qualified though never worked as a clergyman, instead moving into law then politics, then back to law and now, if he's successful in the next election, politics again.

At sundown, we pulled into Evangeline's Beach Resort in Pagudpud, one of those blissful Asian beaches that encourages young, middle-class Westerners to write cult novels. Except maybe not in this exact instance, as I couldn't see a single white face among the students drinking San Miguel under the parasols, the children trying to surf or their parents on the videoke machines failing to master the tricky 'aha-ha-ha-ha' vocal bridge in John Lennon's 'Imagine'. I couldn't envisage these fervent Catholics singing the lines 'imagine there's no heaven,' 'no hell below us' or 'no religion too'.

Leopoldo retired to the drivers' quarters while Frankie and I grabbed a wonky table on the sand. 'Please excuse me,' he said, hooking his glasses into the neckline of his vest. 'Is your birth name Thomas?'

'It is.'

'That is the name of my two favourite saints: Thomas Aquinas and Thomas More. Both Englishmen too, no?'

'More was, yes.'

'You know that I researched my family in both Spain and the United States? In Madrid I discovered that the Salazars came to the Philippines in 1583, and in Salt Lake City I consulted the *Book of Mormon*.'

'Why the *Book of Mormon*?'

'It mentions all the Christian last names of any importance, and Salazar was there.' Frankie grinned and his eyes opened out from circumflexes into grand Italianate archways.

'Does it?' I said, fairly sure that it doesn't. On the journey here, I'd warmed to Frankie and come to believe his testimony – or bits of it. I wasn't sure now I knew he'd placed his trust in the ramblings of a demented sect founded by a convicted conman.

'Please excuse me,' he said. 'I have to prepare my petition to the court to have Miss Vizcocho barred from the mayoral race on residency grounds.' He thrust his hand at me. I extended mine cautiously. He spotted my show of weakness, I think, and gave me the hardest grip so far. 'I am sixty-nine years old!' he exclaimed. 'And I still have this strength. Tom, excuse me, how old is your father?'

'Sixty.'

'Does he have the same strength as I?'

'Not sure. Well, good luck Frankie and stay safe.'

'I am not afraid of death. You know why?'

'No.'

'Because I have always been close to it. Holding the dying persons is just one thing. I also spend time with cadavers, making them look good before the funeral, painting their skin, fixing their holes and all that jazz. I made over my mother-in-law so well that she looked like Marilyn Monroe. My father-in-law was more of a challenge – he had been shot in the face with a revolver. I used cotton wool to fill the gap and, well, by the end he looked like James Dean, trust me.'

That night I dreamed of Frankie leaning over Marcos' embalmed, Madame Tussaud's-like face, needle and thread in hand. 'You taught me so much, sir,' said Frankie to the dead tyrant.

15. AUTOGEDDON

After a late lunch at The Pastry Chef in Malolos, a town 28 miles north of Metro Manila, Leopoldo looked more poorly than before. His eyes were fogged over and the bags beneath them scarlet-sore. He interspersed his usual coughs with sniffs so fierce they made his moustache jitter. When he closed his lips they didn't align properly, the upper hanging over the lower like a loosened fascia. When I asked him if he was okay, his response was more a rumble of the larynx than any recognizable phrase. He tottered over to the Isuzu in the restaurant car park, scrabbling for his keys in the breast pocket of his Adidas sweater.

I followed him, my arms outstretched and ready to catch him if necessary. 'Leopoldo, you put them in your trousers. Are you sure you're alright?'

He grunted once more. Like a cowboy drawing a six-gun, he swiftly tugged the keys from out of his trouser pocket and aimed them at the Isuzu. There was something about these movements that convinced me he was well enough to keep driving. In hindsight, this was prodigiously stupid of me.

The first bad omen was the desperately slow speed at which we entered Quezon City on the hustling NLEX Segment 8.1. We were easily overtaken by a fleet of Phoenix Petroleum tankers, horns bawling as they blazed past us. After them, a bandana-headed tricycle driver slammed a ring-festooned fist against my window.

I reached from the back seat to Leopoldo's shoulder. 'You might want to step on the gas.'

He grunted again.

At a hectic four-directional crossing, I gritted my teeth as Leopoldo accelerated too soon, with ten seconds left on the green traffic clock that gives pedestrians time to cross. Luckily, there weren't any pedestrians, but we did clip the Paisley-design front bumper of a jeepney racing in from our right. A crunch and a clank followed – a piece of that vehicle or ours had fallen off into the road. 'Holy fucking Jesus,' I gasped. If the jeepney had been an inch further forward I'd now be lying in the road twenty feet away, probably covered in glass, probably dead.

'Leopoldo, you *need* to stop the car.'

With another grunt he steered towards the curb. I could feel the tension in my chest easing, my heart rate calming down. But the relief was premature – Leopoldo then steered the other way, not just back into the lane but further, into the centre of the road. A string of oncoming tricycles swerved by us, their horns bleating in grim symphony.

I mustered all the energy I could to shout. 'If you don't stop the car we are going to fucking die!'

It worked. He swerved into the underground car park of a hire-by-the-hour hotel.

I was shaking while I sat in St Luke's Medical Center awaiting news of Leopoldo's fate. I went through a tortuous dialogue in my head.

I feel terrible about this, but what exactly did I do to Leopoldo? How is it my fault?

Well, he was clearly ill from the start of the trip. He shouldn't be working. If he was in England he'd be on disability benefits.

If he was in England they'd be forcing him into work, especially if he has a disability.

I think he has such a strong sense of service that he was too proud to quit. In his mind, he had to get me to my appointment. He's worked for bigwigs before and put up with a lot of shit from them. And now God knows what's wrong with him.

It's not my fault. It's the tour company's. And it's his for not looking after himself.

No, I should have refused to let him drive me the moment we met.

I was interrupted by a dark-skinned doctor with a frizzy pompadour. I surmised he belonged to the persecuted *Negrito* ethnic group that those University of the Philippines students had been killed by the state for researching. He held a clipboard to his chest with both hands. 'Sir, you are the employer of Mr Leopoldo Ramos?'

'Err, indirectly.'

'Meaning, sir?'

'He's employed by the tour company I hired.'

'He is your driver, no?'

'Yes he is. How is he doing?'

'I am afraid to say he is suffering from extreme nausea due to a cirrhotic liver. Did you know anything about this issue?'

'No, not at all. If I had…'

The doctor peered at me austerely, as if I were in a police line-up. 'If you had, you would not have let him drive you?'

'Of course not.'

'He has high blood at the moment. When we have stabilized him, it will be safe to take him home to his family in Pampanga. He has no insurance – all treatments so far will have to be paid for today.'

'Let me sort that out.'

'Very good. Then he will be in God's hands.'

'Can I see him?'

The doctor raised his clipboard up to his chin. 'Sir, this he does not want.'

'Why not?'

The doctor lowered his voice. 'I think he is… ashamed of what happened.'

'He has no reason to be.'

'Sir, he feels he has failed you in some way.'

I stepped closer to him. 'Look doctor, it would mean a lot to me to see him and just, you know, say sorry.'

'Apologies sir, he told me with certainty he did not want to see you. He said only that he wishes you will hurry to your appointment.'

'The appointment was five hours ago,' I sighed.

16. REBEL WITH A SMILE

People on the left are sometimes accused of being humourless, dogmatic and self-righteous. This isn't true of Niva Gonzalez, a cordial woman in her early sixties who, during our interview in the Figaro Coffee Company at SM Mall, peppered her political musings with voluptuous laughter.

I started by apologizing for postponing our meeting due to Leopoldo's illness. I then asked Niva how she got involved in the pro-democracy movement during the Marcos era.

'While a student at the University of the Philippines, I joined Student Catholic Action. Guided by liberation theology, we campaigned on student issues – our civil liberties, the reinstatement of our prohibited newspapers – as well as on matters outside the academy such as the right to strike. On Labor Day, we'd go to workplaces and distribute leaflets. Marcos was bad for students *and* workers.'

Her militancy soon earned her a spot on the junta's enemies list. To avoid detection – and detention – she had to change her name regularly and dash between safe houses.

'Did you ever get caught?' I asked.

She laughed so explosively I couldn't hear the background chit-chat in the café for a good ten seconds. 'Fortunately no!'

'Any near misses?'

'Several. One time in the early 1980s, I was giving out leaflets in Baclaran market. I saw the police coming and had to run. I had to run also from a large Labor Day demonstration in Luneta when soldiers dispersed us with water cannons. Later, after the assassination of Ninoy Aquino (Marcos' leading political opponent), we organized a rally. We thought it would be legal because Marcos had promised to start listening to criticism, but they used tear gas against us. I saw this old man who was in a lot of pain. I thought, "Should I stop to help him?" If I had, we both would have been arrested.'

'Did the old man get caught?'

'Honestly, I do not know. I do not *want* to know.' Niva's lips straightened.

'Was there international support for the democracy movement?'

'Yes, we had many solidarity groups in Europe, in Australia and even in the US because activists like Ninoy Aquino went there to raise consciousness.'

'What was the American government's attitude?'

'Pro-Marcos, of course. For example, one of my friends in the underground could not get a visa for the US.'

'Some say that, aside from his repressive measures, Marcos achieved *some* good things. Do you agree?'

'What good things?' she giggled.

'Some say he improved the infrastructure.'

'No! The problem is we have no movement like the one in Germany after the Nazis to help the populace remember what really happened. The youth here do not know the truth about the Marcoses – they think we had prosperity and discipline then. The newspapers were heavily censored during Martial Law, so it is tough for modern historians to find out the reality of that time.'

'Has there been any attempt at truth and reconciliation?'

'We have a reparations law which is trying to get victims to file their personal stories. These will be collated in museums and archives. Our aim is to get all 100,000 cases documented before the Marcoses re-establish themselves.'

'How will they do that?'

'Ferdinand's son Bongbong may run for president next time.'

'Some people have short memories.'

'*They* do. But *our* slogan is "never again".'

I checked my watch surreptitiously. Niva had only a few minutes before her next appointment. 'Do you think working-class Filipinos are better off today than they were in the 1970s when you started your activism?'

'Well, the left defeated Marcos. After that we had some gains in land distribution. At the same time, old problems persist like the farm workers who can barely eat because they must give most of their produce to landlords. New problems arise like climate change – it hurts the poorest people through flooding etcetera. Then we still have urban poverty and job insecurity. Actually, a contributor to that is the Chinese-Filipino Henry Sy, the wealthiest man in the Philippines. He owns this very mall. Sy started in business near the end of Marcos' time and forbids unionized labour. He gets around the regulations by using a contractor to hire the workers. Now the rest of the service sector in Manila follows the same practice.'

'If there's still all this unfairness why aren't there protests now like in the 1970s?'

Niva sucked in her breath. 'The problem is complex and the solution complex also. Before Martial Law there would be a riot if the price of gasoline went up by five centavos. We were better organized then. We could act quickly and in unity.'

'Why the change?'

'The left fragmented. Now some factions are open to the parliamentary path and others like the Communist Party persist with their armed campaign.'

'Is there much public sympathy for the communists' approach?'

'Yes because country folk starve. Their houses are made from garbage. There are no doctors, no real schools to speak of.'

'What's the attitude of middle-class *Manileños* to the problems in the countryside?'

'Every day, the well-to-do see peasants moving into the city to squat, but they don't do anything. It's like, "Oh we are a poor country, we cannot afford to help them." That is baloney. When some politician plunders 100 million pesos, I ask how many hospitals can we staff with that amount? How many malnourished children can be fed? When the chief of staff of our former President Estrada was in prison for theft, he said the conditions were inhumane. If he'd spent the money he'd stolen on our jails, he wouldn't have ended up in a jail that bad!' More laughter.

'What do you do for a living now?'

'Me, I work on government projects. Ironic, isn't it?'

'You were an enemy of the state and now you work for it?'

'It is a different state now.'

'I'm surprised you think that. You've just been saying it's riddled with corruption and...' I trailed off, curbing my cynicism.

'Sure it has flaws,' said Niva in a defensive tone. 'But at least there are opportunities to make improvements now. This was impossible with Marcos.' She eyed her phone and got to her feet. 'Right, now I have a meeting with the Department of the Environment and Natural Resources. I made for them an environmental impact assessment of five marine protection sites around the country. That is one improvement I can make.'

17. THE PUNISHER'S PARADISE

'If you are doing an illegal activity in my city, if you are a criminal or part of a syndicate that preys on the innocent people of the city, for as long as I am the mayor, you are a legitimate target of assassination.'
Rodrigo 'Rody' Duterte

On 28 March 1945, a second child was born in provincial Leyte to schoolteacher Soledad Roa Duterte and her lawyer husband Vicente Duterte. A few months before, Leyte had been the site of a fierce series of intense air, land and sea battles between the Japanese and US-Philippine forces. The Japanese hid in graveyards and foxholes, emerging only to throw satchel charges at American tanks. It took the GIs days of flamethrowing to clear them out. In late October, Japan's countermove was to send kamikazes day and night into US beachheads, warships and cargo vessels.

It was into this war-scarred society that Rodrigo Duterte came into being. As soon as the boy could walk, Soledad was subjecting him to violent discipline. According to Rodrigo's brother Emmanuel, his mother beat the boy so frequently with a horsewhip that she wore it out. His sister Jo recalls that Soledad would constantly scream abuse at her children and make them kneel down on prickly mung beans as punishment for minor misdeeds. In contrast, Rodrigo's father Vicente was kind and mild, and had great affection for his offspring.

In 1949, the Dutertes moved to Mindanao and, ten years later, Vicente was elected Governor of Davao province. At school, Rody – as he was now nicknamed – was a poor student but a conscientious troublemaker, which meant he received as many thrashings from his Jesuit teachers as he did from his mother at home. The teenaged Rody drank and brawled the night away. Soledad was so infuriated that she kicked him out of the family home and made him live in a mosquito-plagued outhouse. To this day, it is said that Rody always sleeps under a mosquito net.

He developed a taste for risqué gags and pranks. Aged seventeen, he celebrated passing his pilot's test by flying a plane hazardously close to the windows of the family home. Not one to lose his cool easily, Vicente leaped out of his bed and furiously accused Rody of endangering the life of a neighbour with heart disease. Rody was so upset that he hid from the family for three days.

'If you have pain when you are young, you are angry all the time,' his brother Emmanuel told the *New York Times* over fifty years later.

Whenever a suitor of his sister's entered the house, young Rody would stand at the gates holding a pistol. 'It was a miracle if they [the suitor] stayed for ten minutes,' remembers Jo. He would also cramp her social life by gate-crashing parties she attended and demanding she come home with him. His voice was so loud that it often eclipsed the music.

When Ferdinand Marcos became president in 1965, he appointed Vicente his Minister for General Services. Vicente didn't take to national politics and soon went back to practising law in Davao. On 21 February 1968, he collapsed in court from heart failure and died.

The end of his father's life made Rody reassess his own. He resolved that it was time to grow up, cut the mischief and take his studies – also in law – seriously.

From his teenage years up to Vicente's passing, Rody would often say to Jo, '*Malay mo* [you never know], some day I will become mayor.'

The first thing that struck me when I exited Francisco Bangoy International Airport in February 2010 was the overlapping shell design of its roof. It was resonant of the Sydney Opera House. The second thing I noticed was the splendid clarity of the air.

A man from the Ministry of Tourism met me in the car park. He wore a too-tight orange polo shirt buttoned up to his Adam's apple. 'Welcome to Davao, Sir Tom.'

'You must be Arnold.'

Arnold took my bag and marched me to a Toyota HiAce van. He introduced me to Jeps, who would be our driver for the next couple of days. 'Sir Tom,' said Arnold. 'Can you excuse me while I am the one to phone and arrange your interview with the mayor?'

'No worries.'

We drove out on a new asphalt road ranked by black orchids and then into a tidy, low-rise township way more mellow than Manila. Old ladies tilted back on stools behind tables bristling with the chartreuse-hued, spiky-skinned *durien* fruit, a local speciality. Backpack-wearing students huddled around phones and tablets. I saw all the customary – and customized – Filipino vehicles (SUVs, jeepneys, motorbikes), though not many. I didn't hear a single horn honk or a single irate exchange between motorists. Cars froze at crossings, edging obediently off the mark when the lights went green. Pedestrians sloped along the pristine pavements in little herds or stood in hushed attention on bollard-marked traffic islands, eyes skating left and right as they judged the best moment to cross.

I assumed this orderly behaviour was the result of living in a city run by Mayor Duterte. *Time* magazine had dubbed him 'The Punisher' for his stern attitude to law and order.

Arnold finished his call. 'Sir Tom, may I ask you if you will need to smoke?'

'No, not anymore.'

'It is just that if we have a guest who wishes to avail himself of a cigarette then there are designated sectors where we can stop.'

'So you can't smoke just anywhere outside?'

'Yes you cannot. Only in the designated sectors. Nor can you in your home, though you may in your car.'

I opened my mouth to say 'That sounds a bit draconian', but deemed it undiplomatic. 'It must have helped people quit,' I said instead.

Arnold hoisted his eyebrows. 'Actually not. Already sales of tobacco have raised up since the prohibition.'

'The forbidden fruit.'

'Something like that, Sir Tom. By the way, Mayor Duterte's secretary was just telling me that you can perform an interview with the mayor tomorrow.'

'Great.'

'And you will be asking him about the beautiful things we have for tourists here in Davao?'

I hesitated and then nodded. It wasn't very convincing. In truth, I planned to ask Duterte about both tourism – for articles I was writing for some airline magazines – and crime for the political piece I was doing for the *Southeast Asia Globe*. Except I hadn't told Arnold and the tourist board about the latter story, which was naughty of me. (Looking back to this subterfuge – almost a decade ago now – I can't say I'm proud of myself for it. Let's just say that I know things about journalism now that I didn't then.)

In particular, I wanted to ask Duterte about his most controversial policy. Some called it a 'zero tolerance approach to crime', others, mostly human rights advocates, called it 'extra-judicial killing'. From time to time, the peace and quiet of Davao City is disrupted by men in balaclavas and often on motorbikes shooting a suspected offender, many of whom have done nothing worse than smoke crystal meth or steal a mobile phone. Sometimes children and young adults are targeted because it's difficult to prosecute juveniles under Philippine law. According to Amnesty International, over 1,000 individuals have been liquidated in this way since Duterte came to power in 2001. It's alleged that City Hall sends letters to known crooks telling them to leave Davao. If that doesn't work, another letter is dispatched to the crook's mother, threatening the same. If this second missive is ignored, the crook ends up dead in the street.

While 'Duterte Harry', as he's known by some, denies personal responsibility for the Davao Death Squads (DDS), it's perfectly clear where he stands on them. On his weekly TV show he once told any lawbreaker watching, 'You will not survive; you can leave [the city] either vertically or horizontally.' To the *Philippine Inquirer* he said, 'Criminals have no place in the city, except in jails, detention centres and, God forbid, in funeral parlours.' Alluding to the Al Pacino film *Scarface*, Duterte claimed he'd pushed a 'corrupt' personage off a helicopter. When questioned about a wanted rice smuggler, he answered in homage to another Hollywood hard-man, Sam Peckinpah: 'I don't need you to bring the body, just bring me the head of Ryan Yu.' This was no idle threat – Duterte was requesting, quite literally, that Yu's severed head be delivered to City Hall in an ice cooler. The reward was five million pesos.

'Sir Tom, here is your hotel,' said Arnold. 'I will let you have rest now. We will pick you at 7 p.m.'

The Crowne Regency's façade looked frail, angular and yellow, like a cookie-cut piece of dough. My room was as spotless as the streets outside. Unlike bars and hotels in Manila, the wi-fi here was fast and consistent.

I cracked open my laptop and clicked on the links I'd saved to more front-page exposés of Duterte. They read like airport thrillers. Duterte undercover, posing as a taxi driver to monitor police graft. Duterte commanding a tourist caught smoking in a restaurant to eat the offending butt – or else. Duterte forcing a conman to eat the documents he'd counterfeited to extract rent from squatters on land he didn't own. And other incidents that didn't add up: the case of Sally Chua, a rich Chinese-Filipina kidnapped in Manila who somehow persuaded her captors to take her the 600 miles to Davao where she'd get them their ransom. The police were waiting for them. They rescued Chua unharmed after a gunfight that left all three of her abductors dead. A miraculous, Chuck Norris-esque *dénouement* if ever there was one.

I received a text from Bobby, a drinking buddy from Ride N Roll bar: 'How R U in promised land? LOL not so peaceful there owner of ur hotel was killed few months back.'

What did he mean? The owner of the Crowne Regency – where I was staying right now – was murdered? I looked the room up and down. Was he killed *here actually* inside the hotel? I got up and triple-locked the door. Although I'd given up smoking five months ago, I craved a calming cigarette now. Except, if I'd had one I'd be done under Duterte's rules.

I steadied myself. Perhaps Bobby was joking. Then again, if the story were true, Bobby, a well-connected businessman, would know about it. I texted him back to check. He didn't reply. I tried calling him and got his answering service. Before I could Google 'Crowne Regency', 'murder' and 'Davao', knuckles rapped the other side of my door. I unlocked it down to the chain. Through the crack was Arnold.

'Are you good, Sir Tom?'

I released the chain.

'Excuse me, I forgot to give you this before.' He stepped in and threw a tribal necklace made of hemp and an ivory-like material over my head. '*Maayo unta swertihon!*'

'What does that mean?'

'Good luck.'

'Why are you wishing me good luck?'

'The necklace, early on in our history, traditionally gives luck.'

'Oh. Arnold?'

'Sir Tom?'

'Do you know anything about the owner of this hotel being murdered?'

'Of course, but this is a rare thing now in Davao.'

'Did he die *inside this* hotel?'

'No... well, me, I don't think so.' Arnold tipped his head towards the door. 'Come on, Sir Tom, I want to show you the reason why such bad deeds cannot happen here anymore.'

The Public Safety and Security Command Centre (PSSCC) on Aquino Street was encased in tinted glass. We were greeted in a second floor antechamber by a squat, cheery fellow called Angelo. He was clutching a walkie-talkie.

He led us into a darkened room where men were bent over computer screens. The far wall was dominated by a mosaic of larger screens, each relaying CCTV images of landmarks and neighbourhoods in Davao: City Hall, the ferry port for Samar Island, a street of squatters' hovels.

The camera on the centremost screen was following a young woman in shorts and a tight crop top as she walked a bug-eyed Chihuahua through the market.

Angelo pointed the aerial of his walkie-talkie at her. 'Pretty girl, no?'

'Is she a suspect?'

'No,' he laughed laddishly. 'She is just pretty.' He said something in Cebuano to one of his operatives. The wall of screens combined to show a montage of traffic accidents.

A van slamming into the back of a motorbike, the rider flying ten feet into the air before colliding head-first with a wall.
An elderly couple reduced to a crimson puddle by a hurtling juggernaut.
Jeepneys painted with the Madonna and Manny Pacquiao piling into each other at a frenzied crossroads.

Angelo chuckled throughout the show. I had to look away several times.

'You see, the camera does not lie,' said Angelo. 'Since we had them installed these terrible incidents are not happening so often.'

'How many cameras do you have now?'

'157. And in your country?'

'About seven million.'

'Whoa, this is too much, I think.'

He was right, but I was more shocked by Davao's surveillance state because I was standing in its nerve centre right now. If I ever got the chance to visit London's equivalent of this place, I might be several million times more shocked, but that would never happen because the Metropolitan Police surely know that one way of avoiding public alarm about such shifty operations is to stop journalists getting anywhere near them. By contrast, the authorities in Davao were positively proud of their CCTV system and wanted to show it off. The command centre even had its own Facebook page.

'Angelo, do you ever see Davao Death Squad activities on camera?'

He was more than ready for a knotty question like this. He banged his walkie-talkie into the palm of his other hand. 'We have not identified as such these persons who support the mayor's advocacy of extreme discipline. We have invited investigation teams to Davao and they have not pinpointed the perpetrators. What we do in the PSSCC is provide the police with what they need to find felons.'

'So despite all the cameras you've never seen one of these assassinations?'

He'd been well-trained not to give straight answers. 'While all around us here in Mindanao there are problems, not in Davao because we are careful. We have a saying in Cebuano, so let me translate: *Life begins here because crime ends here.*'

On the ride to back to the hotel, I feared Arnold had guessed I wasn't just writing a eulogy to his hometown. 'Why, Sir Tom, are you interested in the lawlessness in Davao when you are working for a touristic publication?'

'It's my duty to give my readers some background. If they get into any trouble here they'll complain that the magazine didn't warn them.'

'I see.'

'Have you ever seen one of these extra-judicial killings yourself?'

'Me, I have not.'

'Do you know how they happen?'

'Oftentimes captured members of the New People's Army will be recruited to slay the wanted men. Their choice is be recruited or go to jail.'

'Who recruits them?'

'I do not know. Sometimes the assassin will already be waiting only 100 metres away from the police station. He waits for the target to be released from custody – and then *blam*! There was a case early on in the year when a target's sister jumped in front of him and she took the bullet. She died, he escaped.'

'How do the killers get away with it?'

'Normally they are not caught. Also, oftentimes when the assassin engages the target with firearms, the target will fire back. Then the law of duelling applies.'

'The law of duelling?'

'Both men are shooting so whoever wins wins, whoever loses loses. And after this the case is closed.'

As he let me out of the van, Arnold said, 'Please only write good things about Davao, Sir Tom.'

In my room I puzzled over his request. If it were sincere, why had he just told me a lot of disturbing things about Davao? Then again, maybe Arnold didn't regard the death squads as disturbing. Perhaps he was as proud of them as Angelo was of the command centre.

Next morning, over a breakfast of *pandesal* (salted bread) and Lipton tea, I tried to situate Duterte politically. His bent for brute force, disdain for due process and his *1984*-ish surveillance set-up was the stuff of right-wing autocracy. But was that too simplistic a verdict?

In preparation for this trip, I'd asked left-leaning *Manileños* what they made of Duterte. All had some admiration for him, but why? In defiance of big business, Duterte had prohibited mining across Davao 'because it destroys our land and our forests' and had created initiatives to uplift the health, education and social mobility of his constituents. He was on good terms with José Maria Sison of the Communist Party of the Philippines, now banished to Holland for his role in a guerrilla war against the Philippine military (assisted by US Special Forces) that was now forty years old. In the febrile atmosphere of the War on Terror, Duterte was negotiating with Islamist *Moro* factions also at war with the state. Rather than taking the absolutist, neo-con line that these terrorists were immune to reason and should be liquidated, he'd listened to their grievances and supported greater powers for their autonomous region in return for them not wreaking havoc in his city. As a result, Davao was mostly exempt from the beheadings and suicide attacks that blighted other parts of Mindanao.

Duterte wasn't afraid, then, to take on both the Manila establishment and US hegemony. For some on the left, this mitigated his more fascistic foibles. But how to explain the contradiction between his self-described socialism and his bullyboy tactics? Perhaps it dated back to his upbringing. While his father Vicente had been a close ally of the Marcoses, his mother Soledad had, after Vicente's death, been a prime figure in the Yellow Friday Movement to replace Marcos with liberal democracy. It seemed to me that the left-right binary means something radically different in the Philippines than it does in the West. In Britain, only people on the far right would agree with Duterte's short, sharp shock treatment for drug dealers. These same people wouldn't also support workers' rights or ecological protection. And I just couldn't picture Nigel Farage negotiating with firebrand mullahs.

Later that morning, Arnold drove us into the mountains outside the city, where the cool wind carried the scent of pine trees. We got out at the Malagos Garden Resort, where amber shrubs dangled like cowlicks over chunks of sandstone and sage-toned epiphytes cuddled old-world *nipa* huts on stilts. We were served *al fresco* some locally-produced, organic goat's cheese and red wine – both firsts for me in Asia.

At the eighty-hectare Eden Nature Park, we meandered among sculpted flower beds. I smiled tipsily at the happy faces of sunflowers and the impish spurts of *sampaguitas*. If a lover's tiff – let alone a gunfight – was hard to visualize on the sedate streets of downtown Davao, it was even harder to visualize one in this idyll. Only dialectical thinking could make sense of the coexistence of beauty and tyranny here, although I assumed where someone stands socially in this situation determines if they see more beauty than tyranny, or more tyranny than beauty.

18. CREATE AND DESTROY

On our way home, Arnold took me to the Ponce Suites Hotel. Its frontage was festooned with silvery rock sculptures. Two Philippine eagles dug their talons into an excessively gnarled branch held up Atlas-style by a bearded figure. I gawked at the depiction of a long-haired man sitting on a toilet. His head was buried in his hands, his trousers pulled down to the shins.

'This I made when I was trying to find myself,' said a voice behind me. I turned to face a guy in a striped bandana with a downy goatee and a moustache that bowed over the corners of his lips.

Arnold pointed at us both. 'Kublai Millan, the famous artist of Mindanao, meet Sir Tom. He is a journalist from England.'

'So it's not a self-portrait?' I asked.

'Ah no, I made it at a time when I was thinking hard about, I don't know, where I was going with my art. Later I overcame my demons and began making sculptures that are smiling always because we are a happy people. Whenever you look at them they smile back. I see that in your Europe the sculptures all look sad, I don't know.'

There was something alluringly humble about the way he inserted the phrase 'I don't know' into his spiel.

'Some Europeans,' I said, 'equate misery with coolness. So how did you get into sculpture?'

'I was a painter before. I was supposed to do a tour in the US, but I have a Muslim name and they cancelled my visa. I was young then and felt so bad about it. After that time, I hated Americans! Instead I decided to stay here and find my purpose doing sculptures. If I had kept on with painting, well, people in Mindanao do not really appreciate this kind of art. In the provinces they do not even have galleries.'

'Is it hard to earn a living as an artist in the Philippines?'

'I cannot talk about the Philippines, I can only talk about Mindanao. I am probably the only one surviving because, I don't know, nobody buys art here. They are not buying so artists are giving their work away on the streets.' Kublai let out a grim laugh.

'So the only real funding is through the state?'

'Even my government projects, I am paid just enough. That's OK. It is a long process to get governments to pay for art. But if there is political will – if the mayor or governor wants it – it will happen. I prefer doing these bigger works anyway; monuments and parks all over Mindanao. I make my pieces big because people cannot ignore them!'

'Have you been to the more troubled areas of Mindanao?'

'Of course.'

'Have you ever been in any danger there?'

'Many times. I was attacked by bandits once and had to be protected by the military. Another time, I was in my house in the mountains when these guys came for me. Recently in Zamboanga one of my team – just a boy – was shot while we were constructing the sculpture. He is lucky to be alive.'

'Who shot him?'

'An NPA sniper. And just this month the mayor of a town who commissioned one of my parks in the southeast was killed by NPAs. Crazy.'

'Why would anyone want to hurt artists?'

'Me, I don't think they want to hurt me as an artist. They maybe want money or they are angry about the amounts spent on these projects, thinking they're worth millions.'

'Are they?'

'Not so much. I use concrete because it is the cheapest material. If we use bronze, we will run out of money. And it's unfair to spend so much cash on materials when, I don't know, people are hungry.'

'It looks bold.'

'We use automobile paints to get a metallic effect. That's the little expensive part, but it's the least we can do.'

'Are there some regions in Mindanao you wouldn't work in?'

'No. My work advocates for the indigenous cultures here so the works have to be here. I don't know, I must take the risk. We do our researches before we go, stay careful while we are there. We have bodyguards too. But sometimes, it's like, "Time to scram!"'

'Do you think your art can help bring peace?'

'What I notice is that, when we make art, people gather. They celebrate, they eat together, they band together. Maybe it works a little.'

'Do you ever do projects in Manila?'

'No, I get sick.'

'From the pollution?'

'From everything. It's very political in Manila. I don't get support there because I'm not a National Artist.'

'Why not?'

'I am from the south, not the north. The north does not take seriously art in the south. Anyhow, I want to stay here in my home province to make change and to give inspiration to local artists. You be careful, though.'

'Why?'

'If I talk too much about Mindanano then you'll fall in love with Mindanao. The waterfalls, the white sand, the forests, the people – I'd do anything for them.'

'Even die for them?'

Kublai stared into my eyes with convincing gravity. 'Even.'

'What are your ambitions now?'

'There are so many tribes here. I want, in my lifetime, to concretize their existence through my art, for my children and my children's children.'

'There's a danger of losing touch with the past, you think?'

'Yes, things are happening too fast. The malls are coming here, the cities are coming here. If we do not build according to nature then it will be bad. There are things to learn from the tribes, as they are the ones closest to nature in terms of their beliefs and principles. I don't know, I try to reflect that in my art.'

'Sir Tom,' interjected Arnold. 'We must be going now, I am afraid.'

As we departed, I asked Kublai a last question. 'Is the Davao government helpful to you as an artist?'

'Yes. So far the mayor has commissioned me to do three works.'

'Is he a good man? A good mayor?'

Kublai didn't answer me. This was the end of our verbal exchange, but the conversation continued, so to speak, in the eyes of Kublai and Arnold. Arnold's pupils dilated fretfully for a second and then returned to their normal size. In response, Kublai's pupils contracted with befuddled caution. Then the men looked away from each other, flustered. I guessed Kublai's subliminal message to be, 'I don't like Duterte, but I need his money and one of his henchmen is here...'

19. THE REST-IN-PEACE SOLUTION

In the Crowne Regency's reception that night I got talking to Eugenio, a cleaner. He must have been older than he looked, as Filipinos born before the 1950s and 1960s are more likely to have Spanish rather than Anglo-American forenames. When I said I was going to interview Duterte tomorrow, Eugenio told me he'd met him a decade ago.

'Me, I was a fire volunteer who rescued a kid trapped on a roof here in Davao. I climbed up to retrieve him and I was electric-shocked at 2,800 volts. I tripped on a live wire, 50 per cent of me was all burned up.'

'You look very well now.'

'I am a type of superhero, no?'

'Did you spend a long time in hospital?'

'Six months. It was there that the mayor gave me a visitation.'

'What was he like?'

'Kindly man. He gave me a medal. He is able to make you feel special when he talks to you.'

'Did he help with your medical fees?'

'No. The fire service did not even. My family and friends put their monies together for me. Actually, I think the electric shock made me more of a man. I had three children since then.'

'Is Duterte doing a good job?'

'I have a family of seven. I work forty-eight-hour shifts in this job to feed them. For a while there were hoodlums making problem in my *barangay*. They beat up on people and tried to sell drugs to my kids. One day, I got back from work and they were gone. It was a relief for me to have this problem no longer. So I support Mayor Duterte's way of doing.'

I went to my room. I dwelled on Eugenio's claim – 'They ... tried to sell drugs to my kids' – and tried to imagine how I'd react if someone did the same to my child, if I had a child.

I got into bed feeling nervous about meeting Duterte. If I worded a question crudely might my mum receive a threatening letter from City Hall? Or worse, would a hitman be waiting for me in the car park?

Other journalists had lost their lives in Duterte's Davao. In 2003, radio pundit Jun Pala was shot nine times in a motorbike drive-by. His brother and bodyguard were with him, but survived the bullets. Pala himself was not a nice fellow – he belonged to a vicious anti-communist cell – but that shouldn't have warranted his extermination. The police never found a witness to the Pala homicide, let alone a suspect for it.

Of course, the interview could go the other way and Duterte might charm me into being soft on him. I have that weakness. As Eugenio had said, Duterte can make you feel as if you are the only person in the world worth talking to.

A phonecall woke me at 5.30 a.m. 'Sir Tom,' said Arnold. He sounded subdued. 'My apologies for calling you so early on. I am afraid the mayor is not able to see you today.'

'Right.'

'And I am afraid I am the one to help him today so I cannot guide you around also. Please accept my apologies for that too. I will send the van to pick you for the airport.'

'Arnold, can we…'

'Goodbye Sir Tom.' The line went dead. Perhaps he'd finally found out I was writing something contentious about Duterte and didn't want to give me any more ammo for it.

Part of me was relieved I wouldn't have to meet The Punisher. But another part of me – perhaps a majority – was disappointed not to get some empirical insights into the man unmediated by what I'd read, heard and seen second-hand.

On the flight back to Manila, I went over the questions I would have asked him. I'd decided there was no point making him repeat his stock ripostes to the death squad criticisms. I wanted more knowledge of his personal life. Then I could understand to what degree his private suffering informed his public actions. Did Duterte share his brother's opinion that an infancy of 'violence in the house, violence in the school and violence in the neighbourhood' accounted for the grown-up Duterte's sick sense of humour and waspish disciplinarianism? And how did he square his obsessive loathing of drugs with his own, self-admitted use of fentanyl, an opioid that is up to 100 times more potent than the street heroin you could get killed for peddling around his city? He'd started using the drug to ease two rare conditions: Buerger's disease, in which the blood vessels become inflamed, and Barrett's oesophagus, where heartburn and indigestion are caused by reflux of bile. The latter affliction was poetic justice, I reckoned. But what if the fentanyl wasn't working and his physical pain – along with the psychological variety – contributed to his lousy temperament? I wasn't sure, though, if I'd have had the balls to ask him about any of this.

One thing I was certain he wouldn't have confessed to me was the state of his mental health. Natividad Dayan, former president of the International Council of Psychologists, has opined that Duterte has Antisocial Narcissistic Personality Disorder. He exhibits 'gross indifference, insensitivity and self-centeredness, grandiose sense of self-entitlement and manipulative behaviours and pervasive tendency to demean, humiliate others and violate their rights and feelings.' If this diagnosis was correct, no doubt the trauma of Duterte's regular beatings at home and school played a role in the disorder. So was he emotionally displacing the aggression he'd endured as a schoolboy onto the desperados of Davao? Was his pharmacophobia an instance of psychological projection given his own problems with fentanyl and the fact that his son, Paolo, had been accused of drug smuggling?

Psychology – of the collective type – might also account for Duterte's allure to the people of Davao. He'd won seven successive elections, after all. Joel had a quasi-Freudian theory about it: 'The populace wants a powerful father figure. They crave someone to tell them off, to spank them. They think that, in return, they receive security.'

I then reflected on Duterte in the wider context of the world. Was he much more awful than other leaders? I found an article on the website of Human Rights Watch, a New York-based outfit that the NGO Monitor website has called out for bias and its 'close links to Western governments'. There were hints of superiority and hypocrisy to the unnamed author's tone, as if the sorts of violations that occurred in Davao never occurred in his own country or under the aegis of his own government. If the dead could talk, 2,500 Arabs killed by drone warfare – itself a species of extra-judicial killing – might quarrel with him. Duterte and President Obama didn't have much in common, but both were trained lawyers who knew the meaning of due process, yet they used illegal measures to – so they believed – foil future harm to their constituents. *Counterpunch*'s Charles Pierson goes further: 'Duterte is an amateur compared with the United States. The US has been in the death squad business for decades. This does not stop the US from lecturing other countries about human rights, much like an 800 lb. man dispensing diet tips.'

At any rate, was the 'violence-to-thwart violence' approach a slippery slope too strewn with blood and guts to be worth going down? If you think you're ethically above your enemies, you don't stoop to your enemies' lowdown methods. Enough innocents had died in both Davao and the Middle East to show that the 'rest-in-peace solution', as Angelo had put it, was futile. And even when the right man is targeted, what about the notion that bad people can be redeemed, or that they deserve mercy because they were compelled to act badly by no-hope circumstances?

I also doubted the 'rest-in-peace solution' was a deterrent. 'Contrary to expectations,' argues human rights activist Kenneth Roth, 'the Davao Death Squad has not reduced crime. In the decade since [the squads] began operating, crime in Davao City has mushroomed ten times faster than the population.' I imagined all those brothers of the slain seeking revenge for their losses. For the same reasons, it could be said that Bush, Blair and Obama's War on Terror had encouraged more terrorism in London, Boston, Madrid and elsewhere.

Later, as I was queuing to exit the plane at Ninoy Aquino International Airport – named, ominously, after a politician who was assassinated in 1983 in the same airport (it was called the Manila International then) – I saw a pundit on ABS-CBN news propose that Duterte run for President of the Philippines in the 2010 election.

Surely he couldn't win, I thought. That's as absurd as, say, Donald Trump being elected President of the United States.

PART 3: 2016

20. TRUMP OF ASIA?

In February 2014, I spotted a social media campaign calling for Rodrigo Duterte to stand in the 2016 presidential elections. This must be a hoax, I said to myself.

At any rate, Duterte dismissed the idea, saying he was 'not qualified for higher office'. But a year later, he revealed on his TV show that he was 'thinking hard' about entering the race after endorsements from friends and family members. Three months after that came another U-turn: 'I am not running. Sorry.'

Then, on 27 November, less than two weeks before the deadline for nominations, he filed his certificate of candidacy. He promised to solve *all* crime in the Philippines using the hardline methods he'd perfected in Davao. The fish of Manila Bay, he said, 'will grow fat' on the corpses of addicts and traffickers. He knew from decades of provincial hustings that such rhetoric would appeal to blue collar male voters – a key demographic in Philippine politics. So would his spectacularly un-PC wisecracks. 'I should have been first,' he said when asked by reporters about the rape and murder of an Australian priestess in Davao in 1989. He crowed about womanizing while on Viagra: 'What am I supposed to do, let this hang forever?' He defended his wolf-whistling a woman journalist on the grounds of 'freedom of expression'.

All of which had echoes across the Pacific, where Donald Trump was embarking on his own shock-populist push for power, his crass gags and tirades aimed at women, Mexicans and pretty much all other foreigners endearing him to the disaffected, post-industrial American male. As with Trump, Duterte harnessed jingoism to laddish belligerence. When asked about the Philippines' territorial quarrel with China over the Spratly Islands in the South China Sea, he promised to 'ride a jet ski [there] while bringing the Philippine flag'. And, like Trump, each new controversy made observers think that this time, surely, he'd gone too far and made himself 'unpresidentiable'. But each time they were wrong.

Castigating the Catholic Church had been the one taboo left for Filipinos until Duterte said of Pope Francis' visit in January 2015, '*Putang ina mo* (your mother is a whore), go home. Don't visit here anymore.' (I remembered Joel telling me on my first night at Ride N Roll that *putang ina mo* was the worst possible insult in Filipino.) Unlike Trump, whose ratings slipped after his 'grab them by the pussy' howler, Duterte's stock grew after this extraordinary salvo. Other notables he has since called sons of whores include President Obama and Philip Goldberg, erstwhile US Ambassador to the Philippines.

Shortly after the former leader of the Ku Klux Klan David Duke endorsed Trump, Duterte hit a fresh nadir when he compared himself favourably to Adolf Hitler. 'There are three million drug addicts (in the Philippines),' he said. 'I'd be happy to slaughter them. If Germany had Hitler, the Philippines would have...' He gestured to himself.

But how spontaneous were these outbursts? Senator Alan Peter Cayetano held that Duterte was a 'master strategist' whose statements were carefully crafted to 'provoke a discussion'. There was evidence of shrewd planning, too, behind his choice of allies. To woo the right-wingers in the north, he spoke of his father's friendship with Ferdinand Marcos and named Ferdinand's son Bongbong as his running mate (Bongbong narrowly lost in the vice-presidential election that is a separate process to the presidential contest). To entice the left, Duterte promised to appoint communists and members of the social democratic Bayan Muna Party to his cabinet. Southerners took to him because he proposed federalist devolution of power away from Manila and was on good terms with *Moro* chiefs.

If he did win – which surely he couldn't – I doubted Duterte could satisfy all of these people all of the time, so incompatible were their values and objectives.

Then, on 10 May 2016, Duterte did win with 39 per cent of the vote, far ahead of his divided rivals. I flew to Manila to investigate.

Although Duterte was yet to be sworn in, the 'war on the poor', as Amnesty dubbed it, had already metastasized from Davao out across the archipelago. In my first week in Manila, police shot dead fourteen putative drug dealers in stings in Manila and General Santos City. The cops claimed they acted in self-defence. This was to become a standard – and increasingly implausible – excuse.

Aside from fattening the fishes, at this stage I struggled to ascertain what Duterte's exact policies would be given his tendency not only to josh around but to flip-flop. Numerous times I watched him on TV strut into midnight press conferences in a pink sports jacket – he'll never don the conventional politician's pin stripes – and make various assertions only to later on retract them or say he didn't really mean them. He pulled away from a confrontation with Beijing over the Spratlys: 'ties [with China] have never been cold ... I would rather be friendly.' After appearing to justify the assassination of 'corrupt' reporters, he then claimed, 'I do not condone nor tolerate killing of journalists.' After his press office released an apology for the rape remarks, Duterte said he wasn't in fact sorry at all. However, he did apologize to the pope and has stood by it.

'We have no way of telling what is true and what is not,' an exasperated editor at CNN Philippines complained to me.

21. CORBYN OF THE PHILIPPINES?

Wqhat did the progressive wing of Philippine politics make of Duterte's extraordinary rise? A contact at CNN Philippines recommended I speak to Teddy Casiño, a former senator for Bayan Muna ('Nation First'), a small democratic socialist political party. I emailed him and received an invite to his cramped office in Quezon City the following morning. True to his name, there was something teddy bearish about the upbeat smile on his round, though not chubby, face. I started by asking if Duterte could bring changes that Bayan Muna – and the left in general – could get behind.

'He has offered to appoint four left members of his cabinet and he promises to resume the peace process with the underground left. Of course, everything remains to be seen – he hasn't assumed power yet. There have always been concerns about his approach to human rights, but we'll continue to pressure him on these issues. And I think they are not a hindrance to good working relations between his government and Bayan Muna.'

'Can he be persuaded to temper some of his more extreme positions if he works with the left?'

'Yes. The experience of our colleagues in Davao City shows that kind of dynamic. In spite of his machismo, he has good policies and programmes for female empowerment.'

'So that joke he made, the infamous joke, was... just a joke?'

'Those who have lived under his leadership know he talks that way.'

'Could you personally work with him, do you think?'

'There are suggestions that I could join his administration..'

'Have you met him?'

'At the airport in 2013, on my way to Manila from Davao. We had coffee and chatted about stuff.'

'What was he like in person?'

'He's down to earth, very practical. No airs. What you see is what you get. His demeanour on TV or at a press conference is the same as when he is talking to you one on one.'

'When you met him you agreed on a number of issues, I guess?'

'He said he would support me. He said he'd advise his constituents in Davao to vote for me.'

'Why do you think he won the last election?'

'Duterte's campaign unleashed a mass movement supporting him. It was not controlled by the big politicians. The question for me is can that electoral mass movement be transformed into a struggle for social reform?'

'You sound optimistic, but isn't there a worry that a lot of the people behind Duterte aren't all that progressive?'

'It is true that Duterte's constituents like his more draconian ideas. Whether there is positive change depends on Duterte himself. I hope he chooses sound, progressive elements for his cabinet. We have to wait and see.'

'One of the main aims of your party is land reform and improving the conditions of the peasant farmers. Is Duterte interested in that?'

'We think Duterte understands the issues. For example, he has promised to appoint one of our colleagues, former Congressman Rafael Mariano, as secretary of the Department of Agrarian Reform. Ka Paeng [Mariano's monicker] is the foremost critic of the previous reforms, and when he was in Congress, he was pushing for something more radical. We hope that's a sign that Duterte is ready to use state power to make positive changes. But we are also cautious because we know that some of the biggest landlords in Mindanao support Duterte. These are owners of large plantations who have resisted redistribution of lands to their workers.'

'I know one of your concerns is tax justice. Is Duterte supportive of that?'

'Bayan Muna's policy is we would cut it by 10 per cent for the middle- and low-income workers. Duterte has said he is amenable, but exactly how much he wants it reduced, we'll have to see.'

'I wanted to ask you about how you got into politics and how you formed your values. It seems to me that most politicians, not just in the Philippines but the world over, are only interested in acquiring money and power. You're different, I think.'

'Thanks!'

'Was there a moment when you were younger perhaps when these principles began to take form?'

'I've always said that I am not a politician – I am an activist who happens to be involved in politics. My awakening was in the mid-1980s, the last years of the Marcos dictatorship. I was in high school and learned about the struggles of the farmers on Negros Island. The hunger, the human rights atrocities appalled me. I took part in the movement against the Marcoses at this time too. And then in 1986, when Marcos was removed, I thought everything was going to be great, so I studied agriculture at state college and learned more about the conditions of the farmers. I realized that the changes I thought would happen were not happening. That got me into the student movement and then the labour movement. In 1998, I took part in what we call a 'multi-sectoral', an umbrella group called Bagong Alyansang Makabayan, featuring farmers, workers, students, and women. And then in 2004, I was drafted by Bayan Muna to stand for Congress.'

'What was that like?'

'We viewed the work in Congress as an extension of the social movement. And it's a very vigilant social movement, and that prevented us from going the way of the usual politicians!'

'No-one has ever tried to induce you to the dark side?'

'There was an incident in my first term when we were trying to impeach President Arroyo. One of her people offered a bribe to my colleague to support a fake impeachment complaint. My colleague talked about it on the plenary, revealing it to everyone. Since then, no one has dared to approach us. They are probably scared we would broadcast it!'

'Sometimes the best policy is just to be open.'

'Our attitude was that we had nothing to lose. If Congress had kick us out we'd be back on the streets protesting.'

'You served three terms as a Congressman yet your party is very small. Who is it that votes for you?'

'We have constituents in practically all sectors.'

'So there are always enough supporters nationally to ensure that at least someone can get elected?'

'We have a bloc of seven seats in Congress, which has been maintained since 2004, consistently. This is down to the party list system of proportional representation, which is particular, I think, to the Philippines. Initially, the system was for the marginalized, unrepresented sectors. Unfortunately, now the big business groups, religious factions and even the political dynasties are allowed to field their own party list.'

'When you were growing up were there politicians, writers or thinkers – Filipino or non-Filipino – who inspired you?'

'There was this one Filipino writer, F. Sionil José. I used to read his books over and over again. Renato Constantino's works were also a big eye-opener for me.'

'No one in mainstream politics?'

'Well probably Ninoy Aquino for the sacrifice he made. But, you know, I'm wary of mainstream politicians, especially now I know many of them!'

'Any current politicians you like? You can say no if you want.'

'I can't think of any.'

'What do you think of José Maria Sison [exiled leader of the Communist Party of the Philippines]? What if came back to the Philippines?'

'His return would be welcome. He'd stir things up, rock the status quo. And his physical presence would help the reform campaign.'

'Politics can be a dangerous business here. Have you ever been in danger yourself?'

'During the Arroyo administration, 1,000 Bayan Muna members were killed. I have never personally received a death threat, though.'

'Do you have a bodyguard?'

'When I was in Congress I had a driver and an aide. They both doubled as bodyguards. I told them that if something bad happened, the best thing to do would be to scream. That would draw attention to the threat. Now I'm not in Congress I don't have a driver. I drive for myself.'

'Do Filipino politicians have any interest in the Filipino diaspora? Do they try and court them in any way?'

'I myself have not been to the US, but I did go to Europe and other parts of Asia. I met with OFWs [Overseas Filipino Workers] through a group, Migrante International. It advocates for the rights and welfare of the OFWs.'

'You found OFWs sympathetic to the Bayan Muna cause?'

'Very much. They have found no opportunities here and are frustrated at the way things have been going in the Philippines. Overseas work started as a stop-gap measure during the Marcos administration but eventually became a permanent policy – we call it the "labour export policy" – because the local economy could not produce the jobs and the incomes needed by ordinary Filipinos. Now in the Philippines we have changed our national education programme to cater to the overseas labour market. This is bad – you should encourage your people to stay in the country. But the free movement of labour is part of the neoliberal framework. You don't have to develop your own industry, you know – just send your workers abroad and they will send the money back.'

'There are so many Filipino nurses in the UK.'

'Very good ones.'

'And it's good for us but not good for the Philippines, presumably?'

'We have a shortage of medical professionals in our hospitals. The social consequences of labour migration are always ignored. Families break up, children do not have parents to look after them. There has been no governmental response to that.'

'Has Bayan Muna had any success in mayoral or council elections?'

'The political dynasties are so entrenched locally that progressive candidates don't make much progress. At that level, you have to contend with the worst kinds of patronage and corruption and electoral fraud. In the national party-list system there's at least a semblance of party principle, party ideology, but if you run for mayor you have to threaten your rivals and behave like a criminal. Bayan Muna won't go that way. In a provincial town the husband is the mayor, the wife is the vice-mayor, the children are councillors – you know, everyone's related to everyone. It's difficult to penetrate that entrenched political structure.'

'In Congress were you able to introduce any bills that would change these entrenched structures?'

'We've been pushing for an anti-dynasty law for years. We want to enshrine it in the Constitution. Everyone supports it, says, "Yes yes, we need that!" and no-one objects to it. But it doesn't get calendared, it just lies there asleep.'

'Someone told me that Filipinos don't like to say no.'

'Maybe that's the problem.'

'I wonder if you have any message for Filipinos in the UK?'

'We shouldn't lose hope!'

'We have a politician called Jeremy Corbyn who says, "Let's do hope not despair".'

'I like that.'

22. A PEOPLE IN BETWEEN

Dusk doesn't last long in Manila – abrupt is the shift from daylight to dark. But this morning, on the Day of the Dead, cloud cover was bringing all the effects of dusk only at 10 a.m. As I surfaced from Abad Santos station, barbecue smoke bore skywards and congealed with the black-grey clouds that were like bubbly nodules of refined and oxidized lead. Women under tarpaulin bivouacs crossed out bingo numbers with pink, green and yellow felt-tips – colours drained of their showy day-gloness by the wan light. Only the burnished Mandarin inscriptions of the Manila Chinese Cemetery's front gates stood out in high-definition against the monochrome of all else.

The cemetery looked less like a cemetery and more like my neighbourhood in Quezon City. The crypts had all the trappings of middle-class homes. Chrome-plated bath tubs sprawled under pagoda roofs, broadband routers twinkled through polished jalousie windows and deftly chiselled hedges bordered a blue-domed townhouse. Between grilles and balustrades I saw TVs, microwaves, espresso machines, refrigerators and air-conditioning units.

I approached a thirty-strong family sitting on deckchairs around an arrow-shaped tower with psychedelic fragments of stained glass for a façade. When the family started opening polystyrene tubs of food, I was hit by twin whiffs: syrupy corn-starch batter and brackish Knorr stock.

'Mind if I ask why you left a TV in the tomb?' I said to a small boy as he was about to sink his argent-braced teeth into a fritter.

'Makes the trip to paradise smooth for my godfather, already,' he said.

'Sometimes I am the one to sleep in the tomb with him,' said his aunt – or possibly his mum.

'Is that very common?' I asked.

'Yes. Some people live here full-time. Others are being born here.' She tendered a greasy paper bag. 'Have you ate?'

I've never been that squeamish, but being around lots of dead people just didn't give me an appetite. 'That's kind, but no thanks. I ought to keep walking.'

I came across other dead people's relatives placing ribbons, tissues and lucky red envelopes of money on marble coffins and memorial stones. As I watched, I posited the cemetery as some place between life and death, where the living interacted with the deceased in ways I'd never seen before. I strained my brain to recall the last time I'd visited the grave of a loved one. Never, I realized. We in the West don't do death very well. We either don't talk about it or we do talk about it – and then we get distraught, nostalgic or sentimental. We certainly don't have the courage to spend long periods of time with the dead.

It dawned on me that this cemetery was not the only aspect of Chinese-Filipino culture to have the quality of 'in-betweenness' to it. The community has long occupied an unstable space amid opposites: hero and villain, native and expat, powerful and powerless; and that middle path between being an object of hatred and an object of esteem – might we call it envy?

The first Chinese came to Luzon in the tenth century AD to import wax, onions, coconuts, cotton and textiles. After the founding of the Spanish East Indies, entrepreneurs from Fujian province brought luxury goods for the Spanish and cut-price food and clothes for the Malay-Filipinos. According to the great Filipino historian Renato Constantino, the Chinese played 'a more vital role than the Spanish colonialists' in 'the growing linkage of the country to world capitalism'.

Seeing two kids fighting over who would pin a red envelope onto a Polaroid of a crumpled forebear reminded me that Chinese integration into Manila hadn't been easy. Chinese prosperity alarmed the early Spaniards. Miguel de Benavides, Archbishop of Manila from 1602 to 1605, cobbled up a conspiracy theory about Chinese

A PEOPLE IN BETWEEN

ambitions to snatch the entire archipelago. The state opted for divide-and-rule, forcing 20,000 *Sangleys* (non-Christian Chinese) into Parián – a ghetto next door to Intramuros – and a smaller number of Chinese converts to the Dominican Order into a place called Binondo – where I was strolling now, 430-odd years later.

I was relieved when a minute but malevolent grandmother inserted herself between the bellicose kids and pacified them with a crooked index finger followed by a thunderous shout. The kids stooped with shame. The conflict was over. The Chinese-Filipinos have seen enough conflict to last them for a lifetime – or rather for six centuries plus an infinite afterlife stuck in their crypts watching *Pilipinas Got Talent* on a 3D 4K Smart TV. Akin to the Jews in Europe, they'd borne demonization, segregation, harassment, expulsion and butchery.

I moved on to Chong Hock Tong, reputedly the oldest Chinese temple in the republic. Without being disrespectful, it seemed to me a tad clichéd with its over-painted terracotta eaves and plasticky emerald dragons stalking the roof. As I stared at it, I wondered idly which cultural group in the world has had the most clichés and stereotypes peddled about it. The Chinese would be candidates. In Hispanic Manila, the upper crust cooked up victim-blaming backbites about the Chinese taste for hard-bargaining and penny-pinching, derived from the fact that, since the upper crust had barred the Chinese from owning land, one of the few vocations left to them was trading. And to be a good trader it does help to bargain and to look after your pennies. A few thousand miles west, the trope of the crafty Shylock had sprouted from Jews working as interest moneylenders because their Christian persecutors were forbidden by their own faith from doing the same job.

After the Spanish confined the *Sangleys* to Parián knowing that few females were among them, they callously spread rumours that sodomy was rife within this crowded, male-dominated slum of heathens who'd spurned Christian sexual morality. For the Spanish to mock the Chinese for circumstances the Spanish had imposed on them was not unlike one of the naughty boys I'd just seen thumping

127

the other and then ridiculing the recipient for having a bleeding eye or smashed nose.

The gay smear obtained until the 1600s, when Chinese men were allowed to marry Spanish and Filipina women. In the same century, Spanish capitalists got rich from galleons transporting silver from Acapulco and spices, ivory, porcelain and silk from China, while the Chinese monopolized trade within the provinces. I passed a column of hawkers selling the same wares as their ancestors would have sold: clothes, shoes, crêpe lanterns, seafood balls on skewers and boxes of rice topped with roast duck.

Later on, Chinese *mestizo* (mixed heritage) business clans did well out of the economic revamp of the Philippines in the late 1800s. Sugar, tobacco, hemp and other lucrative – and often unhealthy – cash crops were grown for the first time and the Chinese earned themselves a fresh reputation for greed by undercutting the competition from European and American merchants. Other Chinese were branded cheats for making loans to native farmers in return for temporary use of their land on the proviso that the farmers could buy the land back later. But so rarely could they afford to buy it back that vast tracts of valuable real estate fell permanently into the hands of the loansharks. The Chinese *mestizos* were not the first to act like this – the Spanish friars had done the same before them. But why let a spot of moral objectivism get in the way of a good solid boilerplate?

As the Chinese *mestizos* gained clout, so they expected more from the Spanish *jefes*, such as the right to apply for government posts reserved for *peninsulares* (100 per cent Spaniards born in Spain). This mild movement for liberal reform snowballed into the 1896 Revolution. Chinese *mestizos* were at the forefront of that movement. Indeed, some historians credit the Chinese *mestizos* with inventing the very concept of Filipino nationality, as something discrete from and at odds with Spanish colonialism. The Chinese had come a long way from their marginal status as the pariahs of Parián.

Going into the adjacent Martyrs Hall, I realized that it celebrated those who had died in World War II. There was a memorial to Dy

Hoc Siu, who had formed the Resist the Enemy League to confront the Japanese. Such credentials should make you the ultimate patriot, but the same men would later be suspected of communist sympathies after Chairman Mao had taken over the mother country. So, again, like the Jews in Europe, the Chinese were paradoxically perceived as both the high priests of capitalism and as its gravediggers. It seemed that whatever the Chinese did they got scapegoated for something.

I took a 360 gaze around the graves. How much pain was inside them? Were there casualties here of the 1603 and 1639 pogroms, bodies shorn of heads because the Spanish had jammed them on to spikes and left them around the city? Were there idealists here punctured by firing squad bullets for dreaming of a free state? Teenage conscripts thrashed to a gory end by the Japanese during the Bataan Death March? Whoever they were and whatever had happened to them, I hoped they'd all found some peace now, at last, among their living kin and their all mod cons.

Spotting a pimply youth picking his nose with one hand and playing a game on his phone with the other reminded me to check the clock on *my* phone. I was late meeting with Charlson Ong, perhaps the country's best-known Chinese-Filipino writer.

23. GENERATION INTEGRATION

'**G**reenbelt Mall, Makati,' I barked at the taxi driver. 'Quick as you like.'

'You been in Chinaman graves, sir?' The driver kept scrunching his nose in a form of tic.

'Yeah. Let's go.' As we zoomed up Ongpin Street, a sand bucket of candles and incense sticks on the pavement blurred into lines of light.

'You like Chinaman, sir?'

'Yeah,' I mumbled.

'You be careful with Chinaman, sir,' said the driver. 'They are already giving problem to my country in South China Sea. They want our islands but they cannot have. Also they have stooges here. You know the Aquinos, the political family from before? They Chinese. Marcos? Chinese. 'Specially Marcos, sir.'

'Really?'

'Yes, all monies plundered by Marcos family go straight to China already. Early on in, they invest in shopping malls in Taiwan and Beijing.'

I switched off. This was all getting a bit *Protocols of the Elders of China*.

At the elevators inside the mall, I met Charlson Ong, a placid man in his fifties with feline lips and a faint grey moustache. He asked if I'd eaten lunch. I suggested Chinese might be appropriate so we went to Chowking, a fast food joint selling flavoursome noodles and *siopai* (steamed, meat-filled buns).

'As a Chinese-Filipino writer are you drawn to aspects of Manila that a non-Chinese writer wouldn't be?' I asked.

'My crime novel, *Blue Angel, White Shadow*, is set in Chinatown. It's a district that interests me.'

130

'Is that where you grew up?'

'Not really. Just after I was born, my family moved from downtown to a suburb called San Juan. I was sent to the Jesuit-run Xavier School at a time when more and more Chinese were settling in the area. I grew up in a sort of Chinese suburb, but I have relatives in Chinatown so I go there often.'

'Growing up, did you feel in any way alienated or discriminated against?'

'Personally, no, because I went to a school that was majority Chinese. And then, our community was Chinese so I didn't encounter a hostile environment.'

'Are there still tensions between Chinese and non-Chinese-Filipinos?'

'I think it is a thing of the past, but you never know. You'll always find tensions if you look for them, if you scratch beneath the surface of any society. Sometimes there are problems when some news story appears such as when China is seen to be bullying the Philippines.'

'Do you yourself have any strong contacts with China?'

'No. We don't have blood relatives because my grandparents emigrated here and my grandfather was adopted.'

'When you started writing were you aware of Chinese-Filipino literary traditions?'

'I'd read Paul Stephen Lim, who was the first to write in English about his experiences as a Chinese-Filipino. He emigrated to the US in the 1960s because he was never actually a Philippine citizen. I was born a citizen because my father was naturalized.'

'So it was difficult in the sixties for someone who'd emigrated from China to be naturalized here?'

'In the old days, it was very difficult even if you were Philippine-born. It cost a lot of money. And you know, the authorities would milk you for all the money they could and make trouble for you. After Martial Law was declared in '72, President Marcos ruled by decree and in 1973 he decided that the Philippines would recognize the People's Republic of China. The result was that all those Chinese in the Philippines, who were nominal citizens of Taiwan, would become stateless. So Marcos decided that all Philippine-born and long-term immigrants could apply for citizenship.'

'Do you as a writer get a sense from your readers that that there's an interest in the Chinese-Filipino experience among non-Chinese, Malay-Filipinos?'

'I don't think there's a big interest in literature in general in the Philippines, especially not in English. There was a series of movies produced by a Chinese, Mother Lily, featuring Chinese-Filipino characters. They have done fairly well at the box office. Many of the actors are Filipinos pretending to be Chinese, so they don't always get it right! But they try. They try.'

'Do they hope the viewers can't tell the difference?'

'These movies have been well received so I don't think there's an issue.'

'Is there a sense that Chinese-Filipinos have different values to other Filipinos?'

'I think we are pretty much integrated, especially this generation. Unless something happens to challenge this harmony, I can't see it changing. Amongst the middle classes in Manila there are no tensions, but maybe in the provinces there could be, I couldn't say.'

'Caroline Hau [a Chinese-Filipino literary historian now based in Japan] has written about a long-standing stereotype of the Chinese being wealthy. Is it just a stereotype or is there some truth in it?'

'There used to more poor Chinese, definitely. That was why the Benevolent Society for the Chinese was formed. Before World War II, much of the blue-collar labour here was Chinese. These guys would move from China to the Philippines firstly to work for someone, a relative usually, and then save up to establish their own businesses. The migration was always steady. They came illegally or legally. In '49, when the communists took over the mainland, immigration stopped. There was this big gap in movement until the 1980s. There was a law that banned Chinese from doing retail trade, so they went into manufacturing and tended to make money at it. The poorer Chinese just died out, in a sense.

'I remember as a boy, when there was a celebration, a wedding or the like in Chinatown, hoboes would always turn up. They would look at the newspapers every day, find out who was getting married and then gatecrash the party! They would sing the hosts their praises in the hope someone would give them money. If they didn't get what they asked for, they'd curse you. And the Chinese don't like to be cursed. It was a kind of extortion.'

'It sounds like the premise for a short story.'

'I recall one beggar in Chinatown who would attach a sign to his head reading, "I am Chinese".'

'But this isn't common now?'

'No, no. Those people were the Chinese who had failed. They came, they failed and they either died – many of them became guerrillas during the war – or went back to China.'

'Which aspects of Chinatown interest you as a writer? Are there certain buildings that have a significance?'

'Well, it's changed a lot. I haven't been there in a while.'

'I've just been to the Chinese cemetery.'

'That's changed a lot!'

'You mentioned Stephen Lim going to the States. Have you been tempted to move abroad yourself?'

'Actually, I was supposed to go on a Fulbright grant in 1990. I was in the same batch as Caroline Hau and got accepted at New York University. And then, at the last minute, they ran out of funding because they reconfigured the application system. Creative writing – my field – was dropped while the guys who were due to read American Studies were elevated. The board said I could re-apply the next year and I would be high on the totem pole, as it were. But then, I thought, this isn't meant to be. Fate has spoken.'

'Why do you think the world doesn't take Filipino literature as seriously as, say, Chinese, Indian or Japanese literature?'

'First of all, I think there are demographic reasons. In India and China the community supports writers more effectively than it does here. Perhaps the main reason, though, is that the Philippines is not in the imagination of the world. Unlike China, India or even Thailand, we don't have a strong identity abroad. It's hard to sell the idea of the Philippines overseas, even if we have figures like Pacquiao and we have many OFWs in the West. These communities aren't as established as, say, British-Indians or Chinese-Americans. Also, it is about history. The British set up the Commonwealth for the nations it colonized and the Booker Prize, until recently, was only open to writers from Commonwealth countries. Obviously, Filipinos couldn't be considered for it. The Americans had this approach of 'reluctant colonialism' which meant that countries they occupied, like ours, didn't figure culturally in the way that British Commonwealth countries did.'

'I guess you have to go to America to be taken more seriously by the literary establishment there. And then you become an "Asian-American writer".'

'Yeah, like Eric Gamalinda and Carlos Bulosan. After World War II, there was some interest in the West, and the Philippines was in the cultural imagination because of Bataan and the other well-reported battles involving US troops. For that reason, Bulosan sold books after the war, but it didn't really last. You could say that, more recently, Jessica Hagedorn has been successful, but I feel she is a "neither here nor there" sort of writer. I don't know why she called her book *Dogeaters*. Perhaps her editor wanted that title.'

'Because it's exotic and would appeal to a Western audience?'

'Right.'

'I've always been disappointed by the lack of coverage of anything to do with the Philippines in the Western media. But then along comes Duterte and...'

'It takes a Duterte!'

'What do you make of his impact?'

'Poorer communities have been very affected by these killings. It's getting out of hand. But you know, he's still popular because he is doing what he said he would do.'

'What's your take on him?'

'Every president has a blind spot. His is his crusade. The last movie he saw, I think, was *Dirty Harry*.'

'They call him "Duterte Harry".'

'Unfortunately, he never saw *Unforgiven* and the later Clint Eastwood movies – he's stuck with *Dirty Harry*. He's stuck in the seventies.'

'Are most writers and artists against the drug war?'

'Yes. Jimmy Abad, Krip Yuson and the Philippine Literary Arts Council are coming out with a book called *Bloodlust: Philippine Protest Poetry*. There have been a lot of movies about extra-judicial killings such as *Ma Rosa*, which won at Cannes last year.'

'The stories you hear about Duterte down in Davao are bizarre.'

'I lived in Davao around ten years ago. I worked for an NGO funded by USAID that tried to promote "growth with equity" in Mindanao. Part of our job was to help MNLF (Moro National Liberation Front) members to transition into civilian life by giving them the equipment they needed to become farmers or fishermen. I used to go to Duterte's favourite bar called After Dark. It was first owned by one of his biker mates, but then Duterte bought it. He liked to sing "To Fill the World with Love".'

'Ironic choice. Have you met him?'

'I saw him once. He drives or roams the city at night. Some journalists would follow him around.'

'Did you get the sense that Davaoans liked Duterte?'

'The cab drivers liked him because, from their point of view, the city was safer with him in charge. And they always gave me change! The Chinese in Davao liked his style too. If you do something he doesn't like, he'll warn you. "You've made your money, so stop," he'll say, "or I'll blow you away." And he does.'

'Does that approach always work?'

'I think it works as mayor, but then, the problem now is that he's president. Running a country is a much bigger job and I think he expected everyone would agree with his *Dirty Harry* way.'

'Do you also do journalism or other kinds of writing?'

'I write biographies mostly, that's my bread and butter. Right now I'm trying to finish a book on Joe De Venecia, the former speaker of the House of Representatives.'

'Is that something that you were commissioned to do?'

'You wouldn't do it otherwise!'

'Have you written any biographies of Chinoys?'

'I wrote the biography of Robert Coyiuto, who founded Pioneer Insurance. He died long ago and his children wanted a kind of document of his life and achievements. And now I'm finishing a book on the founder of Unimart and Makati Supermarket, Henry Ng.'

'Do any of these biographies sell?'

'No, they're usually given away to boost the brand.'

'Duterte's would be a bestseller, wouldn't it? Would you do it?'

'I don't think he'd allow it!'

'The picture on the cover could be him on a motorbike. I'd do it.'

'Oh, go ahead and good luck!'

'Would other presidents' biographies have a market?'

'It depends. I think the unauthorized book on Imelda by Carmen Pedro might have sold well. And then *The Conjugal Dictatorship*, about Ferdinand and Imelda Marcos, might have been successful because the author, Primitivo Mijares, was killed. Primitivo was Marcos' PR agent who left for the US after Martial Law was declared and published this very critical book over there. He threatened to testify in the US Congress. Then he disappeared.'

'Is it still dangerous to criticize the government with these sorts of books?'

'They blame Duterte for the death of Jun Pala. There have always been radio people who get killed in the provinces, but not so much in Manila. If you are well-known, then you are at less risk. Sometimes they're not entirely innocent because they are what we call "blocktimers". They buy airtime and they will ask money from politicians or else they will attack you on air.'

'Sounds like blackmail.'

'Yeah. And usually it is these guys who get killed.'

'Is this true also of bloggers?'

'Well, actually, right now, there are a lot of trolls. The army of trolls who follow Duterte.'

'Working for him?'

'Probably on his payroll. They will threaten opposition candidates and critics. But, again, if you're in Manila, it's pretty safe. Local politics is not so safe.'

'Do you think he'll finish his term?'

'I have no idea. Who knows?'

'I've been trying to arrange a meeting with him, but I don't think...'

'You have to work through his people.'

'He doesn't really like foreigners, I think. At least I'm not American!'

'You have to look for someone who knows him. Actually, there is this poet, Becky Añonuevo. She writes in Filipino and she is pro-Duterte.'

'Do you think she'll be willing to talk to me?'

'Why not?'

24. MYTHS OF THE MACARTHUR SUITE

General Douglas MacArthur was a shrewd manager of his own public image – the MacArthurian Legend we might call it. He rebuilt his reputation time and again, painting over the stains of scandals and filling in the dents made by wrathful critics. So when the tour guide threw open the doors to the Douglas MacArthur Suite of the Manila Hotel, I wasn't surprised to see that it had been impeccably restored to a supposedly Edenic moment in Philippine history, before World War II levelled Manila, before the Japanese trashed the suite just to get back at MacArthur and before the country fell under the heel of Martial Law. Although there was nothing original about the mahogany *chaises longues* or the twinkling brass chandeliers, the impression of 1935 was persuasive.

When as a kid I asked my elderly friends and relatives about what they did in the war, I associated their testimonies with iconic photographs. My maternal grandmother's tales of working as a telephonist during the Blitz will, for me, always be illustrated by Herbert Mason's photo of St Paul's Cathedral framed by thick black bomb smoke, yet somehow undamaged and bathed in a heavenly light. Gran had an American friend called Bob. In my blurred recollections, his white, back-combed hair and icy stare make him identical to the actor Lee Marvin. Bob was one of the first GIs to meet up with the Red Army at the River Elbe at the end of the war. He found out the hard way that a new war, the Cold War, had begun when the US Army promptly court-martialled him for fraternizing with a Russian soldier. That he had, since the 1930s, been a member of the Communist Party of the USA didn't exactly help his case. I don't know if Bob fought in Berlin, but I still equate him with that hunched silhouette of a Red Army soldier waving the Hammer and

Sickle flag from the roof of the Reichstag, the tower blocks in the background shelled down to their rafters.

In the MacArthur Suite, I spotted another classic image of that conflict: a spontaneous snap of the general himself swaggering ashore at Leyte Island in October 1944, at the start of the American liberation of the Philippines. He is fulfilling the highly quoted promise – 'I shall return' – he made two years before, when his spirited resistance to the Japanese floundered and he was forced to retreat to Australia.

Although the claims in the preceding paragraph are widely believed to be true, they are largely false. Mariel, my ginger-dyed tour guide, told me that the photo was far from unplanned. 'It took them three attempts to get it right. The first time, the general believed that he did not look good. The second time, he tripped and fell in the water. The third time, it was a success.'

Moreover, by the time MacArthur arrived at Leyte on that 'historic' day, Filipino guerrillas had already driven the Japanese out of that locality. MacArthur chose this particular beach precisely because he knew it was safe and secure. He could step Moses-like from water to land and play the valiant saviour, without having to be valiant or saving anyone.

As we turned to a cabinet displaying the 'Decorations & Medals of General of the Army Douglas MacArthur', I remembered some of his military mis-steps. As Supreme Commander of the United States Army Forces in the Far East (USAFFE), MacArthur relied on an outdated war plan, ignored a ten-hour invasion warning and neglected to properly clothe and feed his troops. The result was the surrender of 76,000 Filipinos and Americans at Bataan in April 1942. Yet none of this ever came back to haunt him. On the contrary, according to James Hamilton-Paterson, 'Douglas MacArthur's most remarkable achievement was to turn this whole unpropitious series of events into a mammoth public relations triumph such that he ended the war a national hero.'

MacArthur's knack for whitewashing himself was matched by an inflated sense of self-importance. When he accepted the role of

Military Advisor to the Philippine Army in 1935, he demanded to be put up at the 100,000-square-foot Malacañang Palace. 'This was not appropriate,' said Mariel. 'The palace is special for Filipinos. Only our governors and our presidents can live there.' MacArthur's second choice was the entire fifth floor of the deluxe Manila Hotel. The government complained that the bill would be too high. A compromise was reached: alongside his martial duties MacArthur would act as general manager of the hotel. Somehow he was able to finagle exactly the same salary as the then president of the Philippine Commonwealth, Manuel Quezon.

I glanced back at that picture of MacArthur wading ashore. It reeks of theatrical self-consciousness. Like a Hollywood stereotype, the powerful curve of his chin advances out beyond ritzy sunglasses and taut, stoic lips. The uniform unbuttoned at the neck denotes both rebel individualism and Lotharian glamour. As his torpedo-like legs crash through the sea, his beefy hands are clamped to the waist of his billowing khakis. The body language says: 'Nothing will stop me.'

In *Ermita*, F. Sionil José's superlative novel of post-war Manila, a chauffeur names his newborn son MacArthur in anticipation that 'the General's good looks, his noble visage and everything worth emulating about the Liberator of the Philippines would somehow be transmitted to the baby.'

MacArthur needed such hagiography to brace his flimsy ego. During bouts of depression he'd call prostitutes up to the suite. Instead of having sex with them he'd order them to tell him what a wonderful human being he was. He often threatened to commit suicide, only changing his mind after sufficient flattery. Michael Schaller's biography reveals that, on one particular train journey, MacArthur aide T.J. Davis finally got sick of the general's histrionics:

'As we pass over the Tennessee River bridge,' MacArthur said in a maudlin tone, 'I intend to jump from the train. This is where my life ends, Davis.'
'Happy landing,' replied Davis wryly.'

We peeked into a bedroom. In it was an elegant bed made from *nara* wood, the swirling grains of its four posters starkly sepia next to the fulgent white pineapple-skin duvet. 'You know that Bill Clinton stayed here?' said Mariel. 'And before you ask, no he did not bring Monica with him.'

Clinton wasn't the first philanderer to inhabit this room. One cause of MacArthur's blues was his catastrophic love affair with the Scottish-Filipina actress Isabel Rosario Cooper, twenty-six years his junior. MacArthur tried to hide her from public view, first in Manila and then in an apartment in Washington, DC. After two reporters on *The Washington Post* wrote an uncomplimentary profile of MacArthur, the general sued for libel. The reporters got wind of Cooper's existence, tracked her down and persuaded her to stand as a witness for the defence. Fearing disgrace, MacArthur dropped the suit and paid Cooper $150,000 to keep quiet and get out of his life.

In MacArthur's study neither the trademark corncob pipe nor the statesman-like marble-topped desk was ever owned by him. The brass gilded chair was his, though, and dates back to 1939.

'Sir Tom, do you want to sit in the great man's seat?' asked Mariel.

I did so and ruminated on the intimate connection MacArthur's life had with the wider, triangulated narrative of Manila, the Philippines and the United States.

I looked out the north window over Manila Bay. In 1905, a few years after Douglas' father Arthur MacArthur Jr. had briefly served as Military Governor of the US-occupied Philippines, the American architect Daniel Burnham was redesigning the bayside for the twentieth century. He wanted to sanitize, modernize and morally enhance the area with new parks, streets, railways, waterways and a lavish Classical Revival hotel on the waterfront.

But, like Douglas MacArthur's biography, there were flaws and feints in this narrative of beautification. Many Filipinos saw Burnham's civilizing mission as camouflage for the US' uncivilized conduct in their homeland. While refined American gents were strolling around Manila Bay prating about Greco-Roman columns, elsewhere in the islands the US Army was exterminating women and children. For the cultural critic David Brody, the ultimate monument to the myth of American benevolence is the Burnham Memorial in Baguio City, a hill station four hours north of Manila. The inscription on his bust moralizes about 'love, amity and mutual respect' which, for Brody, 'mitigates a tumultuous history that included the bloodshed, loss and cultural trauma that accompanied the Philippine-American War.' Few of Burnham's 'City Beautiful' plans ever got beyond the stage of blabber about progress and harmony. The closest he got to founding a New Jerusalem was a hotel, a highway and a few government offices – the bare minimum required for the US to stamp its authority on Manila.

As Burnham was drawing up plans for the Manila Hotel as an outpost of Western high living amid the boondocks (derived from *bundok*, the Filipino word for mountain), the young Douglas MacArthur was in the Philippines erecting bridges and conducting surveys with the Third Engineer Battalion. On his tour, MacArthur befriended US businessmen and invested in high-yield enterprises like the Benguet gold mines.

On the marble-topped desk was a record of MacArthur's most important encounter from that time: a snap of him shaking hands with a slight, edgy-looking man in a cream suit. This was Senator Manuel Roxas.

The official history goes like this: after the war, the US government charged Roxas and MacArthur with disbursing US$2 billion in aid to rescue the beleaguered nation. James Hamilton-Paterson's account is closer to the truth:

> [In 1945] MacArthur was given a free hand to arrange his former fiefdom according to his taste. His personal support was crucial to getting his old friend Roxas approved by Washington and elected. So also was his capricious withholding of US aid for the reconstruction of the Philippines after the election, thereby making the aid virtually contingent on Roxas becoming President. Thereafter, the $2 billion in aid

was fought over by various groups of vultures who had good links with the new ruling elite of MacArthur and Roxas. Only very little of this fabulous sum (at mid-1940s value, too) actually went into rebuilding the Philippines' shattered infrastructure and economy.

Roxas and MacArthur smashed any dissent to their shenanigans, sending the CIA in to suppress the Huk rebels who saw no difference between this bunch of gangsters and the Japanese, Americans and Spaniards who'd ruled in the past.

I rose from MacArthur's chair and went to the window. Down on Bonifacio Drive a homeless boy, barefoot and caked in tar-black dirt, was holding a quivering hand up to passing cars. He was a reminder that the injustices that shocked the Huks into rising against the MacArthur 'consensus' persist to the present. Costing US$3,300 a night, the MacArthur Suite today is just as alien to the experience of the thirty million or so Filipinos who live on less than US$1 a day as it would have been to the pickpockets and panhandlers of MacArthur's time.

The Philippine economy is still run by a clutch of dynasties, some tracing their roots back to Spanish colonization. The country remains in the grip of dollar imperialism, as proven by the ubiquity of Coca-Cola, McDonald's and basketball, although, perhaps ironically, Japan is now the republic's number one trading partner. The Huks have evolved into the Maoist New People's Army (NPA), which continues the struggle on behalf of the peasantry.

I sat back in the chair where, in the late 1930s and early 1940s, General MacArthur did much of his thinking about war, history, politics and business. If he were somehow to be resurrected and find himself in this chair again, would his thoughts about the contemporary Philippines be all that different?

25. WHITEWASHING THE WRETCHED

It felt wrong to travel straight from the most expensive hotel in the Philippines to one of its most depressed zones, but that's what happened the next morning due to a quirk of scheduling. Isko, a Department of Tourism guide in indigo jeans, met me under the shade of a pure crystal coconut tree in the Champagne Room of the Manila Hotel. If Grandad were still alive and here now, he'd have loved its opulence.

Isko asked how it felt to be in a venue that the Beatles, Michael Jackson, Marlon Brando, John Wayne and John F. Kennedy had all spent time in.

'One day I'll be more famous than all of them,' I quipped. Isko gave me a doubtful grimace.

The history of Tondo is an eloquent refutation of the belief that Western colonialism greatly improved the lives of those it subjugated. From the tenth century AD until the arrival of the Spanish, Tondo was the pre-eminent kingdom in Luzon, spreading across most of the island's 42,000 square miles. It traded with China, Japan, the Indian subcontinent, the Arab World and Southeast Asia, and its people were engaged in mining, weaving, pearl-fishing and wine-making. Most of them, though, were subsistence farmers, which prompted early Spanish observers to libel them as primitive. The *conquistador* Miguel López de Legazpi, who would go on to found Spanish Manila, was appalled by the native preference for growing food over grabbing gold from mines and rivers. But, as that perceptive chronicler of pre-Hispanic life Renato Constantino points out, 'The reason for such behaviour ... is precisely the absence of an exploitative class as such. Everyone worked for an immediate need and that was all.' The Tondolese couldn't eat gold so they focused on rice instead.

Tondo's social structure was in some ways more enlightened than Spain's at the time. A village headman was often chosen by the community rather than born into the role, and he was expected to muck in with farming, hunting, weaving and construction. The next stratum of society was made up of freemen who were each entitled to a plot of land to work. Less progressively, anyone who got into debt or who was taken prisoner after a skirmish with another ethnic group had to work as a slave until the chief deemed their debt repaid or their loyalty proven. However, they were more like 'peons than chattel-slaves', to use Constantino's phrase, and better treated than the Africans the Spanish were trafficking to the New World at the time.

While Tondo wasn't utopian, it did provide food, shelter and a decent living standard for its citizens. That changed when the Muslim rajahs who by that point had united Tondo with its bordering kingdoms, were coerced by the Spanish into handing over Manila. At that moment it was a settlement on a headland between the River Pasig and the ocean based around a fortress made from coconut trunks and defended by twelve cannons. The Spanish brought in the spectacularly unfair *encomienda* system that required all indigenes to pay tributes by way of money, food or materials. Some tributaries had to kill their own children to save enough rice to give to the authorities. Certain officials took the daughters of chiefs hostage until the chiefs could pay up. Those who couldn't pay up at all were press-ganged, tortured or crucified. Until as late as 1884, all Filipino men aged between sixteen and sixty had to join the *polo*, a reserve of labourers forced on pain of death or incarceration to work forty days a year without pay as builders, miners and lumberjacks.

I could trace a clear line from the mayhem those Spanish policies wreaked in old-world Tondo to the mess the district was in today. Our minivan sputtered through a flood coming from a cluster of water butts damaged beyond anyone's means to fix. Most who paused to wave at us had teeth missing, facial scars, tubercular coughs, twiggy limbs. I saw a row of lads sitting on the eight-foot-high blackened steel joist of a burned-out building, white trainer-clad feet swinging casually. Their headgear ranged from bandanas to back-to-front baseball caps. They smoked and chewed gum at the same time.

'They look sort of... better off than the others,' I said to Isko.

'Probably they are gang members already.'

'Can we talk to them?'

Isko looked out the window, paused and then looked back to me. 'I do not advise this, Sir Tom. In fact I am under orders of the tourist board to not let you out at all.'

'Really? But I need quotes for my story.'

'I am sorry, Sir Tom,' said Isko. 'Me, I would not like to be responsible if something terrible will happen after we let you out.'

'What's the worst that could happen? Would someone attack us?'

'These gangs they are only interested of killing each other. It is not worth them to engage civilians. More like you will be invited into someone's house for a gimmick.'

All I knew was that 'gimmick' in Philippine English could mean a night out. 'What do you mean, Isko?'

'You could be asked to drink some local liquors in a competition.'

'Bring it on,' I said. 'I'm from Portsmouth.'

Isko exchanged Filipino with the driver. Then he said to me, 'Okay, we will try to stop at a place of safety for you to explore.'

We followed the route of a stream so heavily slicked with rubbish that it gave the optical illusion of solid ground. Rabbit hutch abodes jutted on stilts out of its opposite shore. I couldn't see any locks on the doors and a toddler could easily kick in the weather-weakened wood.

When he came to Tondo in 1914, the American writer William D. Boyce remarked that its dwellers seemed 'more contented than those in the slums of the big cities in the States'. That the wretched of the earth are happy with their lot is another canard probably invented to make well-off Westerners feel less guilty about adding to the exploitation of these unfortunates by purchasing bargain goods and services from them. The people here were friendly but they didn't look contented to me. Perhaps their ancestors were in 1914, but I doubted it. And why should they have been then and why should they be now?

As Oscar Wilde wrote in his masterful polemic *The Soul of Man under Socialism*, 'the best amongst the poor ... are ungrateful, discontented, disobedient, and rebellious. They are quite right to be so.'

We slowed down as a policeman approached the driver's window. There was something odd about him. Stubble clung to his jaw line like moss on a boulder. His uniform was more creased than a nonagenarian's crow's feet. He was wearing purple trainers rather than shiny black shoes. But why?

The cop had terse words with the driver. The driver produced a licence and a typewritten piece of blue copy paper. The cop sidled off to his Toyota Corolla.

As the driver tussled with the ignition, I asked Isko, who was staring out the windscreen, what that was all about. Before I could finish my question, Isko muttered something in Filipino to the driver. I guessed it was a ploy to avoid responding, so I asked again.

'It was no problem, Sir Tom.'

'I'd be interested to know why he stopped us.'

'Soon we will be coming to a neighbourhood where you may get out and look around.'

'But please Isko, I'd like to know why.'

Isko cleared his throat. 'The officer said we ran a red light. This is true. But our driver told him that our boss, the Minister of Tourism, is buddies with his boss, the Director General of the Police, and it would not be welcome for anyone to begin a fight between them. Lucky we convinced him or the driver would forfeit his licence. I think he was also scared off by a white man in the vehicle.'

'Why?'

'It might bring publicity if he did make arrests.'

'Why was he so scruffy?'

'I do not know.'

'Is there a chance he wasn't a real police officer?'

'A chance, yes. Some bad ones they are stealing police gear and selling it to hoodlums. You can buy a badge for 300 pesos on the black markets. The hoodlums wear the uniforms to do *carnaps* and *estafas*.'

Car thefts and *fraud*, I mentally translated. I wouldn't blame a man for doing such things if he had ten mouths to feed. Or maybe I would if he did these things to me.

We stopped in an area where fragrant sampaguita, gladioli and chrysanthemums grew along the banks of an *estero* (canal) of unusual clarity. Behind the flowers were solid stone houses. Isko walked on ahead and grasped the hand of a youth in check shorts. Isko leaned close to the man and deadpanned him in Filipino. The man then stepped to me, laughing. 'Hello sir,' he said. 'English no good.'

'Don't worry,' I said. 'My Filipino's worse.'

He laughed again, I think not understanding me. This was the first Filipino I'd met who couldn't speak my language well. I guessed that instead of learning English in school he'd worked to support his family selling plastic bottles or *balut* (semi-fertilized duck eggs).

Further up the bank, Isko was shaking hands with other residents and talking to them sternly too. I was waylaid by a drove of ten-year-olds in *X-Men* masks demanding high-fives.

When I finally caught up with him, he told me we were standing in one of the Mayor of Manila's flagship beautification schemes. 'We have dredged the river and allowed nature to come into the equation,' he grinned. 'What are your thoughts? You know we Filipinos like to know what outsiders think of us.'

'It's lovely,' I said.

Isko gave me a thumbs-up. 'Great. Let's scram.'

'What were you saying to the residents before I spoke to them?' I asked later on, as we ploughed through another minor flood.

Isko scratched his head. 'Nothing, Sir Tom.'

'You did seem to be saying *something* to them.'

'Just the small talk. I know the captain of that *barangay* and his family members already.'

That was all I'd get from him. I reflected on how dependent I'd been on translators since coming to Manila and grew a bit paranoid. What if all the data I'd received from translators so far had been filtered through their own preferences and prejudices? There was nothing I could do about that apart from be sceptical where and when necessary. While I couldn't think of a motive for Josefina to mislead me about the comfort women, I had the anxious hunch that Isko had ordered the people we'd met to be on their best behaviour for the Western journalist who shouldn't under any circumstance come away with a negative angle on the locale. And to be fair, this was in his job description: ministries of tourism exist to do puff and PR. If Isko's bosses had been to the West they'd be aware of the repertory of stereotypes the West has of the Philippines. Whenever the country does penetrate the European or American news, positive initiatives like the one I'd just witnessed don't bleed enough to lead. Drugs, rogue cops (real or impersonated), jihadi bombings, overpopulation, Church tyranny – these are sexier headlines to run with.

I was annoyed not to have gone deeper into Tondo, beyond Isko's stage-management and into the jagged realities of living poor. Would my next destination – a squatters' camp under threat of extinction – offer more illumination?

26. SQUATTERS' RIGHTS

In the Philippines 'squatters' is the name given to poor people who move from the provinces to the cities in search of work. They don't always find it. The cost of a dorm bed beyond them, they build make-do settlements out of cadged materials on whatever spare land they can find. Squatters were a hot issue in the upcoming elections. Bourgeois *Manileños* saw them as pests causing crime, disease and overcrowding. The reactionary media had denounced the Mayor of Quezon City for cynically courting the squatter vote by calling for a halt to their evictions.

Meryl met me at the exit of Santolan LRT station. Her plaited, frost-coloured hair and pointy elven ears gave her a sword-and-sorcery vibe. She was an employee an NGO that supported squatters, and knew the way to Concepcion Extension. Just as well, for there were no signs to this officially non-existent neighbourhood. You won't find it on Google Maps or in the *Metro Manila A-Z*. Meryl led me through a labyrinth of food stalls with rags attached to spinning motors to chase the flies away. We cut through an alley where cockerels were tied to door handles and babies slept in cradles hanging from beams. The alleyway opened out into a kind of shadow city, a caricature of conventional Manila. I could tell some of the buildings had once been substantial, but now they were full of holes masked with tarpaulin, polythene netting and polyurethane ad banners. Added to the brickwork of one building was an unpainted *molave* wood balcony shaded by a canopy made from sack cloth marked with the lilac UNILEVER logo. A sweetcorn-yellow strip of plastic reading POLICE LINE DO NOT CROSS was draped around a mountain of sun-hardened earth capped with arbitrary trash: straws, cement, sawdust, ice cream cones, a broken cupboard.

We arrived at a roofless stone chamber with a bamboo table and two female Swedish aid workers within. Before I could say hello we were mobbed by barefoot, greasy-haired kids.

Meryl introduced the aid workers, who were here to teach the kids some English, to the crowd in Filipino and then said in English, 'So do you want to learn?'

'Yes!' came the unanimous cheer from the kids.

While the aid workers produced paints and Play-Doh, I spoke to Nancy, the chair of the residents' association. Concepcion Extension was set up by employees of the Philippine Army who couldn't afford the rooms at a nearby military base. This happened all the way back in 1959, which defied the mainstream assumption that all squatters were new immigrants who moved nomad-like around Manila. Nancy and her comrades had been in the same place for over fifty years and had struggled for the right to remain here ever since.

In 2005, a real estate company won the legal right to sequester the land Concepcion Extension stands on. Since then, all 300 families had been scheduled to leave. Their homes were to be demolished to make way for posh condominiums. 'No one here want to go,' Nancy told me. 'We are work locally in malls serving same people who want us to go to province. Who will cook them *lechon*? Serve them beer? Shine their shoes? Cut their hair? Drive them home at night?'

'For these people,' interjected Meryl, 'relocation will mean destitution.'

'Have you taken your case to the government?' I asked.

'They are too cosy with company,' said Nancy. 'But they make different argument. They say, since Concepcion Extension was flooded after Typhoon Ondoy break river banks, we should leave for own safety case it happen again.'

'Is there any truth in that?'

'No. Scientist from university tell us *everywhere* in Philippines at risk from flooding due to climate change. Besides, if plan is to build apartments here, how will new structures be more protected than *our* structures?'

Nancy then brought up the most preposterous government claim so far: that the *unpeople* of Concepcion Extension were to blame for the river bursting its banks due to a build-up of refuse in the water. In fact, these people were so broke they've never had much to chuck away. It was the nearby pig feed factories that had filled the river with waste.

'Are they offering any assistance with relocating?'

'They offer us 10,000 pesos each, but this not last and we have no employment when we get to new land – wherever new land is.'

The aid workers distributed paper and pens. The kids went quiet while they drew pictures of Concepcion Extension, adding the names of objects in the little English they knew.

I caught the eye of a man working a water pump. Nancy led me over to him. 'One of scare tactics company has use,' she said, 'is arson. After we had fire few years ago, condo company prevent us from reconnecting to power grid. So we build own pumps and generators.'

We walked through more tumbledown dwellings, aerials like pterodactyl skeletons perched on them. We passed shoes hanging by their tongues from washing lines, old women mending clothes, tricycle drivers taking midday naps on the ground. A *carabao* (water buffalo) rolled irritably in the muddy shallows of the Pasig, trying to cool itself down. Above it on the bank was a field of corn and cashews. 'We try to be self-sufficient,' said Nancy.

We returned to the derelict classroom. The lesson was winding up. Meryl looked glumly over a newspaper cutting about a new bill called '6405' soon to be put to Congress. 'If it becomes law,' Meryl explained, 'it will punish all *barangay* captains in the Philippines with either a 500,000 peso (about US$10,000) fine or life imprisonment if they do not kick the squatters out of their jurisdictions. This is a big incentive for the captains to use any means necessary.'

Nancy told me that last year, in a nearby squatters' camp, a demolition team broke through the human barricade with clubs and water cannons. Scores were beaten. The camp was razed.

'Why is the government so tough on squatters?' I asked Meryl.

'There is no will to assist them. The media and the education system encourage Filipinos to look out only for number one and not care for anyone else unless they are family. I would say even the Church has lost its moral compass – at this moment in time only five bishops now claim to be pro-poor.'

'We once had good friend in Church,' said Nancy. 'Father Frederick. Company they bribe him to turn against us. After, I did not sleep for three days.' She waved her hands in front of her face. At first I thought she was just trying to fan herself. Then she began to weep.

After the aid workers had packed up we were invited into Nancy's home. Though it was small and scraggy, I got the feeling Nancy was as house-proud as any bourgeois *Manileño* wife. Crockery was arranged neatly on shelves below a tapestry of the Last Supper. The floor tiles were so well polished I didn't want to tread my trainers on them.

Nancy cooked us some extraordinarily sweet pancakes on a gas stove. When it was time to say goodbye, she made a simple yet clinching argument for her community's right to exist. 'This is our home. We've been here so long. We don't bother anyone else.'

On the walk back to the station, I decided to ask Meryl a question that had been on my mind all afternoon. 'Do you think they can win?'

'Me, I don't know... I hope.'

'Aren't they up against impossible odds? Someone stands to make a lot of money from that land and money always seems to win.'

'This is true. We must keep struggling, I guess.'

27. SCARY NUMBERS

When I got home, the figure the government had offered each resident of Concepcion Extension to relocate was stuck in my brain – 10,000 pesos was about US$200, a few dollars below the annual bare minimum a Filipino can survive on, according to the Philippine Statistics Survey. If Nancy and her people didn't find employment in their new habitat they'd each have less than a year to live, based on what the government was offering them. For the sake of comparison, I looked up how much you'd need to be considered rich in the Philippines: 2 million pesos (about US$38,000) annually. Then how did this all compare to the total revenues of the foreign corporations many Filipinos – rich and poor – worked for? Walmart, which recently opened for business in Manila, earned a cool US$516 billion in 2015. In the same year, Shell (a British-owned company) scored US$283 billion, Exxon Mobil US$263 billion and Apple US$250 billion. Contrast these obscene figures to the Philippines' GDP for the same year – US$312 billion – and you find that one company is worth more than one of the countries it operates in, and several others aren't far behind.

A parcel plopped through my front door. Inside was a recently published book called *Food Wars* by the renowned Filipino sociologist Waldon Bello. I knew of Bello as a peerlessly energetic activist who'd been at the vanguard of every progressive campaign since the 1960s. As a student in the US, he led sit-ins against the Vietnam War and then spent time in Chile in the Salvador Allende era. Exiled from the Philippines by Marcos, he broke into the World Bank HQ in New York and pinched some documents proving that the World Bank and the International Monetary Fund were working with the dictator to dispossess farmers, restrict wages, devalue the currency, remove protective tariffs and subjugate trade unions. The net effect of these policies was to make life worse for the worst-off. The book Bello wrote based on the stolen papers became a spur for the People Power Revolution of 1986.

I flicked to a chapter in his new book on the latest Western maltreatment of the Philippines. It appeared that age hadn't doused the fire in Bello's belly. He related the unsettling story of how in just twenty years the Philippines went from being a net exporter of food to a net importer of it. As with other indebted states in the mid-eighties that hadn't gone Stalinist, the Philippines fell under the sway of 'structural adjustment'. On the say-so of the IMF and World Bank, the government made the economy more 'productive' by touting for foreign investment and developing the export sector.

The project failed. A global recession and a dive in the prices of Philippine paper, rubber, ceramics and beverages nearly annihilated several domestic industries. Cory Aquino, who was elected president after Marcos fell, started spending 8-10 per cent of the annual budget repaying foreign debt. This too was disastrous for the needy. Lack of cash for the infrastructure caused lay-offs and an exodus from the countryside to the cities like Manila. The pressure on services and resources grew.

I thought of Joel, whom I'd caught up with in Ride N Roll bar a couple of nights ago. When I told him I was off to Concepcion Extension, he said the squatters weren't welcome, they're trouble, they should go home. It was another case of unfairly deeming individuals liable for a situation they couldn't control.

In a bid to preserve the status quo in international trade – in other words, to keep the rich countries rich and the poor countries poor – the World Trade Organization ordered the Philippine government to abolish quotas on its agricultural imports. Filipino rice farmers couldn't compete. Thousands went bankrupt and fled to the cities. The subsequent drop in production forced the government to buy in vast quantities of rice from abroad, which, in turn, diminished the price of homegrown rice, causing further injuries to the rural economy. Other types of farmer suffered the same fate thanks to cheap corn, livestock and vegetables – much of it from trading blocs such as the European Union and North America.

Googling about, I stumbled across another statistic. The West African republic of Côte d'Ivoire produces about 33 per cent of the world's cocoa. Chances are, when you eat a Mars Bar or Dairy Milk, it has Ivorian cocoa in it. In 2010, the US multinational Kraft bought Cadbury's, one of the world's largest chocolate companies for US$16 billion. In comparison, the annual GDP of Côte d'Ivoire is a piddling US$36 billion.

Overwhelmed by big numbers, I browsed YouTube for any televisual coverage of the current state of the Philippine country and city. A British Channel 4 *Unreported World* documentary popped up, Teddy Casiño waxing lucid on the Philippine class system, a rigged game in which social mobility and meritocracy consistently lost out to special interests and archaic elitism.

I thought I'd better talk to him again. He invited me back to the Bayan Muna HQ and I started by asking about the obstacles facing the poorest farmers these days.

'Around 70 per cent of farmers do not own the land they till,' he said. 'We have a law now which is supposed to transfer ownership of the land to the farmers through a mortgage system whereby they pay for the land over thirty years. Unfortunately, 50 to 60 per cent are unable to pay the amortization.'

'So the 70 per cent are very poor.'

'They are the poorest of the poor. The majority are subsistence farmers, but the farm workers in the big plantations grow profitable crops like sugar and bananas. One of the biggest challenges that faced the previous administration was Hacienda Luisita [a 6,000 hectare plus sugar plantation in Luzon] where farmers would be paid as little as nine pesos a day. The farmers are treated basically as modern slaves. Most farming families have to augment their income working in construction, as tricycle drivers, vendors...'

'They're part of the informal economy.'

'Yes. All over the country, people have quit farming. A lot of time and effort goes into the job and what's the point if you're not assured of an income? Better to just drive a tricycle.'

'And these opportunities are mostly available in the cities?'

'In the cities you have all these odd jobs that can provide a daily income. In farming, you will need at least three months before you can grow anything to sell. In the meantime, how do you feed your family? The farmers are also hindered by the government. Under the agrarian reform law, they cannot use their land as collateral so they have to go to the loan sharks. These defects in the system have not been addressed by Congress, because it's not in the interests of the Congressmen who often come from the big landed families.'

'What part has the First World played in this malaise?'

'After Marcos fell in 1986, the debts he'd racked up stayed with us. We have not yet escaped from that trap. Under the USAID programme in the 1990s, US-funded study and lobby groups liberalized the economy, deregulated the oil industry and privatized our utilities. This was the time of President Ramos who, by the way, graduated from West Point, so you can see the "special relationship" between the US and the Philippines right there!

'Under Ramos' administration, protectionist and progressive policies were dismantled. He deregulated mining, banking, telecoms and oil. He privatized the water. Subsequent governments applied spending caps, so there was no money for infrastructure development or for rebuilding industries.'

'What were the effects of these policies on Filipino working people?'

'The government devolved assistance. Health services were placed under the control of local government, which could not cope with the large overhead required to maintain all the clinics and hospitals. When we joined the WTO, we had to import all these manufactured goods from the US and the EU which annihilated our rubber, steel, footwear and garments industries. Unemployment surged and many more Filipinos went to work overseas. Wages have stagnated over the last twenty or thirty years. As a percentage of the budget over the same period, health, housing, and education have not been up to par with world standards.'

'Could these budgets be increased through more progressive taxation?'

'The opposite has happened. In 2005, the government increased value added tax from 10 to 12 per cent. Whether you're rich or poor, you'll get slapped with the same tax on everything you buy. And then just earlier this year they approved another tax: the "sin tax" on cigarettes and liquor. Again, it hurts the poorer drinkers and smokers! And you know, our income tax is one of the highest in the region. Workers get a 30 per cent slap.'

'And if you're rich there are always ways of evading it.'

'Even professionals are able to hire accountants but, if you're a waged worker, your taxes are withheld the moment you get your pay cheque.'

'What's the first action a Bayan Muna government would take to improve things for the farmers and the poor generally?'

'We would interpret the existing laws in a more progressive way. With regard to mining, there are strict parameters on environmental protection. Most of these are ignored because there is collusion between the regulators and the big mining corporations. A more progressive administration could limit the destructive malpractice of these corporations, which negatively impacts on agriculture. In the long term we must reverse these neoliberal policies of deregulation, liberalization and privatization. But, again, that would require acts of Congress. Even if you have a progressive-minded executive, it is another to thing to persuade Congress to share the same vision. That's what we have experienced in our fifteen years in parliamentary politics.'

'I suppose the state-corporate media is also opposed to Bayan Muna, which must be another barrier to reaching the electorate.'

'Last week there was an article in the *Philippine Inquirer* saying that the media has been generous to a fault when it comes to the left. But when push comes to shove, the mainstream press will always endorse the status quo, especially during elections when the political ads come out. Progressives cannot afford the rates of the TV or radio stations. If you don't pay up, you don't get covered. The media says, "We will not cover you unless your PR agent has a deal with the station." And the best PR agents work for the vested interests.'

'Your party is aiming for the parliamentary route to reform even though it seems that these vested interests aren't going to give up their privileges without a fight.'

'Recent history shows that it takes upheavals like EDSA in 1986 to bring change. These kinds of mass movements feed into mainstream politics. We feel that being part of government, if there is an opening there, will complement these movements.'

28. BEAUTY AND TERROR

I'd first heard of José Y. 'Butch' Dalisay when studying at the University of East Anglia, where he'd been a David T.K. Wong Fellow in Creative Writing. Since then, I'd learned that Dalisay had travelled more than most other Filipino writers and had become an international authority on his country, having lectured on Philippine culture, society and politics in the US, Britain, China, Italy, Australia and New Zealand.

Before meeting him, I'd just finished his novel *Soledad's Sister*, which was nominated for the 2007 Man Asian Literary Prize. The story begins with a description of the dehumanizing process by which the corpse of 'Cabahug, Aurora V.' arrives at Manila Ninoy Aquino International Airport in crates, is stamped by apathetic officials and then left to be claimed by relatives. The body, we later learn, has been misidentified and in fact belongs to Soledad, Aurora's sister, who is just one of around 600 deceased OFWs per year shipped back to the airport from foreign lands. The fate of Aurora is synecdochal of the predicament of Filipinos who become second-class citizens when they migrate to the rich world, vulnerable to neglect and molestation. Aurora's remains have come from Saudi Arabia with 'no police report, no autopsy' and no passport, 'which was customarily confiscated from foreign workers by their employers'. We later find out that Aurora, in her quest for a better life, had left behind a 'son many thousands of miles away' in Manila.

It seemed logical, then, to first of all ask Sir Butch about his take on the OFW phenomenon when we met in a small bar on Katipunan Avenue, my old neighbourhood.

'I've met Filipinos wherever I've travelled,' he told me in an authentically twangy US accent. 'Just last week I was in Seoul, South Korea and I met with the Filipino community there. You can see how well they adapt, how quickly they pick up the language, and how effectively they establish support systems.

'I call the Filipino a kind of modern Ulysses. But in every Filipino, no matter how far he or she goes, or how long he or she stays away, there is always the desire to come home. With a few exceptions, we always want to come home. I haven't been to Iceland or Angola, but I know that there are Filipino diasporas there.'

'Yes. It amazes me how many OFWs are in the Middle East where the lifestyle is so different.'

'But they will adjust if they have to. They give primacy to earning money for people they have left behind. And that's another thing about us that I'm sure you will observe: strong family ties. Those millions of Filipinos wouldn't be out there if we didn't put a premium on the family, and on our hopes for the next generation. That's what it's all about. It's not about enriching oneself, it's about creating a nest egg for the people who come after you.'

'I suppose it's some sort of evolutionary drive.'

'Yeah, we *will* survive. You know, when our offices burned down in the University of the Philippines, I tweeted that this doesn't even come close to a Haiyan [a typhoon that struck the country in 2013]. We Filipinos are practically disaster-proof. We will die, we will hurt, but we're used to these things. So how could you complain about life as a maid in Hong Kong or Germany?'

'I've been researching internal migration in the Philippines and I wonder if moving abroad is a natural step after moving to Manila.'

'I was born on a small island in the Visayas and I've written about the transformational experience of coming to Manila in my first novel *Killing Time in a Cold Place*. You'll see in it the typical progression – at least we think it's a progression – of a character from the island to the cosmopolis and then on to the world out there. That's a very typical Filipino journey. So, in fact, in this generation, Manila is no longer the endpoint. The endpoint could be California or New York, or some other part of the world where you feel your destiny is. Manila is just a staging point, preparation for that.'

'I suppose modern Manila is so globalized now, you can find restaurants, bars and commodities that represent the whole world.'

'Exactly. I myself am surprised to go somewhere like Bonifacio High Street, close my eyes, open them and I feel as though I could be in Southern California. I think this is about mimicry, which has its apogee in our call centres where we imitate accents, we create personas to negotiate with the outside world. And so here in Manila we can kind of pretend that we're in California.'

'Are there any disadvantages to being good at mimicking other cultures?'

'The problem of course is that some people forget that it's a game! People actually think, "Hey, you know, if I flew to New York tomorrow I could make it there." But I think most Filipinos understand that it's not easy.'

'What is it about Manila that excites the imagination of writers and artists?'

'Well, I would think it's this blend of beauty and terror. The beauty being easily evident, especially for a traveller who comes in by sea. They arrive in Manila Bay and see the vastness of the sky and the colours of the sunset. This is the romantic side of Manila that generations of painters and poets have explored. The Manila sunset is the most popular staple of Philippine folk arts. There's a whole industry, what we call Mabini – painters from Mabini Street in Manila – who know that this image appeals to, again, the romantic sentiments of city folk who can still look out there and find something marvellous and wondrous despite the terrible state that the city itself and its people may have fallen into. It's a saving grace.'

'So there's something about nature being a corrective to culture?'

'Nature, especially at a distance. A couple of months ago I wrote a column piece about staying on the thirty-second floor of a Makati hotel and looking out at the city from the rooftop. I was reminded of what a beautiful city this is, as long as you are up high, you know? You can see the general contours – the mountains in the distance, the Pasig River winding through, the Marikina Valley in the east.

And that always evokes, I think, again, a sense of relief that we still exist somehow as part of the natural environment, and that we could, with a little effort, travel out there perhaps to Antipolo just to escape the city. *Manileños*, city dwellers here, take staycations in places like Antipolo or Tagaytay to get away from the smog and the busy traffic.

'So it's the old country and city dichotomy, with the country being the place for regeneration. Filipinos have a unique phrase in English that resonates with us in a way that it won't with anyone else. And the phrase is "in the province", which you may have heard before. For instance, if I meet my friend on a Monday after a long weekend, I might ask him, "Where were you this weekend?" He'd say, "Oh I was in the province." That place embodies a full complex of ideas. It's a verbal shorthand for saying, "Well I was sick of the city so I had to take a break and I drove out, rode a bus, to X – name the province –which is probably my hometown, 300 kilometres away where the air is fresh, the food is good. I saw my old friends, and there's peace and quiet, life's more relaxed, and so on." So again, the country for us is a refuge. Never mind that it is very likely not. Nobody talks about feudalism in the province. Nobody talks about hunger in the province.'

'They accentuate the positives.'

'Absolutely. One of our most popular classical painters remains Fernando Amorsolo. He painted loving portraits of pretty, nubile country maidens washing clothes by the stream. Again, because this was his idealization of rustic happiness. And this is what many of Manila's socialites like to hang in their living rooms. Amorsolo, who died in 1972, was our first National Artist, and he evidently appeals to a very big part of our sensibility which wants to go back atavistically to that state of grace. But we know we never really can do it.'

'And how old is that sort of attitude? Does it date from the early industrial period?'

'The sixties onwards, when Makati began developing. That was probably the seminal turning point. When I say Makati I mean Ayala Avenue, which was the first big step out of the old Manila. I have a friend who was offered land there at that time and he said, "Hell, no. Why would I want to live in Makati where there are snakes and mosquitoes?" Of course now, he's regretting his decision!'

'It was gentrified.'

'The city has grown. Makati, and then Cubao, and then Ortigas, and now Fort Bonifacio. And Taguig of course is really sprawling.'

'So in a way, the flipside of this approach is a book like *Manila Noir* [a 2013 anthology of fiction and poetry] which very much focuses on the crime and poverty of the city.'

'Well that in itself is a kind of romanticization. If you were putting together that type of book you would gravitate toward that reading of the city. You know, with the steamy streets and people prowling around late at night. A lot of Manila is like that. But there's also a lot of Manila which is suburban and boring, at least on the surface.'

'And other writers have engaged with that suburban Manila.'

'My own piece in *Manila Noir* is set in Diliman, which is kind of suburban. It's academic and genteel. But you can still find some interesting things going on there. Many of my students write about these settings now, with stories rooted not necessarily in the big gated communities, but in middle-class neighbourhoods.'

'Do you think that aspect of Manila life isn't really dealt with enough? I think there's this perception, at least in the West that Manila is a place of extremes – the decadence of the wealthy versus the squatters and the slums.'

'We've had those extremes representing Philippine society for a long long time. Which wouldn't be too far off the mark because you can see exorbitant wealth and abject poverty existing cheek-by-jowl wherever you go in this city. Personally, I have been much more interested in taking on the middle class as my subject. This is because I'm middle-class myself and because I think the middle class is in many ways the most interesting because it's the most vulnerable class. I mean, of course the poor are vulnerable, but the poor have really nothing to lose.'

'There's no way further down.'

'And the rich can buy themselves out of anything. But the middle class is strongly aspirational. They all want to be rich. And it's the power, that aspiration which intensifies our vulnerability. It's very easy to buy us, to corrupt us. We want power and wealth even more strongly than the truly wealthy and powerful already have.

'As a writer I'm also interested in the millennial generation who are kind of expats from the country. Of course, they are in their own country, but their experience is closer to, say, a Filipino-American family in California – the parents may have come from some small town in Ilocos and the kids have been to UCLA. And you see that dynamic right here in Manila, where the kids are radically different from their parents. More oriented, in fact, not just to Manila, but to New York and to Paris, and wherever the action is. You see a kind of alienation that's based on both place and on class right here in Manila. We have many students who really don't know or appreciate their provincial roots anymore. They tell me they haven't been home in ages. They might not even think of home as home. Home for them is here in Manila. Their parents' home could be Cagayan de Oro, but they're twenty-first-century *Manileños* now. Having said that, there is still that sentimental streak which thinks that Cagayan de Oro is the old hometown where I can always run to if I get in trouble here. If I get sick of this place, then I can always take a plane and stay there for a week.'

'And you think most people who have come from the province would feel that way even if, in reality, they wouldn't go back there?'

'When these kids go back to their hometowns for the summer break, they will identify themselves as *Manileños*. They won't say it, but with every gesture they make, every sentence they speak, they denote themselves as coming from the city. It gives them status. "I'm no longer from here – I am transformed." But here in the city, it's sometimes to their advantage to identify themselves by the province or the region that they come from. You see this at the university all the time. Freshmen from the provinces will identify themselves as being from Ilocos or Davao and they will join regional associations because it gives them a support network. And they will stick by that for as long as it's useful, maybe for life, although they will be more and more acculturated into the cosmopolitan environment of Manila.'

'You mentioned earlier that Filipinos are disaster-proof. Manila must have that disaster-proofing given the number of times it's been razed to the ground.'

'By earthquakes, by fire, by bombs, by massacres. It rebuilds itself. To put it plainly, it's a pretty ugly city. You can quote me saying that! Though, again, from thirty-two floors up, you don't see those things. The minute you get to ground level you see the grime and the garbage. The streets don't line up. The power lines above your head are haphazard. It's totally cluttered, messed up. Then again, I would suppose the Indians feel this too about their own megalopolises.'

'Would you also say that the architecture is not terribly pretty?'

'No. Because, again, it's a mishmash, an overlay, a pastiche of centuries of recreation. You could cram all of our architectural wonders into a small district of, say, Paris or Barcelona. And, having just come back from Seoul, how they cleaned up that place is absolutely astonishing.'

'Do you think it would be possible to clean up Manila?'

'Not without the kind of political will that the South Koreans have exhibited. They went through a pretty brutal dictatorship to get Seoul like that!'

'Would that be a price worth paying? You see, I'm trying to edge towards the subject of your new president who's known for "cleaning up" his home town in various ways.'

'It's not a price worth paying, at least not for me. I don't think Duterte is interested in doing that either. Even if that were on his mind, the people around him are basically opportunists. They will see in his clenched fist an opportunity to tack on whatever agenda they may have. Duterte is a very strange and disturbing phenomenon. He came into power on the promise of eradicating drug crime. Sure, there's a drug menace in this country but I suspect it's not as bad as he makes it out to be. I would see it in my students if it were. I'd see it on the streets too. It's a bogeyman claim that scares people. Drugs are not the biggest problem in this country. The biggest problem is still mass poverty, income distribution. And of course drugs is a kind of a spin-off from that. Desperate people turn to drugs.'

'If he addresses poverty than that will reduce drug-taking?'

'Of course that's what he has to do. But instead he's saying, "I'll take care of the street corner dealers first." Because they are the ones he's been killing. We have yet to see a major drug lord being taken out by his vigilantes.'

'I suspect that would be quite difficult in practice. It's easier to just nab someone off the streets.'

'Sceptics like me would take Duterte more seriously if we found the decapitated body of a corrupt Congressman on the steps of city hall tomorrow. I'm not necessarily saying that I want this to happen, but show me that and I'll know you mean business. Problem is, Duterte is taking out the little guys. And who cares about them? We know that they are just pawns, and half of them maybe aren't even guilty to begin with.'

'A lot of them are just juveniles.'

'They're juveniles. They're easy targets. And my theory is that the anti-crime angle is very popular – I bet most of his supporters voted for him just on that one issue. However, it's a short step from saying "let's fight crime" to classifying political dissent as a crime. And we have seen that this is the textbook prescription for dictators.'

'You feel it's no coincidence that he is friends with Marcos Jr?'

'No. While I'm not saying he's getting pointers from Marcos, clearly their hearts are in the same place. One of my deepest fears about this presidency, given its ideology or absence of one, is that Duterte might set up a popular movement, a masses-based "Dutertismo". It would follow what political scientists might classify as a "third-position ideology": neither capitalist nor communist, but populist and essentially fascist. The question is, you get sixteen million votes, a huge majority, so what are you going to do with those voters? You mobilize them, you organize them, especially at the grassroots. You may go on to arm them, again in the guise of the anti-crime drive.'

'And then suddenly you've got this large standing army.'

'Yes. And the minute people like me go out in the streets to protest, who do you think is going to meet us? It won't be his police.'

'And he will have deniability because he can claim that "the people" have resisted subversives like you.'

'It's okay because it's "the people". That's what I foresee happening. These thugs will come knocking on our doors.'

'We've seen it happen in other countries, in other contexts. I mean, a lot of leftists seem to support him. This might be too optimistic of me, but is there a chance that the popular movement behind him could bring progressive change?'

'Every Philippine president from Marcos to Noynoy Aquino has drawn on former cadres from the left to do their organizing for them. I mean, I was part of the left in this country. But that left has been terribly compromised over time. I mean, to put it plainly, it's become opportunistic.'

'Would you include in that category parties like Bayan Muna?'

'Not everyone in Bayan Muna. You can see the divisions in the left today that date back to the 1980s when there was open warfare between the so-called reaffirmists and the rejectionists. Some supported José Maria Sison, others opposed him. They basically tried to wipe each other out. And for many of us, that was our first inkling that the party we had signed up to wasn't what we thought it was, or should've been. We were part of that Maoist element, but even that party which had ironically set itself up in opposition to what it claimed was the corruption and banditry of the old Moscow-leaning Communist Party, itself became corrupted. How else can you explain Sison saying that it's okay to bury Marcos in the National Cemetery for Heroes?'

'Especially when he opposed Marcos tooth and nail.'

'The left is all too willing to take whatever power it can, knowing that it can't succeed in the armed struggle, knowing that it's increasingly becoming irrelevant. It needs an accommodation with Duterte in order so that its main figures can be given certain portfolios. But I don't think this arrangement will last. Duterte is smarter than all of them. They think they're using Duterte, but Duterte is using them. His strategy is "OK guys, come home." But the minute one of them balks at one of his policies – inevitably that will happen – we'll see whether these so-called leftists will have any principles in them. Once they resist, he'll chop their heads off. And he'll say, "Look guys, I gave you a chance, but now you're fighting me, so I'll fight you." It's a gambit and they're just walking into it, either out of silly idealism or out of crass opportunism.'

'A grim prognosis.'

'I'm trying to look for a reason to be hopeful, but I'm having a really really hard time!'

'Are there any politicians that you feel could offer a more sensible way forward?'

'The only ray of hope in these next few years is Leni Robredo, the vice-president.'

'What do you think needs to happen then materially in the Philippines in order to address poverty and these major problems?'

'If, despite his excesses, Duterte manages to keep his promise of fixing infrastructure, creating new jobs and of engendering growth in the countryside, then that would be something.'

'Would that involve raising taxes?'

'Duterte's pledge is to drop taxes. Our taxes are already the highest in the region. We pay 32 per cent tax.'

'But isn't there a lot of tax evasion amongst the rich?'

'Well that's the problem, it costs billions of pesos. And recouping that money will be a test of Duterte's political will. Can he really do that? If you look at the people who financed his campaign, you will see the usual suspects there. It's big business. So is he going to suddenly go up against them? We can't trust him because he makes these empty promises like eradicating all crime within six months. How the hell are you going to do that?'

'At the best of times politicians make promises they can't keep.'

'It was a foolish promise to begin with, which makes the people who believe him even more foolish. For me it's grim enough that, while my wife and I have resisted our brother's pleadings for us to join him in the States, it's an option that I'm starting to think about.'

'Have you ever relocated before?'

'This would be the first time in my life. I mean, we could have moved to the States a long time ago if we'd wanted to. Although I don't know what I'd do there.'

'You could teach and write, presumably?'

'I don't want to be a "minority voice" and have to deal with a whole set of minority issues. I don't want to have to deal with that discourse. But again, if there's no other choice, then I may have to do it. I'll give it a couple of years, if that long.'

'Would moving from Duterte's Philippines to Trump's America be an improvement?'

'Much as I hate Trump, Duterte's worse. And it's not just me thinking about these things. There's a sense of dread shared by many people now in my position.'

'Are there any forces that might balance Duterte's excesses?'

'I'm not a big fan of the Church, but it's probably the only force out there that is big and powerful enough to.'

'He doesn't seem to care what they think.'

'True, he doesn't give a shit what the Church thinks, doesn't give a shit what the pope thinks. So I don't see anyone exerting moral suasion on him. He seems to be a very self-centred fellow.'

'When I heard him come out and more or less advocate the killing of journalists I wondered how serious he was being.'

'Well, his current spokesman was the lawyer for the defence in the Maguindanao massacre [in which the Ampatuan political clan killed at least 34 journalists in Mindanao in 2009]. How much more bizarre does it get?'

'But then Duterte retracted the threat.'

'Yeah, like Trump he will say, "You're taking me out of context. You misconstrued me." But the damage has been done.'

'Do you think he might have a mental disorder?'

'Did you see the psychological profile released on him?'

'Yes.'

'It showed him as pathologically incapable of admitting fault or blame. That's very very dangerous. I mean, I can understand this in a city mayor, which is like being a warlord. But he's no longer a city mayor, now he has to deal with the Judiciary. He has to deal with the Legislature. Of course he has the Congress in his pocket. And what's going to happen if he runs into problems with the Supreme Court? Although, again, our Supreme Court can also be bought and terrorized.'

'Does he still have an opportunity to solve the insurrections in the south?'

'He has one of the biggest, if not the biggest mandates in our electoral history. That in itself should give him tremendous political clout to do what he thinks is right. Again, unfortunately, so far from what we've heard, he has been fuzzy on federalism. He hasn't showed us a path forward. The only method he has shown us is brute force.'

'Have you ever met him?'

'No. And I don't really plan to. I was asked to join his campaign.'

'Really?'

'Yeah. I said no.'

'If you had, do you think you would have been offered a position in the cabinet?'

'It seems to me that that hasn't been too difficult to do for a lot of people. You just show up in the right place and the right time and... He has made some terrible choices. There alone you can see what kind of trouble we're going to be in. These are *the* most unqualified people. They're his friends, they are the wives of his friends, his former professors. He is going to make Jose David Lapuz the next commissioner of higher education. This guy is eighty-plus years old and a certified windbag who likes to think of himself as the most brilliant fellow on the face of the earth, and delivers long but basically empty speeches. The commission should be focusing on an agenda for twenty-first-century education, and this guy has his foot in the nineteenth century. He gets the job because he taught Duterte at college!'

'Do you think there would be any move to try and impeach him?'

'Yeah, but it won't prosper. His presumptive speaker has already said, "Forget it, folks. You just won't have the numbers." And it's true. I think, personally, Duterte will not last his term. But it won't be due to impeachment. A lot of people think he's really sick. In the debates you could see his right hand trembling.'

'Do you think he has Parkinson's?'

'That's what I suspect.'

'That could explain the contradictions.'

'I think this is also one of the reasons why the Liberal Party and its stalwarts seem to have shifted allegiances wholesale and joined the majority bloc. I think they know he's not going to last, so they're preserving themselves as a party for when he departs. But I also don't think that Duterte's people will allow Leni Robredo to become president. They'll pull something off to stop her.'

'But the Constitution says she would have to succeed him.'

'Of course the Constitution says that, but these people don't care about the Constitution. They'll find a way to make her disappear, so it's going to be a very rocky road.'

'How soon do you think the first major problem will come about?'

'Within a month of his assumption of office. First to go will be the leftists in his cabinet. Either they really won't be able to stand him, or they will appear so compromised that they will have to leave. Judy Taguiwalo, the incoming social welfare secretary, is a hardcore Marxist and she has resisted the moves to bury Marcos.

'The divisions within the left will complicate the relationship with Duterte. There will probably be a faction that will continue to resist, who will never surrender their arms. Duterte will try for a quid pro quo like "I will bring you in but you must give up your arms". It's not going to happen. And that will give Duterte a pretext to sack the left, and to declare all-out war against them. Sison thinks he's coming home to a big welcome party with karaoke, but it's not going to happen.'

29. THE SAVIOUR

To get a clearer impression of what a Duterte presidency might look like, I wanted to talk to someone who'd closely followed Duterte long term as Mayor of Davao. I located an excellent source, a TV newsman who'd been based in the city in the 2000s. He asked to remain anonymous.

I began by asking him what had been the more dramatic events on his Davao beat.

'Davao has always been the victim of a negative perception about the conflict in Mindanao. I was there in March and April 2003 when there were major bombings of the airport and seaport. And I was there again in 2002 when the alleged CIA operative Michael Meiring blew himself up inside the Evergreen Hotel.'

'Why did he do that?'

'Some suspected he was involved in covert operations against the *Moros*. He pretended to be a treasure hunter and had access to the MILF (Moro Islamic Liberation Front) camps.'

'Sounds like an intriguing figure. Are these sorts of special operations still going on now in Mindanao?'

'I do not know for sure, but from what I have heard, yes, they continue.'

'Did you report on the death squads?'

'When I moved to Davao in 2000, the DDS were new. At that time, though, they were inactive because Duterte was serving as Congressman for one of the districts in Davao City. After his three-year term, he went back to being mayor and, within a few weeks, the summary executions resumed.'

'Did you gain any understanding as to why Duterte is so popular with voters?'

'I think they support him because those who are killed – excepting those who are victims of mistaken identity – are suspected criminals.

Some have had cases against them but they defended themselves and walked free. Although the law says you are innocent until proven guilty, I think the view of most Davaons is that these victims are highly likely to have done something wrong so it's no bad thing if they are executed.

'I remember when Duterte read out over 500 names of individuals live on his TV show. He was shrewd because he did not allege they were drug pushers. He said, "These people can help us with our campaign against illegal drugs." This is a lawyer's way of thinking.'

'What happened then?'

'A few weeks after that, he demanded that these people come to the Davao City Police Office, report to the staff, attend seminars and enjoy a free lunch. The following week, a lot of those on the list did exactly what they were told. Those who did not come were hunted down by the DDS. When I was reporting on the executions, I would check the name of the victim against the list. Always there was a match.'

'So this suggests Duterte was quite directly involved in the extra-judicial killings?'

'I would guess so. Another initiative was to send a policeman to knock on the door of a suspected drug lord's house and personally convince him to stop.'

'Are there certain figures in the drug dealing hierarchy that are untouchable, can't be brought to justice?'

'Maybe in Manila but not in Davao, I think.'

'What about police collusion in drug dealing?'

'Well, the other day in Manila the PNP [the Philippine National Police] and the NBI [National Bureau of Investigation] arrested a police officer involved in drug running.'

'But arrests of police don't happen in Davao?'

'I haven't seen that there, no.'

'Were you ever in personal danger reporting in Davao?'

'No.'

'Did you ever witness any of the summary executions?'

'No, but I interviewed some who had. Every time there was an execution, witnesses would be willing to talk to me. But they would never identify the perpetrators.'

'They were scared of retribution?'

'I think so.'

'How were the executions carried out?'

'The assassins usually ride on a black Yamaha motorbike without a licence plate. Some wear a helmet, some do not. Then after the killing, they just ride away casually. They never go fast.'

'Duterte calls himself a socialist so I am surprised that he doesn't believe in solving crime by trying to change the social conditions that give rise to it.'

'No, he doesn't care for the argument that criminals do what they do because of poverty. He believes that criminality is almost instinctual for them. They are born into it.'

'Do the DDS always get the right person?'

'Based on the studies, there were nine to twelve cases of mistaken identity during my beat there.'

'Were there cases of innocent people getting caught in the crossfire?'

'I don't know of any. One fatality was labelled as an error. The target, a suspected robber, was released after two days' detention from Talomo Police Station at 10 a.m. and met by his sister. He and his sister boarded a jeepney to travel home. At 10.25, a man got on the jeepney and drew a gun on the guy. When his sister saw it, she threw herself in front of him as a human shield. When the gun was fired the girl was killed.'

'Was the guy released because there wasn't enough evidence to convict him?'

'What they do in Davao is intentionally not file charges against those they arrest. That way they can be killed outside. That is the most common kind of hit in Davao.'

'Did the guy escape?'

'After shooting the guy's sister, the gunman ran off even though he hadn't got the right person. After that incident, the suspect was captured by the police because there was a pending warrant for his arrest. He was put in the city jail.'

'And where do DDS members come from?'

'Some reports say they are NPA rebel returnees. Some say they are paid at least 30,000 pesos per hit. I was told that it was only 5,000 pesos. We cannot validate this because there are no records.'

'Now Duterte is president-elect he's saying the drug war should go national. How do you think he would implement it?'

'By assigning his own people in every police station. In Davao, the commander of each police precinct is the handler of the hitmen. The incoming Philippine national police chief, General Dela Rosa, used to command three precincts in Davao. On his watch, every time the police were unable to file a case against a suspect, they'd be killed within an hour of their release and only 100 metres away from the police station.'

'Do you think it's feasible for Duterte to install loyalists in every police station in Manila?'

'It's easy to do that in smaller places like Davao City, but if Duterte has no support from the local officials and local police, it cannot work. What I think he'll do is to assign precinct commanders that are loyal to him. And then of course Dela Rosa, who worked closely with him in Davao, will direct the operation nationally.'

'Will that pose a challenge to the established order?'

'It's usual practice for any new president to appoint a new chief of the PNP, but General Dela Rosa is a one-star general which means he will outrank all these three-star generals within the PNP. That could be controversial.'

'What do you make of Duterte's joking around and flip-flopping? How do you know when he is serious or not?'

'When I was in Davao, I got used to it because people there just accept that Duterte speaks like that. So you have to work extra hard as a journalist to check, countercheck, verify. Often I had to ask him, "Mr Mayor, do you really mean this or are you just playing around?"'

'Is this a traditional approach in Philippine politics? Are there precedents?'

'No.'

'It's unique to him?'

'Yes.'

'So why does that appeal to people? I imagine it could be a irritating if you're a voter because you don't know what you're really voting for.'

'He knows how to entertain the masses, the ordinary people. In fairness to Duterte, some of his practices appealed to the public because they were common sense. He banned firecrackers, liquor sales after hours, smoking in many places. Garbage collection in Davao is always efficient. When you wake up in the morning, you won't see any garbage because it has all been cleared overnight.'

'And he is liked for his environmental policies. Didn't he ban mining?'

'That's interesting because Duterte is soon to appoint the next secretary of the department of environment and natural resources. His initially wanted a member of the Communist Party of the Philippines, but he said earlier this week that he had changed his mind because of a potential conflict of interests: the CPP and NPA are heavily involved in small-scale mining and oppose the large-scale type.'

'How did Duterte develop good relations with the communists?'

'In the 1980s, Davao was the killing fields of the NPA. There was a low-level war going on, with the communists and the anti-communist vigilantes killing each other daily. Duterte befriended Leoncio "Parago" Pitao, an NPA chief who died recently, and convinced him to stop operating in Davao City in return for concessions.'

'What kinds of concessions?'

'Every time the NPA abducted a policeman or soldier, they would be exchanged for prisoners held by the other side.'

'Do you know where the NPA get their arms from?'

'I don't know. Lately, a legal gun store sold 1,000 Chinese-made AK-47s to security guards at a mining firm in the Agusan del Sur area. But the firearms were then sold to the NPA! The boss of the mining firm said he was forced to do it because the NPA threatened his life.'

'So the NPA are involved in organized crime?'

'I really cannot speak for the NPA.'

'Do you think there will be a move to unseat Duterte now he's the president?'

'Maybe if the military become dissatisfied with him during his term. But I don't think there will be another coup because the military is already fed up with how many we have had before. And also, members of the media, the police, the army and the civil service voted earlier than the general public in the last election and most of those votes went to Duterte. It suggests that these powerful institutions support him.'

'Why do you think they voted for him?'

'Maybe because people are already sick of government corruption. Some see Duterte as the saviour.'

'Is he a religious man?'

'He said no, he has no religion. He claims he is no longer a Catholic and doesn't believe in religions, but he believes in God. And that's debatable because how can you believe in God and not religion?'

'I was wondering what his beliefs were after he attacked the pope.'

'People around the world are wondering why a Catholic country like the Philippines voted for a president who has lambasted the pope and the bishops, and has renounced his Catholicism.'

'Does that suggest that religion isn't as important to Filipinos as it once was?'

'People here don't mind what religion their leaders belong to. They just want someone who can save them. Because Duterte told the people during the campaign that he is the last chance to rescue Philippine politics. We'll see if he can save the Philippines!'

'He still describes himself as a socialist, so does he think he can save the country through government intervention?'

'Yeah, he believes in the power of the state, and believes in himself. He's somewhat like a dictator because what he wants, he gets. For example, when I was in Davao in 2002, he proposed to create this "dial 911" rescue centre. The problem was our telephone system is not configured for 911. All the emergency numbers, all special access numbers start with 1. We have 116 for the police, 163 for the fire and so on. The PLDT telephone company offered him a 119 number, because it's related to 911. It's a reverse, 119. But Duterte said, 'If you cannot give us 911, I'll have your tower bombed.'"

'Really?'

'He jokingly said that. It worked, though, and he was given the number.'

'You've obviously met Duterte. What is he like?'

'He's really nice. But I was not so close to Duterte when I was in Davao because I seldom went out of the office. I'm not so familiar with his personal life, but I learned about his taste for women.'

'Would you say he's charismatic?'

'Something like that. If you observe the presidential campaign, people are somewhat adoring him. He is like a cult leader. Many people are wearing shirts with his face. He catches the people's emotions like that.'

'He doesn't look like a typical politician. Do you think he'll ever wear a suit?'

'I haven't seen him wear a tie. He doesn't even like the *barong tagalog* because he believes it is for funerals only.'

'And what's with these midnight press conferences?'

'Duterte did that when I was in Davao. He once announced a news conference at 10.30 p.m. on a Saturday. Unfortunately, at that time, we lacked personnel so I wasn't able to send a crew to cover it. Afterwards, I found out that there was no press conference – Duterte had just told members of the media to spend time with him in his favourite bar! He told those who came not to report on a suspected rapist who'd been arrested earlier that day by the police. Because we did not send a representative, we were not party to that arrangement, so we broadcast a story about this rapist. By Monday morning, he had been killed. So Duterte must have known what would happen to the suspect, but the evidence against him was only circumstantial.'

'He's also angry. Where does that come from?'

'He has admitted that, as a young guy, he was mischievous. Three journalists – Leo Diaz, Rudy Alicaway and Michael Marasigan – who were killed by vigilantes during my time in Davao had all said negative things about Duterte's son Paolo. Of course there is no proof that Duterte ordered those murders, but if you ask ordinary people in Davao who is their number one suspect, they will say his name.'

'So nobody would testify against him, if it came to that?'

'Nobody.'

'That's why he can say, "I have killed these people."'

'He's a lawyer and knows how to wriggle out of these things. The Commission on Human Rights investigated the DDS and could not pin anything on him.'

'Do you have a sense of who his supporters are?'

'Before Duterte ran for office, he had no real organized movement behind him. He only had Davao. But he changed the landscape of the campaign by fostering an online discussion. A lot of trolls out there have put out fake information about him and fake information against his rivals, and it has worked.'

'So he's savvy about the internet?'

'No, he's not. He doesn't even use social networks. But in early 2014, he hired some marketing experts from Cebu. They employed an online group of people who, in December 2014, floated this slogan "Bisaya", which means people of the Visayan region. Their idea was to have a leader from the Visayas, but, shrewdly, it did not refer directly to Duterte at that time.'

'If the trolls made up things up about the other candidates, wouldn't it be libellous?'

'There's no libellous during a campaign! There was a lot of fake material out there on his behalf. His rival in the race, Mar Roxas, started an online campaign, but it was very late on in the process, well into 2016. Duterte had started two years before.'

'What kind of president will he be, do you think?'

'Personally, I'm apprehensive. I'm just going to wait and see what will happen.'

'Are you scared for yourself?'

'No. When I was in Davao, nothing happened to me. Though there was of course Jun Pala. He called Duterte's administration a "reign of terror". There were three ambush attempts on Pala before he was killed.'

'I understand that his murder was never investigated?'

'None of those vigilante killings in Davao has been investigated. If you check the records of the PNP, the murder rate and the unsolved crime rate in that region are very high compared to the rest of the country.'

'So you don't think Duterte's approach has worked?'

'No. The DDS reduces the number of small criminals like snatchers, hold-uppers, robbers and drug peddlers. But the process of killing them increases the number of unsolved murder cases.'

'Does Duterte personally intervene in the fight against crime?'

'I cannot validate that. I suspect not because, when I was in Davao, I was told that those pictures of Duterte driving a taxi around were staged for publicity purposes.'

'How do you think international leaders will receive Duterte?'

'Based on reports I have read, the international community is not favourable.'

'Do you think Trump would like him?'

'Duterte won't accept that he's the Donald Trump of Asia because, according to him, Donald Trump is a "bigot" whereas Duterte says, "I am not."'

'Do you think there are similarities?'

'Duterte is different from Donald Trump. Donald Trump doesn't kill people.'

'Do you think you might write a book about your experiences covering Duterte's Davao?'

'I will write about it one day. Maybe I'll just title the book *What I Learned from Duterte*.'

'Watch out for the guys on the motorbikes.'

'I'll use a pen name.'

PART 4: 2017-2018

30. THE TALKATIVE TERRORIST

Ileft Manila in August 2016 both a little more enlightened and a little more confused about the political situation in the Philippines. I'd learned more about Duterte's appeal to the public, his electoral tactics and his iron rule over Davao. However, I was perplexed by his relationship with the left – which was set to be a crucial factor over the next few years of his administration – not least because the people on the left I'd spoken to were ambiguous about both his intentions towards them and their intentions towards him.

In May 2017, I watched from afar as the city of Marawi on Mindanao Island was occupied by the infamous ISIS-affiliated Maute terror outfit. Duterte promptly declared Martial Law in the region, which was scarily redolent of the Marcos period. Named after the maniacal warlord family that runs it, Maute appeared to be better trained and more aggressive than other cells in Mindanao. This may have explained why they were withstanding daily aerial, artillery and ground attacks by the AFP.

There were concerns in the Philippines and in neighbouring nations that the city could become a nerve centre for ISIS activity in the region – it might soon be known as the 'Mosul of Southeast Asia'. After all, Maute was thought to comprise both local and foreign fighters from Malaysia, Indonesia and the Middle East. Duterte's credibility could also rest on the outcome of the siege because, during his election campaign, he'd made much of his cordial interactions with Islamist groups in the south.

While mounting casualties on the jihadist side and the intervention of US Special Forces on behalf of the military suggested the state would likely win this particular battle, it seemed to me that the larger war wouldn't end until the root causes of discord in the south were addressed. The *Bangsomoro* (Muslim community or nation) had been struggling for self-determination since the Spanish Empire first tried to colonize it in the 1500s. The Americans tried the same in the early 1900s. While tensions between Mindanao and the central government in Manila were dampened by the establishment of Islamic autonomous regions in 1989 and 2012, many southerners continued to feel neglected and marginalized. Mindanao contains eleven out of the twenty poorest provinces of the Philippine archipelago and has far fewer jobs, schools and hospitals than the better-off north. 'With poverty, hunger, and the lack of economic opportunity strongly felt in these areas,' argues Lila Ramos Shahani of the *Philippine Star* newspaper, 'the youth are easily recruited to "live by the gun".'

It's a familiar irony across the developing world that great natural wealth can often be found a few thousand feet underneath human suffering. Mindanao is no exception here. In 2011, *Wikileaks* published a US diplomatic cable revealing that the island possesses untapped oil and gas reserves that could be worth up to US$1 trillion if properly exploited. This ought to have been good news for all Filipinos north and south, but would probably instead become another rationale for another conflict.

In late July I contacted José Maria Sison, the most famous figure on the Philippine revolutionary left, to discuss the Marawi question and to find out his angle on the left's dealings with Duterte. Before he was due to chat with me by Skype from his home in Holland, I read that Duterte had said.Sison, now seventy-five years old, was suffering from colon cancer, which Sison irately denied. The allegation appeared to be vindictive, as relations between the two men had cooled since Duterte had suggested that Sison could join his cabinet only a year before.

When the video screen came on, I could see Sison looking blankly at me, buck teeth framed by Churchillian jowls. A woman was sitting beside him, slightly out of frame.

'Hello sir.'

'Hello Tom.'

'Are you well?'

He laughed.

'So there's no truth to the cancer story?'

'I'm okay despite Duterte's confused statement that I am dying. He wants to kill me! Now apparently he has said he wants me to commit suicide. This was after I rebuffed him about the colon cancer. He must be taking a lot of fentanyl.'

'So they say.'

'Don't you know he's the number one addict in the Philippines?'

I laughed. 'You're probably bored of being asked about these recent dwalings with him, so I want to instead ask what are your feelings about Duterte's policies and his actions as the president, especially with regard to the drug war. Is it compatible with socialism or with human rights, and with the sort of dignity that socialists believe humans deserve?'

'Duterte has much experience of cooperating with the revolutionary movement in Davao City. I've been wondering how the comrades managed to deal with him! They say he is capable of saying or doing anything that is left, middle or right on the political spectrum.'

'I just wondered...'

'Duterte has this braggadocio. He's like an adolescent who has not grown mentally despite his university education. When he was my student at the University of the Philippines, he was mediocre. But he could not have risen to his position without a high level of native intelligence. At the same time, he cannot conceal his malice.'

I tried to interrupt him again, worried he was digressing. 'Can I just ask something? Can I just ask...' He continued to talk and then paused after the woman next to him commented in Filipino. I started again, and he cut me off again.

'I have bad hearing,' Sison said. 'Can you increase the volume?'

'I'll try to speak louder,' I said, 'and I'll turn my microphone up. So can you hear me now?'

'Yeah.'

'Can I go back to the question about whether the anti-drugs clampdown in any way furthers socialism? Does it help the revolution in the Philippines?'

'It's counter-revolutionary because the targets are poor. Suspicions are growing that Duterte is protecting the drug lords, that is to say those who own the laboratories, those who direct the smuggling operations. The biggest protectors are the military generals and the governors of provinces. Duterte said publicly that he would kill Peter Lim, an alleged major drug dealer, if he returned to the Philippines from abroad. That was a year ago and only now has Lim been subpoenad. He will probably walk. Why? Because he and Duterte are compadres. Then Duterte accused Governor Espino of Pangasinan, a former general, and General Garbo of the Philippine National Police. After that Duterte fell silent. He is a coward.

'Do you know *juteng*, this illegal gambling game we have in the Philippines? Bored people bet on numbers and the *kubradors*, those who collect the bets, have been used as drug distributors. The *juteng* system is under the protection of local officials. The money raised from the bets is supposed to go into a special fund to make up for shortfalls in the budget. Senator Leila De Lima has accused Duterte of protecting the *juteng* operators and drug bosses he favours in order to put rivals out of business. So far, Duterte has claimed to have killed only three mayors complicit in drug dealing. Three out of God knows how many!'

'Is it fair to say that Duterte is a hypocrite? It's too complicated for him to target the big drug lords so he instead takes aim at the street-level users and mules.'

'For that reason also the programme is not working. Street sales are still strong even in the national penitentiary, Bilibid!'

'I just wanted to move on...'

'Let me give you another insight.'

'Okay then.'

'Duterte claims he has an independent foreign policy. This is camouflage because the US has Duterte in their full control through his secretary of defence Delfin Lorenzana, a long time "Washington man" of the Philippine Armed Forces. He was the one who developed the Balikatan joint military exercises between our country and the US in the 2000s. Duterte's bad-mouthing of Obama wasn't important – Duterte is still a puppet of the US. He has not changed a single treaty, military or economic, that has bound the Philippines to the US as a client state, as a puppet state. He's trying to augment what he can get from the US by approaching China and Russia.'

'You were very active in the resistance against Marcos. Do you think that the left…'

'Your voice was chopped up. It didn't come out well.'

'Let me try again. You were known to be very active in the resistance against... Can you hear me?'

'Hello?'

'Hello. Can you hear me?'

'The transmission is garbled,' said the woman.

'That's strange,' I said, 'because I can hear you fine. Can you hear me now?'

'Yeah,' said Sison and the woman in unison.

'Great,' I said. 'If we can talk…'

'Hold on,' said the woman. 'Your voice seems to be distorted. Are you using wireless internet?'

'Yeah, but the signal is strong.'

'Are you near the receiver?'

'Yeah.'

'Is the image of me for publication?' asked Sison. 'I mean, do I have to look formal? I'd like to open my shirt because it is hot in here.'

'No. I won't be publishing any pictures, don't worry. Did you hear that?'

'Not very well,' said the woman. 'Shall we change to just audio?'

We did and that seemed to solve the technical problems.

'Sir,' I said, 'you made a comparison about the Marcos era, during which I know you were very active in the resistance.'

'Duterte is so many times more terrible than Marcos. In the human rights case against Marcos in the US, we were presented with

3,500 cases of extrajudicial killings over twenty or so years. Duterte has much more than that in only one year. And he has repeatedly threatened to engage the military in anti-drug operations on a local level. If that happens, then this will provide an excuse for massacres of others deemed 'undesirables' such as political radicals like me and my comrades. 'With Marcos, it took time before the resistance got going. By contrast, as soon as Duterte was elected he expressed the desire to become the first socialist president, which made us on the left reluctant to protest him. He told Fidel Agcaoili, the emissary of the National Democratic Front of the Philippines (NDFP), that he would release all political prisoners listed by the NDFP.

'But Duterte's ministers – who have ties to the military – persuaded him not to release the prisoners. Duterte then scuttled the fifth round of formal talks in the Netherlands by declaring Martial Law in Mindanao. This upset the CPP. They thought it unnecessary to extend Martial Law to regions beyond the *Moro* area. Duterte's covert aim, we think, is to further the campaign against the revolutionary forces. When our comrades are killed, Duterte says "Oh, it's the military's fault and I don't have control over them." He's a good swindler, you see? A liar..'

'What do you make of Duterte's approach to the Marawi crisis?'

'He made sustained assaults on the Maute group and dared them to bring it on, do the worst they can do. And so the Mautes combined with the Abu Sayyaf [another ISIS-affiliated militant cell created in 1991]. And then, when he started bombing Marawi City, the local Maranao people were so shocked that they started to support the Mautes. Duterte made the mistake of using the American style of fighting – bombing an entire city, destroying every building in order to save the population, supposedly. It's the shock doctrine.'

'Given Duterte's broken promises, what has the left learnt? What can it do?'

'Guided by historical materialism, the revolutionary forces must unite with the legal democratic forces and struggle whenever there is the prospect of a united front.'

'You mentioned Marxism-Leninism and neoliberalism. I

wondered how these ideologies relate to the modern revolution in the Philippines. The revolutions in Vietnam, North Korea or China produced highly authoritarian regimes. Furthermore, surely they've deviated from Marxism and are now closer to neoliberalism. For example, they're supplying cheap labour to Western corporations. And so, I'm wondering are you-'

'That's an interesting question which involves a long answer!'

'But can I just finish... I'm sorry, if I could just finish the question-'

'In Russia in 1989-1991, the revisionist ruling cliques went full steam ahead with embracing capitalism, but retained all the elements of state capitalism wherever it was necessary. The same happened in China and, by the early 1990s, the US was the sole superpower in the world. It outsourced its manufacturing to China which, by retaining the methods of state capitalism, developed major lines of industry.

'China has succeeded economically while the US failed because, after the US slashed its manufacturing, there was a lot of unemployment. Its reaction was to financialize its economy, which caused masses of debt. Another problem was – and still is – American imperialist wars of aggression. Vietnam bankrupted the US and, later on, Iraq alone cost up to US$3 trillion. The result has been a more multipolar world.'

I had been warned by my contacts in the Philippine media that Sison could be a windbag. There wasn't much time left for this interview and I was eager to halt his digression into the history of Marxism-Leninism. 'Can I...' I managed, but he interrupted yet again.

'Now what has this to do with the Philippine Revolution, you may wonder?'

'Actually yes, that's precisely what I was wondering.'

'In the 1960s, when the revolutions in Vietnam, India and other parts of Asia were taking place, the US was beginning to decline. The Philippines had an opportunity then. But do you know about this theory that we could not become socialist because we were archipelagic with no common land borders with China?'

'No, I hadn't heard that one.'

'I don't agree because the Philippine revolutionary movement was able to develop its own strength, and is still going strong. But of course, a new democratic revolution is not inevitable. No, it will take some time.'

I was disappointed that he'd evaded my question about the long-term desirability of a Chinese or Vietnamese-style revolution, but, again, I wasn't going to get a word in.

'The last good thing that occurred for the Philippines,' he continued, 'was the 2008 financial crisis. The only solution the US had was to take in more poison, by which I mean taking on more public debt as if there were no end to it.'

'So could the Philippine Revolution succeed if it got NDF members into the Senate and used the parliamentary process.'

'There are a handful of progressives in Congress already. Unfortunately, some of them do not understand the importance of the extra-parliamentary movement. They say, "After fifty years, what have you gained?" These stupid guys do not know that the Communist Party increased from eighty to hundreds of thousands of members. These stupid guys do not know that the NPA started with nine rifles only and we now have a national armed struggle. And they forget that the mass movement has created a situation of dual power in the Philippines. There is a government seated in Manila headed by Duterte, and it's a government of big compradors and landlords subordinate to the US. But there is also a revolutionary government in the countryside led by the proletariat. The revolutionaries have gained so much that even the most reactionary governments are compelled to negotiate. However, the problem with reactionaries in the Philippines is that they are very primitive. Unlike their counterparts in other Asian states, Jawaharlal Nehru or Sukarno for example, they have not studied Marxism. They have been fed by the US educational and cultural system. The professors who taught them train in the US and it's a no-no for them to even look at Marx's ideas or engage with his exponents.'

'Where does Duterte fit into this model?'

'Duterte is smarter and more like Nehru or Sukarno so far as he knows how to co-opt elements of the left. He appointed to his cabinet a former Communist Party man, Jun Evasco, in order to create the illusion of a mass movement in his favour. In reality, though, he held only around fifteen meetings during his campaign. These emulated local mass meetings where there are vulgar jokes and macho statements, where the speaker evokes the image of a strongman who offers 'Mister Quick-fix' solutions to political problems through brute force. Desperate people whom the system has failed are attracted to that. The poorest Filipinos come from the south and were induced by Duterte's demand for a president to come from the south.

'Duterte didn't win because of the will of the downtrodden, he won because he enlisted all the reactionary politicians whose bailiwicks he needed to win the election. He offered Bongbong Marcos the vice-presidency and that secured him Ilocos Norte. Chavit Singson's support delivered many voters in Ilocos Sur. Mayor Estrada in Manila came out for him.

'That proves Duterte can never be an ally of the revolutionary movement. We have seen his "man of the people" rhetoric before so many times. When Manuel Quezon used his "social justice" slogan, gullible people believed it. When Ramon Magsaysay said he was the hero of the masses, people didn't think it contradicted the fact that he was busy destroying the revolutionary movement under the guidance of the CIA. You cannot blame the people for their ignorance – the whole system of conditioning minds is controlled by the reactionary forces.'

'Other people, perhaps on the more reformist side of the left, argue that the use of violence doesn't win the hearts and minds of the Filipino working class.'

'There was a lot of violence before the revolutionaries came. It was and still is the violence of daily exploitation. For example, when sick children die simply because their parents cannot afford to pay for the medicine, that is violence. And when anyone tries to dramatically challenge the system, you have the violence of surveillance, harassment and murder.

'As a matter of fact, revolutionaries do more "missionary" work than anything else. Above all, they help poor people to understand that they are not to be blamed for their suffering. I don't agree with José Rizal's statement, "There are masters because there are slaves. Slaves are willing." That is a very petty bourgeois liberal statement. Sure, I have seen with my own eyes peasants weep when they have been given their own land because they think the procedure is disrespectful to the wealthy rentier it has been expropriated from. But such respect is generated by centuries of brutal injustice and institutions indoctrinating everyone to behave in a certain way. They are not "willing" to be exploited in the sense that they have a free choice about it.

'Also, it is not just that you're dumb if you don't know you are being exploited. You simply don't have time to argue. Your first priority is to survive each day, and you will starve if you do not work. And then, while you are resting, you listen to the radio or watch the TV and you are brainwashed by the propaganda. You are made to accept your condition and that you cannot do anything about it. The other problem in underdeveloped countries is that the masses draw on religion and superstition to make them feel better.'

'I wanted to go back to when you were a professor at UP. What was the moment when you decided to sacrifice your academic career to become a dissident?'

'I grew up with seven siblings in a feudal, land-owning family. Our family's patriotism and anti-imperialism were its saving graces. We were proud to have supported the Philippine Revolution and the fight against the Japanese occupation. Myself and two of my siblings were sent to a public school where our classmates were mostly the children of our tenants. In grade four, I had a teacher who belonged to the Philippine Independent Church, which grew out of the revolutionary movement. He taught us the real history of our radical heroes.

'In addition, my mother would tell us stories of our relatives in Pampanga who had been killed by the Hukbalahap. They were probably murdered by our poorer relatives because we had a large, extended family. In those days, the rich would live in the large *sala* (rooms) while their distant relations would live in the kitchen or outside in the yard. So even within one family there was social polarization. That was a political lesson to me. And then I eavesdropped on our tenants, who could not grow enough food for harvest time, and they would support the Hukbalahap because they promised land reform. But when they talked to my parents – their bosses – they played a very different tune!

'After grade six, we were sent to the Ateneo de Manila Jesuit school in Manila, which was run by American priests. One of these Americans said Andrés Bonifacio was just a thug in Tondo. and that Claro Recto, the anti-imperialist senator of the US colonial period, was a crazy communist. That upset me because my father hated the Americans because they bombed most of the stone houses of our extended family in World War II.

'If Recto was, as the priest said, a communist then there must be something good in communism, I told myself. At the Ateneo I tried to do pro-poor things like collecting for the needy at Christmas and distributing the newspaper of the Federation of Free Workers, a Jesuit-organized trade union.

'When I began teaching at UP there was a clash between the religious sectarians, who wanted to introduce a theology department, and the liberals, who believed in the separation of church and state. I had some sympathy for groups like Student Catholic Action because they were a radical movement. UP was known then as a free marketplace of ideas, a place of academic liberty. There was a lot of research on the Philippine Revolution and its glories were being celebrated. I published some articles under pseudonyms because students and professors were under threat of arrest for violation of the Anti-Subversion Law. At that time there was the Committee on Anti-Filipino Activities, a copycat of the House Un-American Activities Committee. We resisted by forming the UP Student Cultural

Association which led a mass action of 5,000, the first demonstration of its time.'

'My last question is just about your status as an exile, if you don't mind me asking you-'

'I left the Philippines as half-friend to Cory Aquino and half-critic. I never imagined she would cancel my passport in 1998! She said she was forced to do it because factions within the Philippine military were threatening her with a coup. I had to apply for political asylum. If you can prove, even with soft evidence, that you are a subject of persecution, as I did, then you can be recognized as a political refugee.'

'Do you hope one day to go back to the Philippines?'

'Before he went crazy with his rants, Duterte assured me that, if I returned, I would not be incarcerated and would have complete freedom of movement. Though he didn't make it public, he wanted me to advise him. So if I was prepared to serve those whom I do not want to serve, it would be easy for me to return to the Philippines.'

After our call, I felt dizzy with ambivalence about Sison. His sideswipes at Duterte's faux populism and his under-reported ties with elites had won me over. Sison's self-portrait of the activist as a young man was also absorbing. But I was less sure of his dogged allegiance to the Stalinist pasquinade of Marxism that had caused such grief across Asia and would probably do the same if it ever took hold in the Philippines.

I idly looked him up on Wikipedia. 'Shit,' I said out loud. I anxiously read the following line over and over again: 'Since 2002, he has been classified as a "person supporting terrorism" by the United States.'

How the hell did I miss *that* detail? I thought I'd researched him thoroughly before our interview. I was reminded of the Edgar Allen Poe short story 'The Purloined Letter', in which the Paris police search frantically for the eponymous document only for it to turn up in the most obvious place of all: in a card rack. I'd read a book of interviews with Sison and a dozen articles, but hadn't thought to spend a few seconds reading two lines of his Wikipedia entry, where most sensible people would look first.

'"Person supporting terrorism,"' I muttered. What if somewhere in the vast meshwork of modern communication lines – telephone, cellular, microwave, fibre-optic, satellite, undersea – the name 'Tom Sykes' had now been spliced with the name 'José Maria Sison' – that 'person supporting terrorism' – like two lengths of copper wire in a fuel tank, and now the situation was about to blow up because some sinister monitoring station that looks like a giant golfball had forwarded this association to the CIA or the NSA or the FBI or MI5 or MI6, who were now poised to kick down the door of my flat and drag me by the testicles to Guantánamo Bay for plotting with Comrade Sison the overthrow of Western civilization.

I dialled the non-emergency police number. 'Can you put me through to Special Branch or whatever you now call it? Please?'

'It's now called the Counter Terrorism Command, sir,' said a chirpy young woman.

'That one then.'

A minute of silence and then a man's voice. 'Hello sir, how can I help you?'

'I'm an academic who's researching Philippine politics and I've just conducted an interview by Skype with José-Maria Sison, who's designated a supporter of terrorism by the United States.'

'I understand.'

'In case you or another security service intercepts the conversation, I just wanted to make it perfectly clear that I do not sympathize with Sison's ideas.' This was a slight untruth – I did in fact sympathize with some of his ideas, though not the ones that resulted in murder.

'The conversation may well have been picked up,' said the man. He paused as if to make me sweat. 'But I'll note down what you've said to me today and give you a reference number.'

I wrote down the number on a post-it note and pictured myself holding it aloft at the men in black as they abseiled through my window, fingers on the triggers of their SA80 assault rifles.

31. DUTERTE PROCESS

By the time I went back to Manila in August 2017, 4-10,000 people had allegedly been killed in anti-narcotics operations, depending on which sources you believed.

I read about the case of seventeen-year-old Kian Delos Santos. A shy student who liked cheese-flavoured crisps, Santos was arrested by two plain clothes cops at his home in Caloocan, a deprived suburb of Manila, beaten up and dragged into a *cul-de-sac* with a disused pig sty in it. According to eyewitnesses and CCTV footage, the cops blindfolded Kian and put a loaded .45 calibre pistol in his left hand. They didn't know that Kian was right-handed. 'Sir, can I go home now?' he pleaded. 'My father must be looking for me. I have an exam tomorrow.'

A cop told him to fire the gun in the air. He did so. 'Now you start running,' said the cop.

Kian started running. The cops shot him. They planted two sachets of crystal meth on his corpse and told their superiors Kian had fired first.

Duterte met Kian's parents and expressed his condolences. 'Bring those policemen who are involved in Kian's killing to jail,' he demanded. In this instance the guilty men have been charged, but hundreds of others continue to kill with impunity.

Thirty-two-year-old Rogie Sebastian was mowed down by masked men at his home while his family begged for his life. Uniformed police arrived at the scene and allowed the masked men to escape on a motorbike.

Ogie Sumangue, nineteen, was found riddled with bullets, a .45 automatic in his hand. Given that his sister paid his rent for him, no-one in his *barangay* believed he could afford a gun.

Why would lawmen all over the Philippines frame palpably innocent people in the shabbiest fashion, especially when there were enough authentic crooks to catch? My CNN contact, who'd received emails and phone calls from anonymous sources inside the police and judiciary, told me the motive was above all financial. 'There are cash rewards for police officers and the civilian hitmen they employ. You get 20,000 pesos (US$400) for a small-time pusher or user – there is no discrimination between the two – and 1-5 million pesos (US$20,000-US$100,000) for a kingpin distributor. Thieves, fraudsters and sex offenders are worth 10,000 pesos (US$200) apiece.'

In a country where the average citizen earns 14,651 pesos (US$290) a month, bounty hunting must be a temptation, particularly if you have no conscience and everyone around you is doing the same and getting away with it.

Other victims have been unlucky bystanders. They include a dozen children. Four-year-old Althea Barbon, who dreamed of joining the police when she grew up, was killed mistakenly by an undercover cop who was pursuing her father Alrick on a motorbike. The cop's bullet passed through her father's back and into Althea's spine. Alrick had fled with his daughter after realizing he'd walked into a 'buy-bust', where cops pose as customers to entrap drug dealers.

Francis Mañosca (six) died in his sleep after a gunman fired speculatively through the window of his cinderblock shack in Pasay City. The gunman was aiming for Francis' father, a tricycle driver who claims not to sell or take drugs. 'I hope the killer grows a conscience,' said Francis' mother.

I tried to arrange an interview with the president through the Malacañang Palace. As with the police, I never heard back. Duterte seemed to have lost all patience with Western scrutiny. He'd just changed his mind a third time about the status of journalists – 'You won't be killed if you don't do anything wrong' – which disturbed the United Nations Special Rapporteur Cristof Heyns: 'A message of this nature amounts to incitement to violence and killing, in a nation already ranked as the second-deadliest country for journalists.'

To which Duterte replied, 'Fuck you, UN, you can't even solve the Middle East carnage … couldn't even lift a finger in Africa … shut up all of you.' Later, when the EU condemned his talk of reintroducing the death penalty, Duterte lashed out at France and Britain's 'gall' – their old empires had slaughtered 'thousands of Arabs' and were nowadays 'bullying small nations'. In his State of the Nation Address, he paid tribute to 'the gallantry and heroism of our forebears' who fought in the Philippine-American War and demanded the US hand back three church bells its troops looted after torching the village of Balangiga in 1901. When the US State Department expressed 'concerns' about the drug war, Duterte countered that in the US today 'black people are being shot even when they are lying down.'

Coming from a more principled statesman, such critiques of First World double standards would be legitimate. But if Duterte steams up about Ferguson or Libya when a foreign reporter tries to pin him down on the death squads, it's not that he cares about global paradigms of accountability – he wants to distract us from his own foul acts.

When I put this to a very bright taxi driver, who'd just been awarded an MSc in Political Science but hadn't yet been able to find a white collar job, he said, 'Duterte would not be able to say such things to you if you hadn't bombed, burned and dominated countries like ours over the years.'

While in Manila this time, I was intrigued to see Duterte open up about his personal difficulties, although it smacked of a cynical ploy to reap sympathy from his critics. He announced that he'd been sexually molested at his Jesuit-run high school by the disgraced American priest Paul Falvey. 'How would you complain?' Duterte said. 'We were afraid.' But was this just another self-serving fabrication? If not, it was surely one more formative event – along with getting whipped senseless by his mother – in the brutalization of the man. In an eerie parallel with Marcos' own early homicide of his dad's small-town rival, Duterte confessed to having shot and wounded a fellow student at San Beda College of Law in 1972. The claim remains unproven.

I asked Joel how long Duterte could last. 'We need a new People Power Revolution,' he replied. It wasn't a far-fetched notion, as Duterte's approval rating had sunk by eighteen points over the first year of his term. He'd also made high-ranking enemies in Congress, the Church, the armed forces and organized crime. The Philippines' biggest drug lords had all donated to a fifty million peso (about US$1 million) bounty on his head. If you live by a Wild West code you might in the end die by it.

32. THE MASS

The total of 10,000 men, women and children 'salvaged' – as the Philippine-English slang had it – in just one year was 7,000 more than had succumbed to the Marcos junta between 1965 and 1986. Duterte harked back to Marcos in other ways too. As José Maria Sison had stated, Duterte's introduction of Martial Law across Mindanao after the Marawi City crisis was a frightening omen: to this day, Duterte keeps warning he will expand Martial Law to the entire country to stamp out what he calls a 'foreign invasion' of terrorists. (The Marawi siege finally ended in late October, leaving 87 civilians, 974 militants and 168 Philippine soldiers dead.)

Duterte's father Vicente would have been proud of Rody's decision to give Marcos' embalmed remains a 'hero's burial' in the National Military Cemetery. On 11 September 2017 – Marcos' hundredth birthday, if he'd lived that long – I was standing outside the cemetery's gates with a CNN news team while dignitaries, their identities hidden by their cars' blacked-out windows, attended a mass in his honour. On the other side of the driveway was a 200-yard queue of mostly older women in white T-shirts clutching pink, green and yellow umbrellas. Some bore signs with these sorts of sentiments on them: HAPPY HAPPY BIRTHDAY LATE PRESIDENT FERDINAND EDRALIN MARCOS, WE LOVE YOU AND YOUR FAMILY. A CNN anchor told me these were Marcos devotees who'd come all the way down from Ilocos on the off-chance of being let in to the mass. Blue uniformed police stood at ten-yard intervals to protect them, if needed, from protestors thronging on the other side of the driveway and at the opposite end to the cemetery gates where I was. They had signs too: BLOCK MARCOS, DEFEND OUR RIGHTS AND HISTORY. At the midpoint of the driveway, two dozen black-clad riot police stood resting their arms, encased in futuristic armour, on the tops of their three-foot-tall transparent shields.

The rain came in hefty drops. I stepped into the shelter of a CNN gazebo. More expensive cars cruised past. The queue shuffled forwards, some of the hopefuls gaining admission to the mass. 'Not much happening,' sighed the anchor.

'Do you think much will?'

'More anti-Marcos types are marching here from downtown, but we don't expect fireworks.'

Not much more to see here, I decided. Walking out of the driveway, I found myself within arm's reach of a man in a red crash helmet as he snatched a banner from a protestor. 'Marcos was a great man!' he yelled. 'In his day the Philippines had prestige in the world!' The protestor lunged back, trying to retrieve his banner. The crash helmet sprinted away. The protestor started after him but gave up with a dismissive wave. Having failed to spot any VIP guests and denied any major crowd violence to report on, the media knew this was the best story they'd get today and formed an impermeable scrum around the crash helmet. Microphones and dictaphones poked out like sudden, unwanted erections. The crash helmet would get his soundbite – his fifteen seconds (maximum) of fame – on the news this evening.

When Duterte heard about larger demonstrations planned for ten days later, he reversed his attitude to Marcos. Once a 'hero', he was, now, suddenly, guilty of 'gross human rights violations, arbitrary state interventions, rampant corruption, and disregard of fundamental civil liberties'. Vicente wouldn't have been so proud to hear that from his son.

33. THE LEADER'S LAUREATE

If you want to understand the full frame of a debate you should seek out the strongest, most convincing arguments on all sides of it, no matter your personal attitude. I'd had enough of knee-jerk homages to Duterte from taxi drivers and menial staff: 'He's cleaned up my neighbourhood'/'He's the strongarm our country needs'/'He's for the common man.' It was time to talk to someone who'd thought a little more deeply about his virtues, if indeed he had any.

On my last trip to Manila, the Chinese-Filipino novelist Charlson Ong had recommended I interview Rebecca T. Añonuevo, more or less the only renowned creative writer and academic who'd got behind the president. I hadn't had time to do it then, but I had time now. I emailed her to request a meeting. Aware that she'd just had several tonnes of mud slung at her on social media, I'd added to the message, 'I'm just interested in hearing your point of view, not challenging in it any way. This is for the sake of balance for the research I am doing here in Manila.'

She responded the following evening. 'I prefer that you email me your questions.'

I wasn't sure about this. For all sorts of reasons, a face-to-face interview is preferable to all other forms. For a start, if she became ambiguous or misleading, I'd have the opportunity to pin her down in real time. But, guessing that she'd been scarred by her dealings online, I acquiesced to her demand. My questions and her written responses to them are reproduced below.

Tom Sykes: What is it about Duterte's policies that appeal to you?

Rebecca T. Añonuevo: From the campaign and on almost all occasions, Duterte emphasizes that he wants to rid Philippine society of three things: illegal drugs; corruption; criminality. Business investments and job opportunities are consequences of a general sense of safety, security and well-being felt by the people. Duterte's policy is hinged on practical common sense and affinity with the ordinary Filipino. Before he came to power, I had no idea that the drug menace is as massive and deeply embedded in basic communities we call the *barangay*. But more seriously, I did not realize that drugs are a big industry, worth billions, the profiteers being criminal elements disguised as authorities, including elected officials and people in uniform who are supposed to protect the population but have been coopted by the interests of those who have ruled the country for decades.

I also like that he has broadened foreign policy relations to include countries relegated or effectively dismissed by previous administrations, for example, China and Russia, with whom we have renewed relations. He has also seen to it that ASEAN [Association of Southeast Asian Nations] ties are strengthened, especially with the Philippines as host of various ASEAN events this year. His travels to different countries during his first year have yielded millions to billions worth of investments, not bad for someone his critics decry as too *probinsiyano* [parochial], unpresidential, uncouth. Leadership hinges on credibility. No matter the whiplash he gets from the mainstream and international media, Duterte comes out in the polls as the most credible and most trusted, and recently, most loving, caring and decisive, as far as Filipinos are concerned.

I appreciate that he has thought of the one-stop shop for the Overseas Filipino Workers – all documents they need can be processed in one go, and in less time. He has instructed offices to answer requests in reasonable time. He made instantly available the 8888 and 911 hotlines for citizen complaints and emergencies, respectively. I like that one of the first things he signed into an executive order is Freedom of Information, whose counterpart bill in Congress has languished for years. He has also increased the budget for the sectors of education and health. I have to add that the government's largest hospital, the Philippine General Hospital, is now the recipient of 100 million pesos' worth of monthly subsidies from the president so it can procure equipment and gadgets, like pacemakers, for the poor. He is quite bold to sign into law the bill that grants free tuition in college. Congress has to find ways to establish a budget for that to be realized. Maybe they can start by cutting down on the expenses they have been enjoying, which the public doesn't know. I am excited at the prospects of a new infrastructure improving in the next five years. I agree 100 per cent when he announced that lifestyle checks on government officials and workers in government should be used as a measure against graft and corruption.

It may look like he is pampering the police and military to a fault, but I think he wants these institutions to regain the respect of the citizenry, and for the ordinary citizens to realize that a nation is as strong as their defence and security forces whose principal duty is to defend the Republic first of all, against all enemies, within and without, at the cost of their lives. The military and the police have been corrupted since the Marcos years, and had the reputation of building a record of human rights violations. Today, I hear a different command from men and women in uniform, and because President Duterte goes around to spend time with them in camp visits, and in hospitals where soldiers and police recuperate from their wounds and amputated limbs, I sense they are recovering from the trauma of the past when they became instruments of oppression, and are now working hard to bring back the honour that the honest and brave soldiers and police deserve.

Finally, Duterte constantly reminds government workers that they are public servants, and thinks of himself no higher than anyone of us, but a public servant, a government worker who owes his loyalty first to the Filipino people. When you consider a man like Duterte, you can't ask only about policy, and separate it from his demeanour, whether in Malacañan, or in Davao City. People are pissed off with the lordship of hypocrisy that has been with us for a century.

His singular policy I will sum up in a cliché: 'Actions speak louder than words.' The despised misogynist brings back the dignity of women prisoners and widows by providing them the conditions of home and opportunities to make their lives useful and the future worth pursuing. The madman likened to Hitler (I had to watch Hitler documentaries to see the parallelism that critics insist) fails to convince me as a demagogue and fascist who enjoys the world's attention and believes himself God, although he jokes around saying he will establish the 'Church of Duterte' (this joke grates his critics). I wish he was not bombing Marawi, but how else do you neutralize the armed rebels who have established their foothold in the city and are replacing our national flag with their flag? I may not agree with everything that Duterte does, but he is the elected president, and I trust his decisions for the good of the country.

TS: Critics say that the extrajudicial-killings Duterte encourages violate human rights. Others think his public comments are aggressive and sexist. How would you respond to these criticisms?

RA: President Duterte has been clear from day one when he delivered his first State of the Nation Address: 'I know the limits of the power and authority of the president.' He was a prosecutor for several years before he became Mayor of Davao City. He cannot be a loose cannon – although he is – when he makes outrageous statements that are not at all politically correct, and spices up his public statements with expletives that are uncalled for. Of course he is aggressive. He is sexist. He is not a model to children in terms of proper communication, so adults should caution them. But this president, despite his foul mouth, is in charge, acts right away, listens to the people, allows criticisms and street protests against him. He does not meddle with the courts even if he is obviously quite impatient with the slow wheels of justice. He does not meddle with the Legislature, unfortunately at the expense of former Cabinet members like former environment secretary Gina Lopez and former social welfare and development secretary Judy Taguiwalo, who were performing very well to the discomfort of oligarch interests in Congress. I'm speaking for myself, but one thing I have learned is to put more weight on the actions of a leader than his words. As to EJK, who in their right mind would subscribe to it? Duterte's message to the police and the military is to make sure that you come out alive in a legitimate operation; you don't shoot at suspects when they raise their arms in surrender, or kneel, or plead for mercy. Uniformed people and vigilantes who kill helpless civilians do not have the sanctions of government; they are enemies within, and they are traitors to the Filipino people.

TS: Have you written poetry that explicitly endorses any of his policies or attitudes?

RA: No, but I have reflected on the idea of killing a killer, in the form of a prayer, entitled 'Pangamuyo,' the Hiligaynon term for prayer.

TS: Are there many other writers and artists in the Philippines who would describe themselves as pro-Duterte? Is the general view amongst creatives for him or against him, would you say?

RA: I am one of those writers who are open in voting for and supporting the president. I know of some, especially from the regions, but I don't know how many we are. I would say among the loud ones who lash at him on Facebook, or join protests, are generally against Duterte, because that is how I hear them. Now, the question should be: 'Who do writers support in their quiet corners?' I cannot speak for them.

TS: What sorts of public reactions have there been to your statements of support for the current administration?

RA: The writers in my own poetry group, LIRA, are against me for supporting Duterte. I make them crackle more by calling myself a Dutertard (a moniker redefined by Duterte supporters, with no apologies). One time I posted a photo of the president's assistant secretary of communications, Mocha Uson, a popular blogger who campaigned for Duterte, and captioned it excitedly with, 'Mga ka-DDS.' ['You are Davao Death Squad']. As I expected, these young writers got fuming mad with me. I knew what to expect because I had read their rants and threats to unfriend the 'idiots' who voted Duterte. One even lampooned and rewrote my signature poem, 'Bago ang Babae' ['New Woman'] into a parody. They were jumping about with their loathing because I was openly admitting I continue to support Duterte, despite the burial of the dictator Marcos at the Libingan ng mga Bayani [Heroes Cemetery]. I think they were devastated that the poet they read and looked up to for so many years had crumbled as an illusion. And so even as I never wished to see Marcos laid at that place supposedly reserved for heroes and wrote my little poems of protest to express my position, I would have to concede that Marcos did not lay himself there, the Supreme Court ordered it. Does Duterte control the SC? Far from it. He even said that if the SC ruled against his position, he would respect their decision.

My own critics – it feels weird to say this as if I had any influence – were perhaps asking, 'What of those poems she wrote against injustice and lies and corruption and abuse of power?' They asked, 'How could a poet do this?' in reference to my decision to work within the administration in its first year, an opportunity I was grateful for because it was my first time to have a taste of government work (someone invited me to join the Presidential Communications group). For the record, I chose to be part of government, despite the brief period. I decided not to renew any contract for personal reasons as I had to find time for my spouse who had to undergo brain surgery. A lawyer, he too, by the way, is a Duterte supporter – so that's times two of the hate rants against us.

You should ask, 'How have I responded to the attacks?' I write. On my own. My time, my space. I continue to write my poems as furiously and as lightly as I can, against oppression and killing, in all forms and from all corners. I think they still read me, no matter what they say, or else why continue the rant? Do I feel a disconnect between what I say and who I support? I do not write my poetry for any personality, then and now. I commiserate with upset readers when they attack me, or pretend that they attack only what I write (and not me personally), insinuating that I pretend to attack what

I attack. To each her own. I do not miss my target – they are not the sophomores in life's real battles. The enemies are lurking, and I grant that the so-called idiots that voted Duterte, despite their own excesses, can read the age-old enemies of our country – the small percentage that controls our resources; druglords who have bought the brains and souls of ordinary Filipinos so that out of poverty, illiteracy, and lack of jobs, they enter this dangerous illegal trade that Duterte hates; terrorism, but especially the kind that invades, disrupts, and destroys lives of innocent civilians in another land; the system of corruption that has seeped into the different agencies and branches of government; foreign powers that meddle in the affairs of sovereign nations.

TS: Aside from Duterte, are there other Filipino politicians – past or present – that you admire?

RA: I am no fan of politicians. At the least they amuse me. Distrust is something I reserve for them, for having the temerity to make promises during elections and the lewdness to forget about them once elected. Filipinos are a hopeful people anyway; we still go out to cast our votes for the next set of leaders who will join Congress and the local seats. I have no illusions about Duterte; he showed himself early on to be capable of everything I would never relish in a leader. As a poet, I am expected to show my reverence first for language. Duterte has no room for lovely metaphors. He is the paradox I have put my stakes on to unsettle me, and my conscience, first as a Filipino, and why not, as a writer caught between her light and shadow.

It seemed from Añonuevo's answers that she was not an unequivocal fan girl for Duterte. I was intrigued by her mention of his progressive policies, but unconvinced that, in his moral ledger, these outbalanced all the people who'd died for no good reason.

In the final analysis, though, I was more inclined to agree with a comment made by Conchitina Cruz, another Filipina poet, in an interview in the Australian literary magazine *Cordite*, which Rebecca linked to at the end of her email to me:

'Earlier today, I read some posts on Facebook by Filipino poets expressing outrage, indignation, disappointment, and sadness over a fellow poet (an older writer whom they admired) whose latest status update was a photo of herself and a notorious Rodrigo Duterte mouthpiece of misinformation, with a caption that disclosed, in no uncertain terms, the poet's collaboration with the regime. I'd already heard months earlier that this poet was in the employ of the president, so neither her expressed loyalty to the regime nor the anger it elicited surprised me. What struck me was this recurring sentiment among the poet's critics: *how could a poet do this?* [italics supplied by Rebecca]

'We are so accustomed to thinking of poetry or art as a bastion of resistance that we are so unsettled when we see that it is also a bastion of complicity. It can be an accomplice of tyranny and oppression. It can be co-opted. If you serve the administration of our misogynist and fascist president, then you are a tool for enforcing and extolling this regime's violence against Filipinos. You can't undo that (both the violence and your complicity in it) with your poetry, no matter how feminist and anti-fascist it is.'

34. FATHER OF TIME

Now ninety-three years old, F. Sionil José is, globally speaking, the most successful Filipino novelist ever – his books have been translated into twenty-eight languages. He has also been one of the country's most overtly political writers, having grappled with corruption, land reform, American imperialism and the revolutionary movement in over thirty books of fiction, poetry and essays since the 1950s. He told the BBC in 2003, 'Authors like myself choose the city as a setting for their fiction because the city itself illustrates the progress or the sophistication that a particular country has achieved. Or, on the other hand, it might also reflect the kind of decay, both social and perhaps moral, that has come upon a particular people.'

I met Sir Sionil, a bald, rotund, Buddha-like man, in the office above the Solidaridad bookshop he owns.

'Were you in Manila during World War II?' I ask him.

'No, before the war.'

'Did you serve in the armed forces?'

'Oh, yes, but not as a regular soldier. I was a civilian medic in the American Army. I was not a guerrilla, though, but I knew some. I was involved from December '44 to – when was the atom bomb dropped? August '45. Then two months after the A-bomb I mustered out.'

'I've seen photos of Manila in 1945 after the end of the war. It looks like Hiroshima.'

'Oh yes, yes. All the houses were shelled.' He pointed out of the window. 'See those trees there on the street? They were broken by shellfire.'

'Had you started writing by then?'

'Oh, yes. Way way back. My first novel was actually written when I was in my late teens and early twenties. And then, Rody Vera – he was a very good playwright – made it into a play, *The Pretenders*. I read it again later and I was surprised. The war really matured us.'

'In your novel *Ermita* (1988), which is set during World War II, one of the plotlines involves a Japanese soldier raping a Filipina. Did you witness atrocities like these?'

'I did not, but I saw their results. During the liberation I was not in Manila, I was in the Cordillera, in the US Army.'

'The other book of yours I like very much is *Dusk* [alternative title: *Po-on*] (1984) which is set in the 1880s and chronicles the flight of a group of *remontado* peasants from friarocratic oppression. You have one of these oppressed characters say, "There is so much the world does not know, how the Americans have tortured our people, committed the most brutal crimes against humanity." I took this as a self-conscious nod to how the full grisly facts of the Philippine-American War will never be properly remembered in the real world beyond the fictional world of the novel.'

'Many Filipinos are forgetful. We don't remember, but why not? One reason, I believe, is that we don't have ancestor worship like the Muslims and the Buddhists. The Muslims maintain a kind of lineage whereas I don't even remember my grandfather's real name. Do you remember your grandfather's name?'

'Yes.'

'Oh, you are fortunate. All I know is that we called him "*Ba-ak*": Ilocano for "old". I don't even know his first name.'

'You're one of the few Filipino writers who's had a lot of success outside the country.'

'Oh, I wouldn't say success! If I were successful, this building would be much much bigger. And like I always say, if I depended on my income as a writer, my family would have starved a long time ago.'

'But nonetheless, there must be something about your writing that appeals to an international audience.'

'You ask very interesting questions. We Filipinos write in English and mainstream literature is in English. It's also the lingua franca of the world. English writers in the Philippines should have a global audience precisely because of that. But we don't. Way way back in the late seventies I asked my Russian translator, "Igor, why are you

translating me? Is it because you find some Marxism in my work?"'
Sionil descended into laughter for a minute.

'What did he say?' I asked.

'He howled. He didn't just laugh, he howled. He said, "Kiko" – he
called me Kiko – "there are thousands of brilliant Marxists in Asia, in
Eastern Europe and here in the Philippines. So why should we publish
you?" So I asked him why and his exact words were, "Because you
write about the Filipino condition beautifully." That's all he said. I did
not ask him to explain. And then he said, "You're for the underdog. If
you read our literature, we Russians are for the underdog too."

'Igor studied at UP and was an authority on Rizal. I first met him
in 1967 when I was the only Filipino invited to attend the fiftieth
anniversary of the October Revolution in Moscow. I opened the door
of my hotel and here was this tall, young, strapping Russian with a
crew cut. And he greeted me in the most archaic Tagalog! What I told
him was, "*Pare, hindi ko naintindihan ang mga sinabi mo*" ["Dude, I
didn't understand what you said"].'

'So old Tagalog is really different to the Filipino you speak now?'

'Like Old English, the "yays" and the "nays". Incidentally,
speaking of Old English, I came across the original *Beowulf*. I couldn't
understand a single word!'

'Was Igor also referring to the sense of social justice in your work?'

'Yeah. That's my major thing.'

'When you start writing a novel do you have some topic in mind
that you want to explore? Whether it's poverty or oppression of some
form, do you base your story around that?'

'I start with pure ideas, you know. I'm working on a futuristic
novel now called *Esperanza* about a man who, first of all, loses his
integrity. And then he loses his sexual prowess. Then he loses his mind.
The final loss is his sister who has supported him throughout his life.
She dies. Both this man and his sister believe in political revolution
except, for the man, it is just an idea whereas, for his sister, it is more
concrete than that.'

'What's futuristic about it?'

212

'The man has a secretary who is a sex robot. She is very beautiful and has been programmed to be loyal only to him. Towards the end she becomes human. And that's when the revolution fails – the man is tortured, the sister is killed. I've been working on this idea for a long time, ever since I first read the Bible way back. Job is my favourite character in the Bible. He suffers a lot, he loses his wife, his family, but God redeems by giving all these things back to him. My Job-like character doesn't find redemption, but he remains loyal to his faith. I think that's a lot better than the story of Job!'

'I read *Dusk* as an allegory of Philippine nationhood. The peasants kill their local friar, reject Spanish authority and find refuge in a romantically rejuvenating vision of the countryside. They seem to find some sense of identity and belonging in rural Luzon, is that right?'

'Yes. And those peasants represent wider history. Yesterday, there was a conference of historians concerning the seventy-fifth anniversary of the war with Japan. And they were rambling about what happened to this, what happened to that, and who did this, and who did that. It was such a narrow, constipated view of history. They remind me of the *Rizalistas* collecting all the laundry bills that ever belonged to Rizal. So I asked these historians, why history? What do you learn from it? I told them that there is nothing definitive or conclusive about what we are saying now because it is difficult to understand the past especially when new evidence about it is unearthed.'

'That's a theme of your fiction, I'd say. Competing narratives about the past.'

'Yes.'

'Do you like Renato Constantino's work?'

'I knew him personally. But there was something wrong with "Tato", as he was known. Because he's a communist, he's highly selective. I mean, he gets his facts right, but you know, he had a narrow view.'

'What was he like one-to-one?'

'Well, for a communist he was petty bourgeois. Like me. I like good food. To hell with proletarian food!'

'So what do you think of the political situation in the Philippines now? Have things improved in your lifetime?'

'I wrote an essay recently called "Why Our Leaders Failed". Remember, I'm ninety-three years old. I've seen sixteen presidents from Laurel during the Japanese times to this Duterte.'

'What do you think of Duterte?'

'I think he takes too much of that fentanyl drug. They say he did a good job in Davao. I wouldn't know because I've never been there. Apart from that, I don't think of him at all. When he decided to team up with the Marcoses that's when I stopped thinking about him. But I can understand why a lot of people like him. That woman downstairs selling cigarettes, the taxi drivers and so on, and then even some upper-class Filipinos like him.'

'During the Marcos time were you living here?'

'I never left Manila.'

'I imagine your politics and your writing would be in conflict with the Marcos ideology.'

'Not really, not always. That's why he didn't imprison me. I just got harassed.'

'How so?'

'The silver Schaefer fountain pen downstairs in the shop is one of my most valuable possessions. Marcos sent his men to break into the shop one night and they took the pen from my desk and smashed it up. It was weird because they opened the drawers and a filing cabinet, maybe read some papers, but didn't steal anything else. They didn't take my Swiss watch that was in the room either, nor my Nikon camera, nor the money stashed away.'

'They were just trying to scare you?'

'It was harassment. They did also take a letter I had from Bill Blair, who was the US Ambassador to the Philippines at the time, and placed it on the chair. I think they meant it as a kind of warning not to criticize Marcos because he was close to the Americans.'

'What do you make of the Filipino literary scene today? Do you think it's thriving?'

'I think it's thriving in its way. But I'd like our writing teachers to look at why we don't we have a global audience. I think a lot of young writers are very passive, they have nothing or very little to say.'

'I think it's true in England too.'

'Also?'

'Well, a poet friend of mine said that 90 per cent of poetry is about nothing of any importance whatsoever.'

'I think the way it works is good times, bad literature and bad times, good literature. When people suffer physically, they also suffer internally. Western literature today – and that includes England, the United States and Europe – has very little melancholy or heroic in it. These modern writers don't move me like the old writers did. I noticed the same about Singapore writing: it is very passive, with hardly any melancholy about it. Is it in *Merchant of Venice* where someone says that the rich also bleed? So, if the rich also bleed, they need to bleed in order to write about bleeding.'

'So why is it you think Indian writing in English has a global appeal, but Filipino writing in English doesn't?'

'Our critics should acquire an understanding as to why. I always cite Japan and the Meiji restoration when it comes to this topic. You know that the Japanese modernized their culture on the bases of Western technology and Japanese spirit? In the nineteenth century, the American poet Ralph Waldo Emerson argued that Americans should forget the European tradition, Romanticism in England, realism in France and all that. Let's celebrate America instead, he thought, and there started this conscious focus on American ideas, attitudes, landscapes. Then you have Whitman and Melville and Wharton and my favourite American novelist Willa Cather. After them O'Neill, Hemingway, Steinbeck. In creating American literature they defined America. That hasn't happened here yet.'

'Because?'

'Because American influence on the Philippines is constricting, you know. And worse, many of the writers who go to America are influenced by the New Criticism that was popular in the fifties, and they come back here citing the same models. So they imitate E.M. Forster or Henry James – these are very dull writers.'

'They are hanging on to late nineteenth-/early twentieth-century realism?'

'Yes, and this has been the theme of my talks, but nobody listens to me.'

'But there have been modernist and post-modernist Filipino writers?'

'Like who?'

'Krip Yuson for example?'

'I like his poetry.'

'The *Great Philippine Energy Jungle Café* was experimental.'

'Good point. It's not only that, though. I am waiting for a very good critical tradition to develop like you have in England. Boy, the way your critics lambast one another, it's so wonderful reading them, you know.'

'So people are too kind here?'

'I don't know if they are too kind. I think they are just – how would I call it? – too shallow.'

'You've got academic literary critics in the Philippines, though.'

'It's the same thing with the academics. And almost every writer wants to be an academic, I don't know why.' Sionil found that worth laughing out loud about as well.

'What do you make of Western writers who have dealt with the Philippines?'

'Some ten years ago, I read an English novel. I forgot who the author is because I put the book down immediately. It was about the Philippines before World War II. The opening paragraph stated there was a traffic jam in Manila. But there were no traffic jams at all then, so I didn't continue. I was so amused, because he didn't know. He should have done more research.'

'Yeah, I've noticed many Westerners get basic facts wrong and deal in terrible stereotypes. Do you think some of us get it right, though?'

'Most of them are very accurate, except that guy who wrote about the traffic. You know, they're professional journalists. The Japanese stories on Manila are very accurate too, very attentive to detail. James Hamilton-Paterson was very good on the Marcoses.'

'In *America's Boy* he argued that Marcos played a double game: he wanted to be close to the Americans while appearing to the Philippine people as a nationalist.'

'Oh, that's the game every politician here plays.'

'Duterte included?'

'I don't know. He seems to be selling the country to China or something. But be careful because everybody likes to say there are a nationalist.'

'How do you define nationalist?'

'Oh, easy: love of country. But then you must ask, what is the logic of love?'

'Does being a nationalist mean you have to love *everything* about your country?'

'It depends.'

'Do you still love the Philippines?'

'I don't consider it love. It's the kind of affection that someone feels towards a distant family member. I wrote about this in the sense that I said that the peasant is the real nationalist. I come from a village. I know how to plough, I know how to plant and harvest rice. You know the historian Reynaldo Ileto, who wrote about the Pasyon, the story of Christ and how it affects the peasants? I told him, "*Alam mo Rey* [you know Rey], you've never lived in a village." He's very urbanized. His father was a general. You know these PhDs, rarely do they come from the village, because they have to be rich to get that PhD. So I said, "You know, Rey, you're all wet! The Pasyon, the book, is brought out only during the Holy Week. And then it is put away in a wooden chest."'

'So you're saying that these pre-Christian, pagan beliefs are more important than the Pasyon?'

'The peasant knows that, if the rainfall doesn't come on time, he's going to be hungry that year. So he takes care of the land, he worships it. The Ilocano peasant calls the sound *Apo Init*. *Apo* is for something that you venerate, like *Apo Diyos* or God. The earth is *Apo Daga*. Moon is *Apo Bulan*.'

'Whereabouts in Ilocos do you come from?'

'About two hours from Rosales City. The most industrious ethnic group among the Filipinos is the Ilocano. You look at the land in Ilocos and it's well-tended. Nowadays I look at the land and think, Oh, this is really like Japan or Korea, especially during the planting season.'

'Carlos Bulosan [Filipino social novelist of the 1940s and 1950s] was also Ilocano. Did you ever meet him?'

'No, but I was responsible for setting up the Bulosan Museum in his hometown. I told the local authorities, "One of the most famous Filipino writers is from here and you're not honouring him."'

'Bulosan's *America is in the Heart* is another world classic, or it should be. It's both poignant and fast-paced. It's astonishing how much abuse and harassment he and the migrant workers received while they were in the US during the Depression. The violence in it strikes me as very contemporary, still relevant.'

'It's moving. Busolan very much wanted to get published in America. And that has been the dream, and still the dream of so many Filipino writers up to now.'

'Well thank you sir, that's all my questions.'

'You know my favourite cheese is English.'

'Which one?'

'Stilton.'

'I love Stilton. You like to eat it while drinking port wine?'

'Yeah, with whatever. My daughter always brings Stilton from San Francisco.'

'You should have told me. I could have bought you a whole wheel. My stepfather is really into cheese and he bought an entire wheel of Stilton last summer.'

'Really? That big? I never saw it this way.'

'Quite a lot of it was eaten at my mum and stepdad's wedding and then he used the rest to make soup, a sauce, etc.'

'Well, you can always come back with some, although I might not still be around.'

'I hope you are!'

'If I'm not, think of me when you enjoy your Stilton.'

35. SELECTIVE
MEMORIALS

The clamour of bombs and the fetor of corpses. Under a giant toadstool of smoke a gang of Japanese soldiers, eyes shaded by the peaks of their caps, swoop on a nun in habit. They circle her and throw punches till she's prone. One unzips and forces himself inside her. Behind them, on a shredded fairway of Wack-Wack golf course, other Japanese bayonet civilians tied by their chests to the trunk of a molave tree. I turn to the southwest and picture the lethal fireworks display that is Shaw Boulevard. US marines have knocked out two of the sandbag walls of a machine gun nest, but the few Japanese still inside will never retreat.

I removed my sunglasses. Like a tacky photo on an estate agent's website, vestal clouds streamed over the pastel greens of Wack-Wack golf course as it was today. There were no bombs or corpses now. All I could hear was the rattle of the zephyrs in the trees. All I could smell was freshly trimmed grass. This was a dimension away from what my imagination had just conjured about the Battle of Manila, 3 February to 3 March 1945. Nowadays, I guessed the only chance of Japanese-instigated violence happening here would be if a Tokyo businessman on a golfing holiday was short-changed at the club-hire station. That was progress, I supposed.

I moved along the perimeter fence to a pillbox manned by a goon in a hard hat with in-built shades. 'Excuse me, could I look round the golf course?' I asked.

'Are you member, sir?'

'No.'

'Then you are prohibited.'

'But I'm a journalist.'

'You are journalist? Then you are *extra* prohibited.'

I had to concede that the goon was right to be wary – my aim was to find out how and why Filipinos remember some facets of their history, but not others. That might annoy someone somewhere.

Looking back over the course, I realized that my earlier mental reconstruction had rested too much on the narrative the West likes to tell itself about the Battle of Manila. After invading Luzon the day after Pearl Harbor, the Japanese occupied the Philippines for three years before the Americans took back the archipelago, island by island. The strategy was called 'leapfrogging'. Some 280,000 troops – the largest number used in any US campaign in World War II – fought their way onto Luzon just before Christmas 1944. Loath to give up Manila, the Japanese threw everything they had left at the Americans. They raped, tortured, stabbed, shot and burned civilians. Over 100,000 innocents perished.

This account isn't all wrong, but it *is* selective. Whereas my mind's eye had seen only Japanese war crimes at Wack-Wack, even a conservative annalist such as Max Hastings admits that 'for every six Manileños murdered by the Japanese defenders, another four died beneath the gunfire of their American liberators.' The explosions I'd fantasized came from just a smattering of the 42,153 missiles fired at Manila by the US over that appalling month. Preserving American lives, reasoned a US official at the time, was more important than preserving 'historic landmarks'.

Proponents of the Western side of the story may say that, had the Japanese not seized Manila in the first place and then held it to the death, the Americans wouldn't have needed to shoot it up so heavily. Was it that simple, though?

I went to the Manila American Cemetery in the district of Taguig to learn more. Its clean-shaven lawns and disciplined rows of marble tombstones make it a doppelganger for the Arlington National Cemetery in Virginia. The American Battle Monuments Commission, a US government sub-agency, owns both. Maybe this is why the detailed maps and inscriptions in the limestone memorial rooms in the Manila branch offer a slanted view of the Pacific war.

THE REALM OF THE PUNISHER

The righteous defence of democracy in the Far East begins as a response to Japan's 'surprise attack' on Pearl Harbor. The only accurate part of that last sentence is that Japan attacked Pearl Harbor. Many historians know that the raid was no surprise – the US was on a war footing with the Japanese long before 7 December 1941. Earlier that year, President Roosevelt had placed oil sanctions on Japan knowing full well that the US serviced 80 per cent of its petroleum needs. Predictably, the Japanese started eyeing up the massive oil reserves of Southeast Asia, which Dutch, British and US companies had been looting for decades. American ships and aircraft were patrolling Hawaii expecting strife right up to the end of November when the Honolulu *Advertiser* newspaper stated, 'Japan may strike over the weekend.' On 27 November, the aptly-named Admiral Howard Stark had warned in a memo, 'An aggressive move by Japan is expected within the next few days.'

Another problem with the Western line is the proposition that the conflict in the East was between democratic good guys and autocratic bad guys. As the armed forces scholar John Dower writes, 'Japan did not invade independent countries in southern Asia. It invaded colonial outposts which the Westerners had dominated for generations, taking absolutely for granted their racial and cultural superiority over their Asian subjects.' There was no democracy in the Philippines for the Americans to defend because the Philippines was an American vassal state. The idea that the Allies were out to eradicate dictatorship and imperialism is laughable when you glance at a map of who owned what in Asia on the day of Pearl Harbor. The Japanese empire consisted of Manchuria, Taiwan, the Korean peninsula and parts of China's east coast. The Western empires ruled – and not by popular consent – what is now India, Pakistan, Bangladesh, Myanmar, Vietnam, Cambodia, Laos, Malaysia, Singapore, Hong Kong, Indonesia, Papua New Guinea, Fiji, Samoa, Vanuatu, New Caledonia and, of course, the Philippines.

It was time to see the Philippines' largest collection of World War II memorials on Corregidor, a spermatozoon-shaped island in the mouth of Manila Bay. As the ferry set off from Esplanade Seaside Terminal near the Coconut Palace, I got back to reading the American media magnate William D. Boyce's reflections on Manila from 1914. He wrote that the Spanish 'did not make the most' of Corregidor's position as probably the best natural defence to a harbour in the entire world. He was right.

In 1574, shortly after the creation of Spanish Manila, the Fujianese pirate Limahong anchored sixty ships between Corregidor and the northern bank of the bay, and sent 3,000 heavily armed thugs to sack the city. They came close enough that they killed the most senior Spaniard in town, Martin De Goíti (an ancestor of post-independence Presidents Disodado Macapagal and Gloria Macapagal-Arroyo).

By May 1898, when the US Navy cruised in at the height of the Spanish-American War, the Spanish had taken to mining that same northern channel. It didn't work. Admiral Dewey knew all about the mines and so sent his ships through the southern channel instead. Within a few hours, the entire Spanish Pacific fleet was resting in pieces on the seabed.

Boyce's rebuke of the Spanish failure to weaponize Corregidor implies that the new American regime wouldn't make the same mistake. This too is part of a jingoistic tall-tale that Boyce didn't live to see refuted in the space of a mere twenty-four hours when, between 5 and 6 May 1942, a 75,000-strong Japanese army came at Corregidor from the direction of Manila, and overcame forty-five pieces of heavy artillery and 13,000 US and Filipino troops.

As with Wack-Wack golf course, it was hard to picture such carnage when gazing across the magnificent, palm-bordered cove of puff-pastry sand that our ferry pulled in to. We were ushered off the boat into a retro tour bus that resembled a 1940s tram. We clunked through the jungle past the spectral ruins of mess halls and barracks. Although they were still erect, pediments hung loose and columns were missing in action. As we drove, the tour guide held up items he'd found hereabouts: a Coca-Cola bottle from 1912 and currency as old as the revolution. He then showed us the *pièce de résistance* of local atrocity memorabilia: a laminated black-and-white photo of a Filipino baby skewered on a Japanese bayonet. 'Bad people,' declaimed the guide. A Japanese couple sat to my right swapped edgy glances.

We stopped at Battery Way, a gun emplacement that still had bullet holes in it. The guide told me to look down the barrel of a mortar. I did so and saw a bomb nestling in the base. 'That's still live,' he said, 'but it is harmless.' I backed off anyway.

The centrepiece of the Pacific War Memorial complex was a forty-foot-tall abstract sculpture representing the eternal flame. I asked the guide if any other conflicts were commemorated hereabouts. He pointed me to the nearby Filipino Heroes Memorial, a much smaller park and museum. There I could only find a brief and vague tribute to those who died between 1898 and 1902 in the Spanish-American and Philippine-American Wars. Perhaps briefly and vaguely was how the Americans and the modern Americophile rulers of the Philippines wanted to remember this rampage of arson, torture, disease, war crime and racially-driven genocide.

I recalled Noam Chomsky's quote on the double standards of US foreign policy: 'When they do it, it's a crime. When we do it, it's not.' The relative size of the two memorials here showed that, in the popular consciousness, when the Japanese had annexed the Philippines, it was a crime, but when the Americans had done the same forty years before, it wasn't.

I closed my eyes and recreated the Philippine-American War in my head.

A naked rebel hangs by his thumbs from the branch of a bani tree, yelping as two US privates in khaki tunics light a bonfire under him.

Firing squad mouths chew tobacco above fiery muzzles that send pubescent boys to ground like whits of eroded chalk toppling into the sea.

In a gutted barn, four officers of the Tennessee Regiment pin a captive on his back and stick a bamboo tube between his lips. They pour half a barrel of water into the tube. The captive's eyes and belly inflate. 'Tell us where that goddamn swine is,' says one of the officers. More water is decanted. The brawny lieutenant stamps on the captive's stomach. A private removes the tube. Blood-tinged water eructs a foot into the air.

'Welcome to the suburbs of hell,' laughs a plump colonel as his men force choleric peasants at Krag-point into a reconcentrado *(concentration) camp. Occasionally, they pick one out of the crowd to be executed on the bridge and tossed into the river.*

I felt the guide's finger against my elbow and quit my day-mare.

'Time to go, sir.'

'Do you know much about the Philippine-American War?'

'Not really.'

He wasn't the only one. Professor Dylan Rodriguez argues that modern Filipino identity is based upon a 'strategic undertheorizing and misconceiving' of the 'technologies of race, violence, and global white supremacy' that found its apogee in the Philippine-American War.

But why keep neglecting this critical event a century after it happened? As the leftist Senator Teddy Casiño said to me, 'The classic post-colonial relations with America are still with us. We are a source of materials and a market for their goods and services. Since the approval of the Enhanced Defense Cooperation Agreement, American bases have been making a comeback and any party that gets into power here in the Philippines must bow down to US foreign policy.' It doesn't suit elites in either nation to sour this special relationship by dredging up a 'genocide' (Rodriguez's strong but apposite term) that undermines the rhetoric of aid, partnership and mutual respect beloved of generations of politicians on both sides of the Pacific. President George W. Bush was often lampooned for public misspeaking, but when he addressed the Philippine Congress in 2003, nobody picked him up for his shifty assertion that the US had teamed up with the Philippines to destroy colonialism in 1898. Nor did anyone but a few academics notice that, when riffing on Uncle Sam's 'part in the great story of the Filipino people', Bush cited the Spanish-American War, World War II, the Cold War and the so-called War on Terror... but not the Philippine-American War.

As historiographer Reynaldo Ileto has noted, amnesia about that conflict started early. The US colonialists outlawed veterans' clubs, libelled rebel chief Emilio Aguinaldo as a scheming autocrat and obliged schoolchildren to read David P. Barrows' textbook *A History of the Philippines* (1905), which dismissed the rebellion as 'a great misunderstanding'.

Although in recent years Filipino writers and scholars, from Ileto to Luis H. Francia to F. Sionil José, have explored the genocide in-depth (in *Dusk*, Sionil renders the marauding American infantrymen as 'a ruthless enemy who defiled women and bayoneted children'), the few Western fictions dealing with it have usually done so badly. Starring Gary Cooper and David Niven, *The Real Glory* (1939) is swashbuckling cant of the tackiest order. In the first scene, nervous natives watch a gaunt Spanish *padre* beg a US army officer to keep his men on Mindanao Island, for 'as soon as the American troops are gone, the *Moros* will come down from the hills. They will kill all the men and carry away all the women and children for slavery.' If there was an Oscar for Most Number of Historical Errors Contained in a Single Cinematic Scene, *The Real Glory* would have won it that year. Spanish clergymen weren't renowned for giving a fig about the natives they'd spent 300 years thrashing, swindling and coercing. Mindanaons did not slay or shackle other Mindanaons – they were fighting in self-defence against foreign incursion. And the lie that American firepower is the only way to staunch chaos in some bedevilled backwater has been repeated so often since then we now have a respectable-sounding name for it: 'humanitarian intervention'.

Another reason why so many are keen to forget the Philippine-American War is that the American and Japanese occupations were too similar for comfort. Both needed the collusion of native leaders to succeed. Many of the *ilustrados* who collaborated with the Americans circa 1900 did exactly the same with the Japanese in 1942. Both the US and Japan used propaganda to swivel public opinion against rival empires – for the US Spain was the enemy, for the Japanese it was the US. Moreover, 'the final six months of the war with Japan,' Ileto observes, 'were very similar to the final six months of the war with the United States forty years earlier. Homes and buildings were razed; civilians suspected of aiding guerrillas were tortured and executed; disaster accompanied the path of the contending armies.'

On the ferry back to Manila, the sun withdrew and the rain came down hard against the cabin roof. It was like listening to industrial quantities of rice sieved through a huge tin strainer. After two minutes it was all over. Abrupt shifts in nature are peculiar to Philippine life – earthquakes, typhoons and volcanic eruptions strike from nowhere, cause harm and then life returns to normal. That the tour guide continued his diatribe against the Japanese throughout the micro-storm suggested to me that attitudes to the past don't change as easily as the weather.

While disembarking, I received a text message from Joel: 'Look at this pic x x.' Attached was a photo of a Filipino toddler with endearing moptop hair. His hands were outstretched, palms turned skyward, the forty-eight-foot-tall Manila Cathedral perching on them. At first I thought this was a still from a sub-par B-movie in the mould of *Attack of the 50 Ft Woman*. Then I assumed it was an example of 'forced perspective' – the cathedral was, in reality, small because it was far away, but someone clever on *Photoshop* had made it seem like it was right next to the boy and petite enough to be picked up easily.

For me, the juxtaposition of the young child and the old building (established by the Spanish in 1571) said something about history – and its contrasting interpretations – always being close to the present. Indeed, they are continually graining and warping the present. Wars are picked up, handled and manipulated by politicians after the fact in order to craft a present and a future that will aid their agendas, be they the Japanese viceroy in the forties or George W. Bush in the noughties. And perhaps even a critic of this enterprise like me was guilty of exploiting the past – or at least reading the past selectively. But if this were true, I hoped my motive – to write something fair and humane – had some integrity to it.

36. THE COCK WAVE

When I sat down to watch a cockfight (local term: *sabong*) at Roligon Mega stadium in Parañaque City, I realized that the Duterte sensation wasn't new, or not as new as some pundits held it to be. In the taxi there I'd been reading about *caciques*. This was what the first Spanish adventurers called the headmen of indigenous societies they encountered in Asia and the Americas. Incidentally, cockfighting had been a popular pursuit in these societies since perhaps 3000 BC. The Italian intellectual and explorer Antonio Pigafetta, who accompanied Ferdinand Magellan on his voyage around the Philippines in 1521, wrote of the Luzon natives he met, 'They have some rather large domestic cocks, which, from some superstition, they do not eat, but they keep them for fighting; on such occasions they make bets and offer prizes, which are acquired by the owner of the conquering cock.'

In the Philippines, the term *caciquismo* came to mean government by strongmen or warlords. Throughout the twentieth century, foreign commentators viewed the *cacique* as a cross between Don Corleone and Saddam Hussein. Feared and respected, he had unquestioned dominance over a village or province. Macho and charismatic, he'd steer the public consciousness by whipping up envy, resentment and vengefulness, as well as pride, compassion and community spirit. *Caciquismo* was no meritocracy. If you sought political influence, talent or qualifications were less important than having blood ties with the *cacique* or belonging to his faction. The *cacique* kept his constituents happy through bribery and patronage, and controlled them with threats both covert and overt. His first loyalties were to these parochial supporters, which was why he thought in local rather than national or global terms. Selfish and survival-oriented, the *cacique* could be callous and vindictive, and would indulge in the 'routine use of violence', as Reynaldo Ileto puts it. Ileto also argues that these Western *idées fixes* about the *cacique* are condescendingly simplistic and have been used to excuse years of foreign meddling in the 'pre-political' Philippines.

That said, it was difficult not to think of some of these characteristics when the cock fight commenced. Two beefy men in their twenties strutted into the ring and placed their respective cockerels – one white, one red – on two painted circles about ten feet apart. Looking confused, the birds flapped their wings and skittered in a clockwise direction for a good thirty seconds. Then they appeared to notice each other's presence. Red took tentative, jerky steps towards White and the game was on. With poor coordination, the cocks jumped up and kicked each other with their spurs, which resemble scaled-down elephant trunks. Red kept overjudging his leaps, flying straight over White and landing behind him. The pair would often collide breast-to-breast like frat boys doing chest-bumps. As the scrap wore on, after these collisions the cocks would, like boxers clinching, take a break, nestling in each others' hackles. And, not unlike a boxing match, the shaven-headed *koyme* (referee) would separate them by picking them up by their backs, bumping their beaks together several times in quick succession and then setting them back down to get on with it.

A minute later, White looked diminished. He couldn't be bothered to jump. He couldn't flap with the same gusto. He was keen to rest in the bosom of his opponent whenever the option arose. When White lost the use of his little legs, Red – rather unsportingly, I thought – trampled all over him and then, for good measure, turned round to savage him with a few pecks. The *koyme* seized the birds and banged their heads together. When he put them down, White didn't move. He stayed face-down, his handsome tail feathers aloft and shaking faintly. That was a kill, or near enough. Red's owner ferried him over to the *koyme* who lifted Red's right leg and attached to it a plastic victor's tag.

There was something pathetic about the whole affair. The fluster, ungainliness, bad sportsmanship, miskicks and mis-pecks felt like a parody of a drunken brawl between two human males who, despite their bungling, believe they are heavyweight champions or kung-fu black belts. I returned mentally to Duterte, whose spiritual fragility and moral weakness grew more evident with each brag, taunt and snarl.

After the bout was over, the crowd constructed a seething wall of sound around the glass fencing of the ring while men with shoulder bags in white polo shirts, 'bet taker' written on the backs, offered a medley of gestures to the patrons, also all men, as far as I could see. The bet takers pitched 'OK' signs, waggled their forefingers, held up multiples of digits, made Hitleresque salutes and waved downwards as if drying nail varnish (this vaguely messianic move has earned these men the nickname *kristo*). The frantic transactions happened in every part of the stadium: along the fawn stucco balconies at the top, amid the red and blue plastic seats ranging below them and at ringside, where the frenzy of windmilling arms, rotating waists and tiptoe reaches took on the impression of an elaborate dance.

These hand-and-arm permutations made me think once more of Duterte. Seldom is he pictured without pointing accusatorily, giving the middle finger or waving cockily to his fans. The cock wave, you might call it.

37. THE DUMMY RUN

Two days before I was due to fly home, Tropical Depression Maring hurtled in from the easternmost point of the Philippines and crashed down in Manila about 8 a.m. After an hour of abounding rain, the street below my hotel room balcony was flooded. Flotillas of bin bags, tin cans and cigarette packets drifted past kids up to their chests in the water playing Frisbee with a CD. A tricycle driver hauled his vehicle by a length of rope like someone struggling with a lethargic mule on a lead.

I waited and grew hungry. There was no kitchen or restaurant inside the hotel. I was tantalized by the trays of golden muffins in the bakeshop window across the road. It surely wasn't safe to wade or swim there. I searched my room for something to eat and devoured two complimentary packets of peanuts I'd kept from the plane over.

Later on, when the water levels were at knee-height, I went on to the balcony and spotted an old-timer in a cream vest and Nike shorts being helped across the road by a schoolboy in a crisp white shirt. The old-timer was shivering and his head was bent forward. There was a dribble of what looked like dried blood down his chest. Had he fallen foul of the war on drugs?

Once they'd splashed their way onto my side of the road, the schoolboy helped the old man into the sidecar of a stationary pedicab. The schoolboy then went to join his mates to wait for a jeepney. The old man lay back in his seat and closed his eyes. Was he sleeping or dying?

'Should I help him?' I asked myself. 'I should help him.' I put my flip-flops on, quit the room and called the lift. As the numbers corresponding to each floor ticked by I fretted about how precisely I, with no medical training, could help him, whatever was wrong with him. What if he hadn't been shot by a rogue cop and was dying of some contagious disease? Did I want to catch that? No. What if

231

he asked me for money? What if he and the schoolboy were part of an audacious sting and I'd be ambushed by muggers the moment I reached him?

I stepped away from the lift and went back to my room. My cynical friend Bobby's voice was in my head: 'People die every day in Manila. Nothing you can do about it, man. *C'est la vie.*' Guilt gripped my stomach. What if I read in tomorrow's Manila *Bulletin* that some poor, vulnerable geezer was left to die by people who didn't give a damn? But I like to give a damn where and when possible so I returned to the lift and descended to the ground floor.

When I saw him he was still in the pedicab, conscious but delirious, his features clenched with anguish. He pulled his penis out of his shorts and pissed into the foot well of the sidecar. The schoolboys were staring at him while they waited for a jeepney.

'Do you know what's wrong with him?' I asked.

'Drinking liquor all night,' the one who'd helped him shrugged.

'But isn't he wounded?' I asked. I looked at the man again. This close, I noticed that the trail of blood led all the way up his neck and chin to his nostrils. More probably a nosebleed than a slug from a .45.

38. WHERE THEY DIE

As I climbed out of the taxi and onto the road where a former police officer was gunned down by anti-narcotics agents, Duterte's recent warning to deport foreigners who 'malign and defame' him was ringing in my ears. A few days ago on 23 May 2018, Australian nun Patricia Fox had lost an appeal against the cancellation of her visa for, as Duterte colourfully put it, treating the 'Philippines like a mat to wipe your feet on'. A lifelong human rights campaigner, Sister Fox had joined demonstrations on behalf of maltreated farmers and indigenous people. A month before, Giacomo Filibeck of the Party of European Socialists, had been kicked out of the country for daring to challenge the Punisher's war on drugs.

My British friend Richard Peirce, who was in Manila before travelling on to Mindanao, got out of the taxi's passenger seat and said, 'This is one of the nicest neighbourhoods I've seen in the Philippines.' I agreed. Thick, lush trees dotted with scarlet flowers poured into Dingle Street on one side while fragrant pot plants in old, half-cut mineral water and Coca-Cola bottles hung from the frontages of bourgeois houses on the other.

On this stately street back in summer 2016, ex-cop-turned-drug-dealer Pelito Basan Obligacion succumbed to a classic buy-bust sting when undercover policemen, acting on a tip-off, tried to arrest him and an unnamed companion. Obligacion opened fire with a .45 pistol and the policemen shot back. Obligacion's companion survived, he did not. Sachets of crystal meth were recovered from his corpse. That was the police force's side of the story anyway.

At the end of Dingle Street, Richard and I came across an enormous, fortress-like home with twelve-foot-high iron gates and a steel grille so chunky that it looked like it could withstand a direct hit from a rocket launcher.

'Do you think the people who live there heard the gunshots that night?' I asked.

'Probably,' said Richard. 'I wouldn't want to live like that, though. I'd feel too isolated and paranoid.'

We moved on to the UP Arboretum, a 493-hectare forest within the campus of the University of the Philippines (UP). It was easier to imagine criminality taking place amid the weatherbeaten cinderblock shacks and drowsy, mangey dogs that marked the outskirts of the forest. As we moved deeper into the mahogany, monkey pod and *tagutagu* trees, I thought of the two men who drove into the area at 2.45 a.m. on 24 September 2016 to meet with who they assumed to be addicts in need of a fix. These people turned out to be plainclothes policemen. According to their boss, Anonas Station Police Chief Wilson Delos Santos, when the dealers realized they'd been tricked they threw a firecracker onto the ground and fired a shotgun at the cops. One of the dealers was shot dead as he tried to drive away, the other was arrested.

'Surely there'd be too many witnesses for something like that to happen without controversy,' I said after we'd encountered a horde of boys playing basketball, two jeeps full of environmental protection workers and various older women sitting on plastic chairs asking if Richard and I were single.

'Well it happened in the middle of the night,' said Richard, 'and they probably went into a remote corner of the forest.'

Our next destination was Barangay Botocan, about a mile south of the Arboretum. Although this too seemed like a friendly, low-key part of town and the events I was interested in had happened eighteen months ago, I was growing anxious about two risks. Firstly, what were the chances of us wandering into a crime-in-progress? Botocan was notorious for drug-related gunfights and arrests. Secondly, I feared that Richard and I, as Westerners snooping around sites connected to the drug war, would now be under state surveillance. I had no desire to be jailed and deported.

We got out at Bliss 2 Building on Mapagkumbaba Street, a double-fronted structure with corrugated iron cornices looming from behind a fire-blackened concrete wall. It was outside this very wall that Leandro Kanahashi and an unidentified accomplice were shot to death by police, but not before they'd wounded Officer Julius Albao. Kanahashi was the prime suspect in the investigation into the 2016 vigilante slaying of Aurora Moynihan, daughter of the disgraced British peer Lord Anthony Moynihan. A sign reading 'Pusher to the celebrities, you are next' had been left next to Aurora's bullet-riddled body. Kanahashi was her boyfriend at the time of her demise and the police later established that the .40-calibre pistol used to slay Aurora was the same one recovered from Kanahashi's corpse.

As we stood outside Bliss 2, the syrupy-fishy scent of deep-fried squid snacks from a nearby vendor's cart congesting my nostrils, I wondered how dependent all the news reporting I'd read on these murders was on the official police records.

The following morning, I went to Pasay City Hall Press Office. I was greeted by a tabloid columnist who asked for a pseudonym, so I will refer to him as Ray. Ray's smouldering cigarette and straggly mullet gave him a Gonzo mien. He showed me around the pokey portacabin-style room where up to thirty journalists at any one time will sit and wait for reports from the Southern Metropolitan Police District to come in. They then either turn them into stories for their respective newspapers – in Ray's case he has to translate the information into Filipino before filing – or travel out to the scene of the crime.

'Are the police reports always accurate?' I asked.

'I don't think so,' said Ray. 'The war on drugs is really...' He paused to think of the correct wording. 'We don't know if what we are told about it is true because, honestly, so many people are making money out of it.' Ray handed me a freshly issued memorandum from the acting chief of the Pasay Police. It outlined an *estafa* (fraud) case in which a South Korean suspect had allegedly conned an anonymous 'complainant' out of 1.5 million pesos (just over US$28,000). 'The reports look like this,' said Ray.

'How do you write the truth if you don't believe the reports?' I asked.

'We have to interview the persons involved in the case.'

'How do the police react if your articles differ from their reports?'

'They are always complaining. They don't like that, in my own column, I often attack the police for their wrongdoings, their abusive arrests.'

'They can be violent?'

'Mostly.'

'Can you give me some examples?'

'Sometimes they will find one who is urinating in the street. They will frisk him and plant *shabu* on him. Then they beat him and build a drug case against him. And of course the policemen will make extra cash for these sorts of grabs.'

'When you journalists are first made aware of an operation what happens next?'

'It is dangerous for us to go on the operations, so after they are completed and the police lines have been put up, my photographer goes out on his motorcycle to the scene.'

'It's safe by that time?'

'Yes.'

'Does the photographer see the dead bodies?'

'He always sees the dead bodies.'

'How long do the police lines stay out?'

'They have to allow time for scene of the crime operators to process the incident. Sometimes they are very slow because they come from other districts. It can take an hour or more, but we really don't know if the police tamper with the evidence in that time.'

'What would they tamper with?'

'Maybe they add the *shabu* or they will plant it on the person they have shot or detained.'

'How many incidents happen per day in the southern region of the city?'

'Sometimes there are three or four per day, mostly in Taguig, Makati and Parañaque.'

'Overall, is the number of extra-judicial killings going up or down?'

'I think down because the cops are now knocking on the door of the suspect and begging them to surrender. This doesn't always go to plan, though, because these suspects sometimes get killed.'

'From what you know is it always the police who do these killings?'

'Sometimes we are not sure if the perpetrators are police officers, a private individual or members of a crime syndicate. I myself do not think there are independent vigilantes.'

'The syndicates are hired by the police?'

'Maybe.'

Ray broke off from our interview to say hello to a middle-aged woman journalist for the *Philippine Star*. I asked her if she travelled to the crime scenes.

'Anytime, anywhere, any place,' she smiled.

'Do you expect to travel to a scene this afternoon?'

'Yes.'

'Do you ever have foreign reporters going out with you?'

'Sometimes.'

'But it's dangerous for them,' chipped in Ray.

'It could become a hostage drama,' said the woman.

'So they might take a foreign reporter hostage?' I clarified.

'Yes. Anyway, I have a deadline, sir. Sorry!' The woman marched off to her desk.

I thought back to our little tour of Quezon City's hot spots yesterday and counted myself lucky not to have got into any trouble.

The next day would be my last in Manila, as in the evening I'd be journeying north with Richard to Sagada Mountain Province to learn about the aboriginal Igorot people for a novel that I planned to write, if ever I found the time. I rose early and had a breakfast of fruit salad on the delightful terrace of the University Hotel. I heard an almighty bang from above. 'What the fuck was that?' I said out loud, terrified that the drug war had come to find me.

A nearby waiter overheard me and explained that mangoes often fall from the trees surrounding the terrace and land on the steel roof. I turned my attention back to my fruit salad. The final piece of mango tasted peculiar.

I took a taxi to the sleek, modern Leong Hall lecture theatre at Ateneo de Manila University for a conference on 'world Englishes'. By midday I was feeling sick and could only manage a few spoonfuls of rice and vegetables at the buffet lunch laid on for delegates. The nausea mounted as I walked in the 38° heat over to the classroom where I was scheduled to give a lecture on my research into British and American travel writing on Manila. I struggled through my talk, suppressing the urge to puke, downing water to irrigate my barren throat and hoping my heart rate would return to a sane pace.

Any hopes that I'd merely been suffering from performance anxiety were dashed after my talk was over. I still felt wretched. As I lurched back to the main hall for the final meeting of delegates before the conference finished, Richard texted me to say that he'd join me in an hour so we could go on to Cubao Station and catch our bus to Sagada.

Outside the hall, menacing thoughts swirled around my head while my heart thumped faster and my stomach grew more bloated. 'The Philippines has finally taken its toll on me,' I kept saying to myself. I couldn't rid my mind of everything sad and painful I'd seen or heard over the last nine years: my near-car accidents; my watching car accidents at the Davao CCTV centre; the artist Kublai Millan's colleagues shot by NPA snipers; Kian Delos Santos and all those other luckless quarries of Duterte; Duterte cackling; Duterte joking about rape; Duterte giving the middle finger; Duterte putting my name on a hit list for being a white, imperialist son of a whore who despises him and, by extension, his country. The fear, the suffering, the carnage, the death.

'Excuse me,' I croaked to one of the conference's organizers. 'Is there a doctor on campus? I feel really really ill.'

39. THE DEATH LIST

Twenty minutes later, I was inside a minibus-sized ambulance trapped in the traffic on Aurora Boulevard. The driver's decision to switch on the flashing lights didn't aid our progress. 'In Manila everyone wants to get in front of everyone else,' said the young female paramedic while she listened to my heart with a stethoscope.

'I don't want to die,' I squeaked. 'Please tell me I'm not going to die.'

'Don't worry, sir. It is not serious.'

The ambulance pulled up outside World Citi Medical Center. I was led into the outpatients' ward where a clerk asked me to fill out some forms. 'Could we establish whether I'm dying first and then I can do the forms later?' I asked.

I was shown to a bed and, within half an hour, I'd undergone blood, diabetes, blood pressure and electrocardiogram tests. A doctor, also young-looking, came later to tell me that I was in good physical health.

'Why is my heart still beating like a speeded-up record?' I demanded.

'Sir, there is nothing we can see that is wrong with your heart. May I ask, sir, are you feeling anxious?'

'Yes. Very.'

The doctor produced a pill. 'Please take this for calm.'

I did as bidden and texted Richard to instead come to the hospital. The pill kicked in as he arrived. I hugged him. 'It's good to see you, mate.' I then drew the curtains and wept like a foundling.

I felt considerably better after that. 'We have less than an hour before our bus leaves,' I said.

'Tom, do whatever you like,' said Richard. 'No pressure if you're not feeling up to it.'

After I paid for my treatment, we hopped in a taxi and arrived at the station just as our bus was leaving. Thankfully, for a few extra pesos we were able to book seats on the next one.

Twelve hours later, I awoke to stunning alpine scenery, cauliflower clouds kissing pine tree-cloaked ridges. After the hothouse that is Manila in June, the cooler temperatures were welcome too. Gwen Gaongen, our hostess for the next three days, picked us up and took us back to her attractive, self-built and wood-panelled home on the uphill road to Sagada town. After showering and breakfasting we were taken to our guide, a slight Igorot woman who, for reasons soon to become apparent, prefers not to be named in this book, so I will call her Judith.

Our interview began with Judith explaining the history and culture of the Igorots. Given their inaccessible location in the mountains, the Spanish never properly colonized them. At the dawn of the twentieth century, American Protestant missionaries managed to penetrate the community. They took a pragmatic approach to conversion by allowing the Igorots to retain their animist beliefs alongside their newfound Christian values. The conversation soon turned to politics given that, according to Judith, the Igorot way of life is under threat from the central government in Manila and from national and multinational corporations.

'The government tramples on indigenous peoples,' she told me. 'Duterte has used Presidential Decree 705 to stop us harvesting the trees and plants we need. He is also closing all the small-scale gold and copper mines across the Cordillera region which will mean more unemployment and poverty. At the same time, giant mining companies are operating here and sending their profits back to Manila. There is also the TRAIN [Tax Reform for Acceleration and Inclusion] Law that imposes high taxes on poorer Filipinos [on fuel, sweetened drinks and other goods and services] and low taxes on big business. Duterte pushed this legislation so he could raise collateral for loans from the World Bank and to fund his new infrastructure project which will not really benefit provinces like this one.'

'Are there people affiliated to the indigenous rights movement in Sagada who have criticized the current government?'

'Yes, there are many. I am one of them!'

'Have any been killed?'

'A lot previously, but not yet under the Duterte regime. Some are on his list, though.'

'This is a list of people Duterte wants to kill?'

'Yes.'

'Is he serious?'

'I think he is. He wants to destroy anyone who goes against him. The people on the list have been called terrorists but they are not. They only protest on the streets, that kind of thing.' Judith then mentioned several local activists by name who are reputedly on the list.

'Have they ever done anything terroristic?' I asked.

'They have never hurt anyone. They are peaceful.' Judith then hesitated for a moment, as if weighing up the risks of saying more. 'Actually,' she said, 'I am also on the list.'

Richard and I traded fearful looks. My inner voice said, 'If she's in grave danger might Richard and I now be for associating with her?' I discovered later that Richard had had exactly the same thought at the same moment.

'Last week,' continued Judith, 'an intelligence operative confronted me with some photographs of me and those others I mentioned. He said to be careful.'

'Are you scared?' I asked.

'Really scared.'

'Does that mean you'll now stop attacking Duterte's policies?'

'No, I will intensify my shouting!'

'How did the operative locate you?'

'He is the son of my close friend. My friend said to his son, "You'd better kill me first before you kill Judith and these others."'

'Would your friend's son be the one who'd assassinate you?'

'No, his role is to prove that we are terrorists.'

'They wouldn't be able to, surely? Or maybe it doesn't matter, as with the drug suspects in the lowlands?'

'The photo the operative had was of me up in the mountains with the NPA. I was invited there as a member of the media to get a statement about their first anniversary of working in this region. That is all.'

Richard leaned forward and looked Judith in the eye. 'By saying all this you're putting a lot of trust in us.'

'Just to be clear,' I said, 'I don't have to publish what you've told us, but if you wanted me to tell your story without mentioning your name, I could do that.'

'Yes. okay.'

'Or I could not tell the story at all. The last thing I want is to endanger you in any way.'

'Well,' said Judith, 'I want the world to be aware of what is happening in the Philippines.'

'Will you stay in Sagada or go into hiding?' I asked.

'I will stay and show them that I'm no terrorist. Anyway, it's stupid going somewhere else. Nobody is safe anywhere.'

'Did you have any prior warnings that you were on the list?'

'Last month, the mayor called me into his office to tell me that the police had accused me of extorting money from someone. This was not true either.'

'Was this an attempt to smear you?'

'Yes.'

'Did they think it would stop you from speaking out?'

'Maybe. The police here have a problem with me because, some years before, I was involved with a group of women who made a citizen's arrest on a known paedophile and delivered him to the police station. For reasons we don't understand the paedophile was released and went on to abuse more children in other places.'

'Have the police regarded you as a troublemaker since then?'

'I think so.'

'But why do you think the state sees you as a threat?'

'Because I am involved with any organization that is against the government and that wants to change the Philippine political and justice systems.'

'So it's not just the current president you oppose?'

'No. All presidents here are puppets. They sell the Philippines to foreign business. And remember that every president has had indigenous people murdered.'

'Do you have a family?' asked Richard.

'I have children – a boy who is twenty-four and a girl who is fifteen. I was separated from my husband ten years ago.'

'Have you told your children about the list?' I asked.

'Yes, two days ago.'

'What did they say?'

'Nothing. I guess they just accepted it because they know they couldn't change my mind about my activism.'

'I've met a lot of very good and very brave people around the Philippines working for NGOs and other outfits. You're one of them, Judith, and I just hope that my writing about you can help in some way. But I'm not always sure it can.'

Judith smiled. 'Of course journalists will always help by letting the world know.'

On our last afternoon with Judith, the police set up a checkpoint at the entrance to Sagada town. We waited in a line of vehicles to be examined – and possibly interrogated – by an armoured cop cradling a CAR-15 assault rifle like a Shetland fisherman showing off a prize turbot. I couldn't help but glance at Judith nervously. Her expression of utter serenity made me feel ashamed of myself. The Robocop waved us through, no questions asked.

Back at the house, Gwen told us that, last night, one policemen had been killed and nine wounded in a firefight with the NPA. I imagined the police were thirsty for revenge. I fretted for Judith again.

EPILOGUE

Despite the optimism of some leftists about Duterte in the early phase of his presidency, the majority now seemed to abhor him. On my last two visits to the Philippines, I asked various individuals what could be done to get rid of him. Graduate student and socialist campaigner Taja Villanueva said to me, 'It is not as though the killings started in the Philippines the day Duterte took office. No, we had them with Aquino and Arroyo and Marcos. All our premiers, actually. The danger of personalizing the resistance, of saying "if we can only eject Duterte then things will be hunky-dory once more", misses the structural problems of our society: the poverty, the inequality, the democratic deficit.'

She then drew an analogy with the US. 'The issue there is not just the one man, Trump. These issues of racism and sexism and fascism have been brewing in the US for centuries. The liberals there are pining for Obama and the Clintons, when apparently all was well. They forget that these leaders were almost as bad. They only got away with it because they used the language of civil rights and equality.'

Her points were plausible. *Al-Jazeera* journalist Mehdi Hasan has found that Obama 'deported 2.5 million people – more than every single US president of the twentieth century combined'. In addition to his drone programme, Obama extended the Afghan war and air-raided Syria, Iraq and Libya. According to Michelle Alexander, Bill and Hillary Clinton 'embraced former president Ronald Reagan's agenda on race, crime, welfare, and taxes – ultimately doing more harm to black communities than Reagan ever did.' The Clintons, too, had an attachment to attacking punier nations like Haiti, Serbia, Somalia and Sudan, in which thousands died outside of due process.

'My view,' continued Taja, 'is that the unelected institutions in any society are more powerful than elected figureheads like Trump and Duterte. Primarily, we are talking about business. Then there is the media, the education system, state religions. These must be dismantled before real change can come. Real change cannot come from marking a ballot paper.'

I had tea again with Niva Gonzalez, the veteran of the anti-Marcos movement. 'Next to Duterte,' she quipped, 'Marcos is like Martin Luther King!' But then she added in a sullen tone of voice, 'Duterte has destroyed years of progress, years of good work in human rights, in land reform, in pro-poor initiatives. We travelled so far and now we are going backward.'

'What can be done?' I asked.

'As always, we will fight.'

And Filipinos are still fighting. There have been hundreds of demos and vigils for the victims, some led by former Liberal Party President Benigno 'Ninoy' Aquino and my old acquaintance Teddy Casiño. Retired police chiefs have blown the whistle on the machinations of summary slaughter. On 10 November 2017, the eve of Trump's official visit to the Philippines, Manila riot police scrapped with red-clad demonstrators chanting 'fascist!' and 'fight US imperialism and plunder!' As oblivious to this as he has been to every other rebuke of him, Trump congratulated Duterte on his 'unbelievable job on the drug problem'. When the men had dinner, more cringeworthiness occurred. In a not-too-terrible voice, Duterte sang to Trump these words: 'You are the light in my world, a half of this heart of mine.'

On 19 January 2018, Filipinos appalled by Duterte's ban on Rappler, a news website that has frequently upbraided his administration, gathered in Quezon City with 'defend press freedom' banners and silver masking tape over their mouths. 'We're speaking truth to power,' said Rappler CEO Maria Ressa. 'We're not afraid and we won't be intimidated.' A month later came the 'Youthquake' of thousands of students walking out of their schools and universities in opposition to extra-judicial killings, media censorship and the commercialization of education. On Labor Day (1 May), 20,000 rallied in Mendiola Street in San Miguel, Manila to demand the abolition of the *endo* scheme that allows employers to cancel their employees' contracts just before they are legally obliged to offer them proper benefits.

When it came to the end of my latest visit to Manila, I kicked myself for not having obtained an interview with Duterte. I'd written letters and emails to the Malacañang Palace but to no avail. I'd obtained the phone number of Duterte's official spokesman, Harry Roque, and requested a meeting with him via WhatsApp. 'Okay,' was his rather casual reply. After that I tried calling him several times and on each occasion the phone rang out.

I now doubt that, had I met the president, I'd have gleaned anything novel from him. If he lied, jived and boasted to every other foreign writer why wouldn't he do the same to me? A creature of the age of postmodern politics, where surfaces matter more than concrete policies or convictions, he was unlikely to deviate from his usual style which surely conforms to what Peter Oborne in his excellent book *The Rise of Political Lying* identifies as 'the assumption that political reality [is] not something that exists "out there", checkable and subject to independent verification. On the contrary, it has suddenly become something that can be shaped and used as part of the battle for political power.' As the Trump and Duterte administrations staggered onward, an idiom was coined to describe their discourses: 'post-truth'. I've never been comfortable with the term, partly because there's nothing new about it. For instance, the Oborne quote above refers to the New Labour era of British politics when spin doctors with backgrounds in advertising and tabloid journalism, and beaming, management consultant-like MPs would omit, distort, back-pedal and opine in bad faith on an almost daily basis.

For fear that this was too despondent a note on which to end this book, I forced myself to consider what I had enjoyed and appreciated about the Philippines. I'd never forget the resolute charm and politeness lavished on me. How often had hairy happenings been alleviated by an ice-breaking joke or compliment? Unlike the lonely crowds and competitive 'me-firstism' of Britain and the US, the Philippines was in many ways a more altruistic society – as evidenced by the saintly unpeople of Tondo and Concepcion Extension – that hadn't entirely lost sight of the proto-communitarianism of the pre-Hispanic *barangay*.

However, this cordiality and cooperativeness was far from the cutely stoical, put-up-with-any-old-oppression mindset mooted by starry-eyed Western tourists. Many of the Filipinos I'd met knew how to think critically and stand up for themselves when needed. Unlike Britain, where we'd been whingeing about the lack of a proper left politics since the 1980s, Manila had plenty of brave, selfless activists devoted to the downtrodden, no matter the odds heaped against them. The ones I'd talked to were gracious and selfless in this enterprise, and at quite the opposite pole to J.M. Coetzee's conception of 'politics [as] too convenient and too attractive as a theatre in which to give play to our baser emotions: ... hatred and rancour and spite and jealousy and bloodlust and so forth.'

Shortly after I got back to the UK after my most recent trip, it was the tenth anniversary of my grandad's death. The occasion prompted me to wonder what he would have thought and felt had he walked in my shoes in the modern-day Philippines. Proud, illiberal and quick-tempered, Grandad might have found common ground with Duterte, Marcos and the other alpha males I'd researched. On the other hand, he'd have dismissed idealists like Niva as spineless pinkos. But, whether he'd been to the Philippines in 1940 or in the early twenty-first century, as I had, the city would have become a strong preoccupation and a subject for continual debate. For that abiding passion, at least, I owe Grandad a lasting debt.

ACKNOWLEDGMENTS

This book would never have materialized without the extraordinary patience, honesty, kindness, generosity and knowledge of legions of people in the UK, the US and, above all, the Philippines.

Extra special thanks to those who shared with me their wisdom about the contemporary Philippines and either arranged interviews for me or were themselves willing to be interviewed, particularly Avie Olarte, Joel Toledo, 'Taja Villanueva', Douglas Candano, Keith Cortez, F. Sionil José, Charlson Ong, Butch Dalisay, Victor Paz, Teddy Casiño, Niva Gonzalez, Rechilda Extremadura, Estelita B. Dy, Red Constantino, Kublai Millan, Becky Añonuevo, José Maria Sison, 'Meryl', 'Ray' and 'Judith'.

A different kind of extra special thanks to James Ferguson of Signal, who agreed to publish the book despite its unusual premise and made many useful suggestions for the manuscript.

I am also grateful to the Faculty of Creative and Cultural Industries, University of Portsmouth for funding large parts of my research and to colleagues within – Stephen Harper, Sophia Wood, Sally Shaw, Oliver Gruner and Dan McCabe – for their invaluable advice and for putting up with my pub ramblings about my Philippine sojourns.

Others who greatly helped me include Louis Netter for his dazzling design and illustration chops, Ella Hermonio for her peerless transcribing skills and Richard Peirce for his company on that fateful last trip.

And, last of all, thanks to my family for their unconditional love and moral support throughout the research and writing up of this book.

Due to the increasingly volatile political situation in the Philippines, the names of some of the people in this book and certain identifying details about them have been altered to protect their privacy and ensure their safety.

BIBLIOGRAPHY OF WORKS CITED

ABC News. 2018. 'Australian nun Patricia Fox ordered to leave Philippines after appeal rejected', *ABC News*, 24 May <htttp://www.abc.net.au/news/2018-05-24/Philippines-orders-australian-nun-to-leave-rejects-appeal/9793862> [accessed 10 June 2018]

ABS-CBN News. 2018. 'Duterte: Let Congress decide on TRAIN Law', *ABS-CBN News*, 3 June <http://news.abs-cbn.com/news/06/03/18/duterte-let-congress-decide-on-train-law> [accessed 10 June 2018]

Agence France Presse. 2016. 'Philippines' Duterte offers hands of friendship to China', *South China Morning Post*, 19 May <http://www.scmp.com/news/asia/diplomacy/article/1946067/philippines-duterte-offers-hand-friendship-china> [accessed 2 December 2017]

— 2016. 'Philippines police, vigilantes shoot dead six suspects', *New Straits Times*, 28 May <http://www.straitstimes.com/asia/se-asia/philippine-police-vigilantes-shoot-dead-six-drug-suspects> [accessed 2 December 2017]

— 2018. 'Rodrigo Duterte says he personally ordered arrest of Australian nun', *Guardian*, 19 April <https://www.theguardian.com/world/2018/apr/19/rodrigo-duterte-says-he-personally-ordered-arrest-of-australian-nun> [accessed 10 June 2018]

Agpalo, Remigio E. 2007. *Ferdinand E. Marcos: A Hero in History* (Manila: Marcos Presidential Center)

Alexander, Michelle. 2016. 'Why Hillary Clinton Doesn't Deserve the Black Vote', *The Nation*, 10 February <https://www.thenation.com/article/hillary-clinton-does-not-deserve-black-peoples-votes/> [accessed 4 December 2017]

Alvarez, Ivy and Conchitina Cruz. 2017. 'Archiving the Present: Ivy Alvarez Interviews Conchitina Cruz', *Cordite*, 1 August <https://www.cordite.org.au/interviews/alvarez-cruz/2/> [accessed 07 August 2017]

Anderson, Benedict. 1997. 'First Filipino', *London Review of Books*, 19, 22-23

Arcilla, José S. 1998. *An Introduction to Philippine History* (Manila: Ateneo de Manila University Press)

Associated Press. 2012. 'Mayor in the Philippines offers $121,000 reward for decapitated head', *New York Daily News Online*, 26 October <http://www.nydailynews.com/news/world/filipino-mayor-offers-121-000-head-article-1.1193368> [accessed 20 July 2016]

Barrows, David. 1905. *A History of the Philippines* (Indianopolis: Bobbs-Merrill)

Baudrillard, Jean. 1988. *Selected Writings* (Redwood City: Stanford University Press)

BBC News. 2016. 'Philippines President Rodrigo Duterte in quotes', *BBC News*, 30 September <http://www.bbc.co.uk/news/world-asia-36251094> [accessed 2 August 2017]

— 2018. 'Philippine news website Rappler has licence revoked by SEC', BBC News, 15 January <https://www.bbc.co.uk/news/world-asia-42692723> [accessed 14 June 2018]

Bello, Walden. 2009. *The Food Wars* (London: Verso)

Boyce, William D. 1914. *United States Colonies and Dependencies Illustrated* (New York: Rand McNally and Co)

Brody, David. 2010. *Visualizing American Empire: Orientalism & Imperialism in the Philippines* (London: University of Chicago Press)

Brizuela, Maricar B. 2016. 'New twist in Moynihan case: BF killed', *Inquirer. net*, 11 October <http://newsinfo.inquirer.net/824019/new-twist-in-moynihan-case-bf-killed> [accessed 28 May 2018]

— 2016. 'Gun in Moynihan death linked to slain BF', *Philippine Daily Inquirer*, 13 October <http://www.pressreader.com/philippines/philippine-daily-inquirer/20161013/281685434361488> [accessed 27 May 2018]

Cahiles, Greg. 2017. '17-year-old student gunned down by cops in anti-drugs operations', *CNN Philippines*, 18 August <http://cnnphilippines.com/news/2017/08/18/Kian-Loyd-Delos-Santos-war-on-drugs-Caloocan-police-operations.html> [accessed 2 December 2017]

Chomsky, Noam. 1990. *Necessary Illusions: Thought Control in Democratic Societies* (London: Pluto Press)

Churchill, Winston. 2007. Quoted in Martin Gilbert, *Churchill and the Jews* (London and New York: Simon & Schuster)

Corales, Nestor. 2016. 'Duterte is "master of strategy", says Cayetano', *Inquirer.net*, 6 June <http://newsinfo.inquirer.net/789324/duterte-is-a-master-of-strategy-says-cayetano> [accessed 3 December 2017]

Coetzee, J.M. 2009. *Summertime* (London: Harvill Secker)

Constantino, Renato. 2010. *A History of the Philippines: From Spanish Colonization to the Second World War* (New York: Monthly Review Press)

Crossley, John Newsome. 2016. *The Dasmariñases, Early Governors of the Spanish Philippines* (Oxford: Routledge)

Dalisay, José Y. 2008. *Soledad's Sister* (Manila: Anvil)

Daval Jr., Lean. 2016. 'Philippines President-Elect Rodrigo Duterte now vowing to protect journalists', *Newsweek*, 8 August <http://www.newsweek.com/philippines-president-elect-rodrigo-duterte-now-vowing-protect-journalists-467910> [accessed 3 December 2017]

Debord, Guy. 1967. Society of the Spectacle (London: Rebel Press, repr. 1992)

Dee, Ching. 2014. 'Rodrigo Duterte: Mayor by day, Taxi Driver by night?', *Philippine Canadian Enquirer*, 4 September <http://www.canadianinquirer.net/2013/09/04/rodrigo-duterte-mayor-by-day-taxi-driver-by-night> [accessed 29 November 2015]

De la Cruz, Kathlyn. 2013. 'Why a kidnap victim brought her abductors to Davao', *ABS-CBN News*, 12 July <http://news.abs-cbn.com/focus/07/12/13/why-kidnap-victim-brought-her-abductors-davao> [accessed 13 July 2015]

Deutsche Presse-Aguntur. 2017. 'Duterte slams Marcos ahead of mass protest', *Gulf Times*, 20 September <http://www.gulf-times.com/story/564560/Duterte-slams-Marcos-ahead-of-mass-protests> [accessed 5 December 2007]

The Dish (Rob Sitch, 2000).

Dower, John. 2016. Quoted in Max Hastings, *Nemesis: The Battle for Japan 1944-45* (London: William Collins)

Flint, Grover. 1900. Quoted in Howard Zinn, *A People's History of the United States: 1492-Present*, (New York: Harper Collins), Amazon kindle e-book

Francia, Luis H. 2001. *Eye of the Fish: A Personal Archipelago* (New York: Kaya Press)

— 2014. *A History of the Philippines: From Indios to Bravos* (New York: Overlook Press)

Garcia, J. Neil. 2008. *Philippine Gay Culture* (Hong Kong: Hong Kong University Press)

Garland, Alex. 1998. *The Tesseract* (London: Penguin; repr. 2007), Amazon Kindle e-book

GMA News Online. 2018. 'Journalists, bloggers join Rappler in Black Friday protest', *GMA News Online*, January 19 <http://www.gmanetwork.com/news/news/nation/640349/journalists-bloggers-join-rappler-in-black-friday-protest/story/>

Gonzalez, Yuji Vincent. 2015. 'Davao tourist swallows cigarette butt after reprimand from Duterte', *Inquirer.net*, 3 September <http://newsinfo.inquirer.net/719038/davao-tourist-swallows-cigarette-butt-after-reprimand-from-duterte#ixzz4xkTwNT2C> [accessed 7 February 2017]

— 2015. 'Duterte's final answer: I won't run for president', *Inquirer.net*, 7 September http://newsinfo.inquirer.net/719960/dutertes-final-answer-i-wont-run-for-president [accessed 5 December 2017]

Hamilton-Paterson, James. 1998. *America's Boy: The Marcoses and the Philippines* (London: Granta)

— 1994. *Ghosts of Manila* (London: Random House)

— 1998. *Playing with Water: Alone on a Philippine Island* (London: Sceptre)

Hasan, Mehdi. 2017. 'Barack Obama: The deporter-in-chief', *Al-Jazeera*, 14 January <http://www.aljazeera.com/programmes/upfront/2017/01/barack-obama-deporter-chief-170113105930345.html> [accessed 3 December 2017]

Hastings, Max. 2016. *Nemesis: The Battle for Japan 1944-45* (London: William Collins)

Hamilton-Paterson, James. 1998. *America's Boy: The Marcoses and the Philippines* (London: Granta)

—1994. *Ghosts of Manila* (London: Random House)

— 1998. *Playing with Water: Alone on a Philippine Island* (London: Sceptre)

Harvey, David. 2013. *Rebel Cities: From the Right to the City to the Urban Revolution* (London: Verso)

Hau, Caroline S. 2010. The "Chinese Question": A Marxist Interpretation', in Teresa S. Encarnacion Tadem and Laura L. Samson (ed.), *Marxism in the Philippines: Continuing Engagements* (Manila: Anvil), pp. 156-187

— 2000. *Necessary Fictions: Philippine Literature and the Nation, 1946-1980* (Ateneo de Manila University Press)

Hegina, Aries Joseph. 2016. 'Drug lords raise bounty for Duterte to P50M—incoming PNP chief', *Inquirer.net*, 9 June <http://newsinfo.inquirer.net/789845/drug-lords-raise-bounty-vs-duterte-to-p50m-incoming-pnp-chief> [accessed 7 May 2017]

Holmes, Oliver. 2016. 'UN envoys condemn Rodrigo Duterte for incitement to kill journalists', *Guardian.com*, 8 June <https://www.theguardian.com/world/2016/jun/08/un-diplomats-condemns-rodrigo-duterte-for-incitement-to-kill-journalists> [accessed 19 June 2016]

Human Rights Watch. 2009. 'Clinton Should Press Arroyo on Killings', *Human Rights Watch*, 9 November <https://www.hrw.org/news/2009/11/09/philippines-clinton-should-press-arroyo-killings> [accessed 3 December 2017]

— 2017. '"Licence to Kill": Philippine Police Killings in Duterte's "War on Drugs"', *Human Rights Watch*, 2 March <https://www.hrw.org/report/2017/03/02/license-kill/philippine-police-killings-dutertes-war-drugs.> [accessed 5 December 2017]

Iaccino, Ludovica. 2014. 'Child Sex Abuse: Top 5 Countries with the Highest Rates', *International Business Times*, 12 February <http://www.ibtimes.co.uk/child-sexual-abuse-top-5-countries-highest-rates-1436162> [accessed 20 March 2014]

Ileto, Raymundo C. 2017. *Knowledge and Pacification: On the U.S. Conquest and the Writing of Philippine History* (Manila: Ateneo de Manila University Press)

Jacobsen, Barry C. 2017. 'Juramentado: Moro Suicidal Assassins', <https://deadliestblogpage.wordpress.com/2017/04/19/juramentado-moro-suicidal-assassins/> [accessed 22 January 2017]

Jacques, Martin. 2012. *When China Rules The World: The End of the Western World and the Birth of a New Global Order* (London: Penguin)

Joaquin, Nick ('Quijano de Manila'). 1980. *Language of the Street and Other Essays* (Manila: National Bookstore)

José, F. Sionil. 2013. *Dusk* (New York: Modern Library), Amazon Kindle e-book

— 1988. *Ermita: A Filipino Novel* (Manila: Solidaridad Publishing House, Inc.)

Kramer, Paul A. 2006. *The Blood of Government: Race, Empire, the United States, & the Philippines* (Chapel Hill: University of North Carolina Press)

Kipling, Rudyard. 1899. 'The White Man's Burden', in *Collected Poems of Rudyard Kipling*, ed. by R.T. Jones (London: Wordsworth Editions; repr. 1994)

Kwong, Peter and Dušanka Miščevic. 2006. *Chinese America: The Untold Story of America's Oldest New Community* (New York: The New Press)

Lacorte, Germalina A. 2015. 'Duterte names priest who allegedly molested him as teen' *Inquirer.net*, 4 November <http://newsinfo.inquirer.net/744824/duterte-names-priest-who-allegedly-molested-him-as-teen> [accessed 1 March 2016]

— 2013. 'Duterte tells criminals: Leave Davao City vertically or horizontally' *Inquirer.net*, 30 June <http://newsinfo.inquirer.net/435783/duterte-tells-criminals-leave-davao-city-vertically-or-horizontally> [accessed 26 July 2017]

— 2007. 'Jun Pala's Ghost Still Haunts Duterte', *Davaotoday.com*, 26 April <http://davaotoday.com/main/politics/press-freedom/jun-pala%E2%80%99s-ghost-haunts-duterte/> [accessed 26 July 2017]

Lee, Clark. 1943. *They Call it Pacific: An Eyewitness Story of Our War Against Japan from the Bataan to the Solomons* (New York: The Viking Press)

De Legazpi, Miguel López. 1570. Quoted in Renato Constantino, *A History of the Philippines: From Spanish Colonization to the Second World War* (New York: Monthly Review Press)

Lima, Karen, and Manuel Mogato. 2016. 'Philippines' Rodrigo Duterte likens himself to Hitler, wants to kill millions of drug users', *Reuters.com*, 30 September <https://uk.reuters.com/article/uk-philippines-duterte-hitler/philippines-duterte-likens-himself-to-hitler-wants-to-kill-millions-of-drug-users-idUKKCN1200BD> [accessed 6 December 2017]

Lopez, Eloisa. 2018. 'Filipino youth lead nationwide "walkout" for freedom and democracy', *Rappler.com*, 23 February 2018 <https://www.rappler.com/move-ph/196750-filipino-youth-lead-march-freedom-democracy>

Lopez, Ron. 2016. '2 patay sa drug bust sa UP Diliman campus', *ABS-CBN News*, 25 September <http://news.abs-cbn.com/news/09/25/16/2-patay-sa-drug-bust-sa-up-diliman-campus> [accessed 2 June 2016]

Lozada, Aaron. 2016. 'Understanding Duterte: What a psych report says', *ABS-CBN*, 20 April <http://news.abs-cbn.com/halalan2016/focus/04/19/16/understanding-duterte-what-a-psych-report-says> [accessed 26 July 2017]

Malik, Kenan. 1996. *The Meaning of Race: Race, History and Culture in Western Society* (London: Palgrave MacMillan)

Manahan, Josefina P. 2001. *Street-Bound: Manila on Foot* (Manila: Anvil)

Mogato, Manuel. 2017. 'Philippine leader's opponents turn historic event into protest march', *Reuters.com*, 25 February <https://uk.reuters.com/article/uk-philippines-duterte-protests/philippine-leaders-opponents-turn-historic-event-into-protest-march-idUKKBN164062?feedType=RSS&feedName=worldNews> [accessed 6 December 2017>

Moore, Charlie. 2017. 'Violent anti-Trump protests erupt on the streets of Manila ahead of US leader's arrival as the president has a 'short but cordial' meeting with Philippines counterpart Duterte', *Mail Online*, 11 November <http://www.dailymail.co.uk/news/article-5072407/Anti-Trump-protests-erupt-Philippines-arrival.html#ixzz50TM4GUT7> [accessed 6 December 2017]

National Historical Commission of the Philippines. 2011. *Colonial Accounts* (Manila: New Day)

Nightingale, Carl H. 2012. *Segregation: A Global History of Divided Cities* (Chicago: University of Chicago Press)

Nkrumah, Kwame. 1965. *Neo-Colonialism, the Last Stage of Imperialism* (London: Thomas Nelson & Sons)

NGO Monitor. 2017. 'Human Rights Watch (HRW)', *NGO Monitor*, 4 December <https://www.ngo-monitor.org/ngos/human_rights_watch_hrw_/> [accessed 4 December 2017]

Oborne, Peter. 2005. *The Rise of Political Lying* (London: Simon and Schuster)

Paddock, Richard C. 2017. 'Becoming Duterte: The Making of a Philippine Strongman', *The New York Times*, March 21 <https://www.nytimes.com/2017/03/21/world/asia/rodrigo-duterte-philippines-president-strongman.html> [accessed 3 December 2017]

Parreño, Al A. 2011. *Report on the Philippine Extra-judicial Killings 2001-2010* (Manila: Supreme Court of the Philippines)

Phillips, Kristine. 2016. 'Philippines' Duterte keeps lashing out at the United States – over atrocities a century ago,' *The Washington Post*, July 24 https://www.washingtonpost.com/news/worldviews/wp/2017/07/24/philippines-duterte-keeps-lashing-out-at-the-united-states-over-its-atrocities-a-century-ago/?utm_term=.b41b08eeb3ae [accessed 8 December 2017]

Pia, Renada. 2016. 'Rody Duterte: The rebellious son, the prankster brother', *Rappler.com*, 20 May <https://www.rappler.com/newsbreak/in-depth/133595-rody-duterte-rebellious-son-prankster-brother> [accessed 4 December 2017]

Pike, Francis. 2015. *Hirohito's War: The Pacific War, 1941-1945* (London and New York: Bloomsbury)

Pierson, Charles. 2016. 'Duterte's Death Squads, and Ours', *Counterpunch.org*, 5 October <https://www.counterpunch.org/2016/10/05/dutertes-death-squads-and-ours/> [accessed 2 December 2017]

Quiros, Judy, and Karlos Manlupig. 2013. 'Davao 'Death Squad' strikes again', *Inquirer.net*, 27 June <http://newsinfo.inquirer.net/434243/davao-death-squad-strikes-again> [accessed 14 October 2017]

Rappler, 'Oldest alliance of college editors to stage nationwide protests February 23', *Rappler.com*, 22 February <https://www.rappler.com/move-ph/196585-cegp-stage-nationwide-protests-duterte-attack-press-freedom> [accessed 24 February 2018]

The Real Glory (Henry Hathaway, 1939).

Reuters Staff. 2016. 'Philippines' Duterte to allow burial of Marcos at heroes' cemetery', *Reuters.com*, 8 November <http://www.reuters.com/article/us-philippines-marcos-court/former-philippine-dictator-marcos-to-get-heros-burial-three-decades-after-death-idUSKBN1330PX> [accessed 14 October 2017]

— 2017. 'Philippines' Duterte sings love song for Trump: 'You are the light'', *The Guardian*, 13 November <https://www.theguardian.com/world/2017/nov/13/you-are-the-light-philippines-duterte-sings-love-song-for-trump>

Rey, Aika. 2018. 'Labor groups dismayed by signed "employer-backed" EO vs endo', *Rappler.com*, 1 May <https://www.rappler.com/nation/201511-groups-dismayed-employer-backed-eo-labor-day-2018>

Richard, Claire. 2011. 'Dérive and Psychogeography: Situationist practices of urban spaces', *Immediacy: An Online Media Journal*, 3, <http://immediacy.newschool.edu/?p=397> [accessed 2 March 2015], (1-3)

Ripley, Will and Jay C. Croft. 2016. 'Philippines drug war's wide net claims 6-year-old shot dead in his sleep', *CNN.com*, 16 December https://edition. cnn.com/2016/12/15/world/philippines-duterte-killings/index.html [accessed 13 May 2018]

Rizal, José. 1912. *The Social Cancer (Noli Me Tangere)*, trans. by Charles Derbyshire (Project Gutenberg: Salt Lake City; repr. 2004), Amazon Kindle edition

Rodriguez, Dylan. *2010. Suspended Apocalypse: White Supremacy, Genocide, and the Filipino Condition* (Minneapolis: University of Minnesota Press)

Roth, Kenneth. 5 May 2009. 'Philippine Death Squads: A Murderous Plague', *Far Eastern Economic Review Online*, <http://www.feer.com/ politics/2009/may56/Death-Squads-A-Murderous-Plague> [accessed 30 January 2015]

Rufo, Aries C. 2013. *Altar of Secrets: Sex, Politics, and Money in the Philippine Catholic Church* (Manila: Journalism for Nation Building Foundation)

Santos, Eimor P. 2016. 'Other vehicles accused of sudden acceleration problems', *CNN Philippines*, 21 January <http://cnnphilippines.com/ news/2015/12/02/sudden-unintended-acceleration-problems.html> [accessed 5 April 2016]

Sauler, Erika. 2016. '5-yr-old boy shot dead along with drug-using pa', *Inquirer.net*, 15 December <http://newsinfo.inquirer.net/853751/5-yr-old-boy-shot-dead-along-with-drug-using-pa> [accessed 13 May 2018]

Schaller, Michael. 1989. *Douglas MacArthur: The Far Eastern General* (Oxford: Oxford University Press)

Seagrave, Sterling. 1988. *The Marcos Dynasty* (New York: Harper and Row)

Sison, José Maria and Ninotchka Rosca. 2004. *José Maria Sison: At Home in the World, Conversations with Ninotchka Rosca* (Greensboro: Open Hand Publishing)

Spear, Andrew. 2017. 'Hypocrisy and Responsibility: On the Uses and Abuses of tu quoque for Life', in *Grand Valley State University News* <https://www. gvsu.edu/seidman/ethics/module-news-view.htm?storyId=CD0BC3F2-D254-A741-C4495405CDC5B795&siteModuleId=9C6681B1-92E9-F4F1-7B4DF17EDBE5D2DC> [accessed 27 July 2017]

Tempo Online. 2016. 'Dismissed cop killed in shootout', *Tempo.com* <http:// tempo.com.ph/2016/07/16/dismissed-cop-killed-in-shootout/> [accessed 10 June 2018]

Twain, Mark. 1901. Quoted in Howard Zinn, *A People's History of the United States: 1492-Present*, (New York: Harper Collins), Amazon kindle e-book

Udtohan, Leo. 2016. '4-year-old Althea dies in drug war, together with her dream to be a cop', *Inquirer.net*, 7 October < http://newsinfo.inquirer.net/822667/4-year-old-althea-dies-in-drug-war-together-with-her-dream-to-be-a-cop> [accessed 13 May 2018]

Wells, Matt. 2017. 'Philippines: Duterte's war on drugs is a war on the poor', *Amnesty.org*, 4 February <https://www.amnesty.org/en/latest/news/2017/02/war-on-drugs-war-on-poor/> [accessed 4 December 2017]

White, T.H. 2014. Quoted in Brayfield, Celia and Duncan Sprott, *Writing Historical Fiction: A Writers' and Artists' Companion* (London and New York: Bloomsbury)

Wilde, Oscar. 1891. *The Soul of Man Under Socialism and Selected Critical Prose* (London: Penguin, repr: 2007)

Zabriski, Phil. 2002. 'The Punisher', *Time*, 19 July, p. 17

Zinn, Howard. 2001. *A People's History of the United States: 1492-Present*, (New York: Harper Collins), Amazon Kindle e-book

FURTHER READING

Buruma, Ian. 1988. *God's Dust: A Modern Asian Journey*, (London: Vintage, 1991)

Carpenter, Frank G. 1929. *Through the Philippines and Hawaii* (New York: Doubleday, Doran and Company)

Clegg, Jenny, *Fu Manchu and the 'Yellow Peril': The Making of a Racist Myth* (Stoke-on-Trent, Trentham Books, 1994)

Connell, John. 1999. 'Beyond Manila: Walls, Malls, and Private Spaces', *Environment and Planning*, 31: 15-24, <doi: 10.1068/a310417>

Damrosch, David. 2008. *How to Read World Literature* (New York: Wiley-Blackwell)

Fanon, Frantz. 1990. *The Wretched of the Earth* (London: Penguin Classics)

Fee, Mary H. 1912. *A Woman's Impression of the Philippines* (Manila: G.C.F. Books; repr. 1988)

Feleo, Anita and David Sheniak. 1998. *Two for the Road* (Manila: Anvil)

Fenton, James. 1989. *All the Wrong Places: Adrift in the Politics of Southeast Asia* (London: Granta; repr. 2005)

Filipinas Heritage Library. 2007. *Filipinas Heritage Library Catalogue* <http://opac.filipinaslibrary.org.ph/> [accessed 7 December 2017].

Goncharov, Ivan. 1965. *The Voyage of the Frigate Pallada* (London: Folio Society)

Guerrero, Amadis Ma. 1994. *Traveler's Choice: North to South* (Manila: Anvil Press)

Gunter, Archibald Clavering. 1898. *Jack Curzon (Being a portion of the Records of the Managing Clerk of Markrtin, Thompson & Co., English Merchants doing business in Hong Kong, Manila, Cebu and the Straits Settlements)* (New York: Hurst)

Hagedorn, Jessica. 1991. *Dogeaters* (London: Penguin)

Hagedorn, Jessica. 2013. (Ed.) *Manila Noir* (New York: Akashic Books)

Huggan, Graham. 2001. *The Postcolonial Exotic: Marketing the Margins* (London: Routledge)

Iyer, Pico. 1988. *Video Night in Kathmandu* (London: Black Swan; repr. 1998)

Jagor, Fedor. 1875. *Travels in the Philippines* (London: Chapman and Hall)

Kelly, M.G.E. 2015. *Biopolitical Imperialism* (London: Zero Books)

Kidd, Benjamin. 1898. *The Control of the Tropics* (New York: McMillan)

King, Charles. 1901. *Ray's Daughter: A Story of Manila* (Philadelphia: J. P. Lippincott)

Kram, Mark. 1975. 'Lawdy, Lawdy, He's Great,' *Sports Illustrated Online*, 17 January 2012, <https://www.si.com/boxing/2012/01/17/muhammad-ali-70th-kram> [accessed 28 September 2017]

Loney, Nicholas. 1964. *A Britisher in the Philippines or the Letters of Nicholas Loney* (Manila: National Library)

Mailer, Norman. 1948. *The Naked and the Dead* (London: Harper Perennial; repr. 2004)

MacKenzie, Duncan Alexander. 2012. *The Unlucky Country: The Republic of the Philippines in the 21st Century* (Balboa Press: Carlsbad), Amazon Kindle e-book

MacMicking, Robert. 1851. *Recollections of Manilla and the Philippines During 1848, 1849 and 1850* (London: Richard Bentley)

Manguel, Alberto. 1994. 'Gouging Out Hell's Entrails: Ghosts of Manila – James Hamilton-Paterson', *Independent Online*, 3 June <http://www.independent.co.uk/arts-entertainment/books/book-review-gouging-out-hells-entrails-ghosts-of-manila-james-hamilton-paterson-jonathan-cape-pounds-1420229.html> *[accessed 25 September 2017]*

McKinley, William. 1899. Quoted in James H. Blount, *The American Occupation of the Philippines 1898-1912* (New York: G. P. Putnam's Sons)

Miller, George A. 1929. *Interesting Manila* (Manila: Philippine Education Company)

Mo, Timothy. 1997. *Brownout on Breadfruit Boulevard* (London: Paddleless Press)

— 2000. *Renegade or Halo²* (London: Paddleless Press)

Nelson, Raymond. 1968. *The Philippines* (London: Thames and Hudson)

FURTHER READING

Netzorg, Walton J. 1990. 'The Philippines in Mass-Market Novels', in Robin W. Winks and James R. Rush (ed.), *Asia in Western Fiction* ed. by (Manchester: Manchester University Press), pp. 175-195

O'Rourke, P.J. 1989. *Holidays in Hell* (New York: Grove; repr. 2012), Amazon Kindle e-book

Pagan, Andrew. 2012. 'From the Darkness to the Family: Evolving Orientalist Representations of the Katipunan in Euro-American Travel Literature, 1899-1917,' *The Forum: Journal of History*, 4: 87-102

Phelan, John Leddy. 2010. *The Hispanization of the Philippines* (Madison: University of Wisconsin Press)

Robb, Walter. 1926. *The Khaki Cabinet and Old Manila* (Manila: Sugar News Press)

Roh, David S., Betsy Huang, and Greta A. Nui. 2015. 'Technologizing Orientalism', in David S. Roh, Betsy Huang, and Greta A. Nui (ed.), *Techno-Orientalism: Imagining Asia in Speculative Fiction, History, and Media* (New Brunswick: Rutgers University Press), pp. 1-20

Romein, Jan. 1962. *The Asian Century: A History of Modern Nationalism in Asia* (Berkeley and Los Angeles: University of California Press)

Rowland, Dr. Henry C. 1902. 'Fighting Life in the Philippines', *McClure's Magazine*, July

Said, Edward. 1994. *Culture and Imperialism* (London: Vintage)

— 1985. *Orientalism* (London: Peregrine Books)

Sardar, Ziauddin. 1999. *Orientalism*, (London: Open University Press)

Sayles, John. 2011. *A Moment in the Sun* (San Francisco: McSweeney's), Amazon Kindle e-book

Spurr, David. 1993. *Rhetoric of Empire: Colonial Discourse in Journalism, Travel Writing and Imperial Administration* (Durham: Duke University Press)

Stratemeyer, Edward. 1900. *The Campaign of the Jungle or Under Lawton through Luzon* (Boston: Lee and Shepard)

— 1898. *Under Dewey at Manila or The War Fortunes of a Castaway*, (Boston: Lee and Shepard)

— 1902. *Under MacArthur in Luzon or Last Battles in the Philippines*, (Boston: Lee and Shepard)

Stevenson, DeLouis. 1956. *Land of the Morning* (St Louis: The Bethany Press)

Stuntz, Homer Clyde. 1904. *The Philippines and the Far East* (New York: Jennings and Pye)

Sykes, Thomas. 2018. *Searching for Manila: Personal and Political Journeys in an Asian Megacity* (unpublished PhD thesis)

Tan, Antonio S. 1986. 'The Chinese Mestizos and the Formation of the Filipino Nationality', *Archipel*, 32: 141-162

Teixera, Pedro. 1610. *Relaciones de Pedro Teixera del Origen, Descendencia y Succession de los Reyes de Persia y de Harmuz* (Manila: publisher unknown)

Temprano, Pablo Feced. 1888. Quoted in Paul A. Kramer, *The Blood of Government: Race, Empire, the United States, & the Philippines* (Chapel Hill: University of North Carolina Press)

Thomes, William Henry. 1875. *Life in the East Indies* (Boston and New York: Lee and Shepard)

Westling, Megan. 2011. *Empire's Proxy: American Literature and U.S. Imperialism in the Philippines* (New York: New York University Press)

Wickberg, Edgar. 1997. 'Anti-Sinicism and Chinese Identity Options in the Philippines', in Chirot, Daniel and Reid, Anthony (ed.), *Essential Outsiders: Chinese and Jews in the Modern Transformation of Southeast Asia and Central Europe* (Seattle: University of Washington Press), pp. 153-183

Wilkes, Charles. 1842. *Travel Accounts of the Islands (1832-58)* (Manila: Filipiniana Book Guild; repr. 1974)

Williams, Maslyn. 1979. *Faces of My Neighbour: Three Journeys into East Asia* (Sydney: William Collins)

Workman, Daniel. 2017. *Philippines Top Trading Partners* <http://www.worldstopexports.com/philippines-top-import-partners> *[accessed 25 September 2017]*

Zinn, Howard. 2001. *A People's History of the United States: 1492-Present*, (New York: Harper Collins), Amazon Kindle e-book